ME FATHER WAS A HERO

AND

ME MOTHER IS A SAINT

The extraordinary story of an ordinary Irish working-class family

by Eamonn Sheridan

Strategic Book Group

Strategic Book Group
P.O. Box 333
Durham CT 06422
www.StrategicBookClub.com

ISBN: 978-1-60976-820-1

Book Design: Suzanne Kelly

To my wife Linda, our children,
Tara, Aisling, Philip and Ross
and our grand-children,
Cameron, James, Sophie, Jason, Eoin and Aaron.

Remembering also
Catherine, Eamonn Jnr., and Martin.

To, my good friend John Cable
with my very best wishes.

Eamonn

30TH. December 2011.

INTRODUCTION

This is the story of an ordinary working class Dublin family, some of whom had one or two extraordinary experiences. I trust that the reader will enjoy our story and perhaps even manage a smile at times. I have deliberately avoided using names in some instances to save embarrassment to those still living. Our story starts with my father's birth in the year 1900 and takes us right up to date. The story hasn't finished. Most of the family are still living and there may be more to come.

For some years before my father died in 1977, I had pleaded with him to write down his experiences with the Irish Republican Army during the "War of Independence" or the "Tan War" as he called it. He was very reluctant to do so, but I finally managed to persuade him. Although it is by no means comprehensive, it will give the reader some idea of the man and those he served with.

I was also curious to know why he never attended any of the commemoration parades, for example, and when I enquired about his reason for this, he looked me straight in the eye and said, "Have you seen any of these parades?"

I answered in the affirmative.

"You've seen the guy who carries the flag, in that case."

I nodded again.

"Well, in the first place, he and many of his colleagues never fired a shot in anger. Although they were members of the IRA, they were never involved in any action. There was some excuse for those who didn't turn out during 1916; due to confusion when the mobilization order was cancelled. There was no excuse this time, however. Everybody knew what was happening, but some of them chose not to show. More importantly, a Republican Court tried the fellow who carries the flag, and found him guilty of sexually interfering with a child. His sentence was a bullet in the scrotum and that's what we gave him. So, there's no way that I would march with a swine like that. On another occasion," he continued, "as I was making my way along the quays, I came upon two of these brave warriors. They were about to throw a drummer boy dressed in his British Army uniform, into the Liffey. The lad was about fourteen years of age and he was scared to death. I pulled out my gun and ordered them to let the boy go or I would shoot both of them on the spot. It is this sort that gives an organisation a bad name."

My father was a devoted follower of Eamonn De Valera all of his life. He, like many of the men who stayed with the Republican ideal of a united and free Ireland, remained true to this ideal to his dying day. My mother named me after his hero and though there were twelve children in the family, we spent more time talking than any of my siblings. He later served with the British 8th Army during the Second World War, but this didn't change his original belief in a United Ireland. I have included some photographs that I believe will be of interest to the reader. The 1st Battalion memorial, shown here, is located opposite the Public Library in Phibsborough Dublin-7. The sculptor was a friend of my father and told him that he modeled the figure after him. I have also included pictures of his medals and the certificate of service that the government issued together with other photos I have in my collection.

I dedicate this book to both of my parents. To my father, who was a hero as far as I am concerned, and took up the gun to play his part in freeing our country from the oppressor. To my mother, who stood by him in good times and bad; whose dedication to the family was nothing short of saintly. She had twenty-three pregnancies (contraception wasn't considered, they were devout Catholics), and this in turn led to her untimely death at the age of sixty-three years. We still sadly miss her. If I have any regret it's that she didn't live long enough for the family to return in kind some of what she did for us.

I have told this story as honestly and frankly as I can. It relates the joys and sorrows of being brought up in a large but proud working-class family in Cabra and Cabra West. It tells of the effects of emigration on the family and how we coped with living apart and in different digs in Birmingham. It was an old industrialized city and it still hadn't recovered from the effects of the bombing that it had suffered during the Second World War. I found it strange compared to Dublin. The houses had been built during the industrial revolution. They were jammed together in narrow streets and the toilets were in the back yard. They did at least have a modern sewer system, unlike Oldham where the system was primitive. I had no sex education whatso-ever. Because of this and my Roman Catholic upbringing, I felt obliged to marry the first girl that I had sexual relations with. This, I discovered, is no basis on which to build a marriage and it led to divorce eventually. I tell of my disappointment with the Army and the Gardaí after I reported the plot to blow up Nelson Pillar. As a result, I received threats to my life; and then there was the killing of my old school friend Billy Wright. Then, there was new love, new life, and stability at last.

CONTENTS

*The beginning of our story
is told in my father's own words . . .*

Chapter One

Birth of a Hero

“ I was born on the seventh of June 1900, to Thomas Sheridan and Alice Gaffney-Dunn. We lived in 61 Upper Dominick Street. The house was a tenement and was occupied top to bottom by relations, on both sides of the family. I attended St. Mary's Boys School, which is located in Mary's Place, just at the top of Mountjoy Street and at the back of the "Black Church." My father was a coachbuilder with Great Southern Railways and he wore a bowler hat to distinguish himself as a tradesman. He was also a member of the church choir in Halston Street. He won the gold medal in the Feis Ceol in the same year that I was born. My mother was a down to earth, plain, and simple woman with a wicked sense of humour.

On Easter Sunday 1916, I went with my sister Molly to have our photos taken in Keogh's of North Earl Street. The studio was near what is now Lloyds Public House. I was fifteen and a half years old at the time. On our way back home, we saw the men of the Irish Citizen Army marching into Sackville Street (O'Connell Street). They were dressed in full uniform and we wondered what they were doing. After asking some of the people who had stopped to watch, we learned that they were on their way to the Wicklow Hills to carry out an exercise.

Next day Monday, I went for a walk with my pal, Jim Brady. We walked up Mountjoy Street and on up Berkeley Road and into Phibsboro'. We carried on, out the Cabra Road and enjoyed the surrounding green fields that were either filled with grazing cattle or growing vegetables. Once we reached the railway line at the top of the Cabra Road, we turned around and headed back towards home. Just as we reached St. Peter's Church at the junction of Cabra Road and the North Circular Road, we noticed a group of men formed up in ranks, carrying rifles and bandoliers of ammunition. They were under the command of a man I recognised, called Joe Gogan. He was the brother of Richard Gogan, who later became a Fianna Fáil TD. I also recognised a Mr. John Falconer, whom I knew very well. After a short time a car drove up and stopped near us. The man who got out was dressed in the uniform of the Irish Volunteers. It was Commandant Edward Daly, who was later executed by the British for his part in the Rising. A Mr. Sean Howard, dressed in the uniform of the Fianna Scouts, accompanied him. I had no difficulty in recognising him as he lived in Upper Dominick Street, not far from where I lived. Sean was later killed in the fighting in Church Street. The armed men moved off in the direction of the city centre.

Not long after they had left, another body of armed men came down the Cabra Road and asked us for directions to the General Post Office. We knew by now that there was something big about to happen, so we showed the troop all the way to the door of the GPO. We hung around waiting to have our curiosity satisfied and witnessed a troop of British Lancers on horseback, charge down O'Connell Street from the direction of Parnell Street. Just as I was wondering who or what they were charging, a volley of shots rang out from the GPO and several of the Lancers, including the officer leading them, fell to the ground. Some of the horses were also hit and the screeches as one lay dying were unnerving.

All hell seemed to break loose and in the ensuing confusion, several shops were looted. My pal and I were sheltering in a shop doorway when a stray bullet struck the doorpost just above my head. We decided it was time to leave, and Jim and I took off down the road like jack-rabbits. On my way home, I met a volunteer named Mr. Mulcahy who knew me. He gave me a pair of grey flannel long trousers. I didn't ask where he had gotten them and accepted them gratefully. I pulled them on over my short ones and they fitted me fine. They were the first

pair of long trousers I ever had and I was so pleased with them
that I helped the volunteers build barricades wherever they were
needed in the area. I was fifteen years old but looked younger.
So they sent me home because of my age; though I was reluctant
to go despite my earlier experience with the bullet in the doorpost. They told me that it was too dangerous to hang around. All
of this and what followed left a very deep impression on me,
and I was determined to get involved if the opportunity arose
in the future.

Following the "Rising" the police tried to keep people out of
O'Connell Street. This didn't deter one of my pals, who climbed
the ruins of the GPO and retrieved the Tricolour. Jim Brady,
from Upper Dominick Street, the Frongoch Barber Jimmy Mullen, and I were in the street waiting for him. We all ran with
the flag to Mullen's Barber Shop in Lime Street off Sir John
Rogerson's Quay.

In 1917, following the amnesty, I went over to Westland
Row (Pearse) Station to welcome the returning hero's from British gaols. Despite the hundreds that had gathered, I managed to
get right up near the exit; as the men came out of the station,
I found myself face to face with my schoolmaster. I knew now
why he had been missing from school. Nobody had told us
anything, though I suspected that he had been involved in the
Rising. He took my hand and shook it as I muttered, "Welcome
home, Mr. Lynch." His first name was Finnian and he was later
to become Minister for Fisheries in the Free State Government.
They received a tremendous reception as they walked over to
Flemings Hotel, just across the road. There wasn't enough room
to cope with them all so some went to Barry's Hotel in Little
Denmark Street. Following this and on hearing that the fight
wasn't over, I joined the 2nd Northern Fianna Scouts, which had
been reorganised. My superior officers included Countess Markievicz, Garry Houlihan, Theo Fitzgerald, Comandant Roddy
Connolly, Liam Murphy, Dan McArt, and Liam Langley.

We met in a hall in Skipper's Alley near to the Francis-
can Church on Merchant's Quay. Although it was a boy-scout
organisation, we drilled at night and learned military tactics.

3

On Sundays we would head off on route marches, usually out the Wicklow Road towards Kilmacanogue. The main purpose of these marches, apart from keeping us fit, was to act as decoys and keep the Royal Irish Constabulary busy and away from the areas where the Volunteers were drilling. The British had declared it illegal for anyone to belong to an Irish Military Organisation and we were constantly harassed. On one occasion the RIC drew batons and attacked us in Dundrum in South County, Dublin. Some local people tried to come to our rescue, screaming at the police that we were only boy-scouts but they were beaten with batons to the ground.

Having reached my eighteenth birthday and just before the Anti-Conscription Act of 1918, I was transferred to "E" Company of the 1st Battalion, Dublin Brigade. The Battalions remit was to occupy the Four Courts, Broadstone Station, the terminus of the railways from the west, and of covering the approaches from the Royal (Collins), Islandbridge (Clancy) and Marlborough (McKee) Barracks. I was the youngest member of the company at the time and Captain Donaghy, the unit commander, took me under his wing. Unfortunately, he died soon afterwards we then elected Paddy Garland to be our new company commander. Captain Bill Corri succeeded Captain Garland after he was arrested by the British and sent to Ballykinlar Prison Camp.

We carried out manoeuvres at the rear of Messrs Craigies' milk yard, situated between Cabra West and Finglas. It was all green fields in that area then and we used it extensively. One day while we were holding a range practice with the .22 rifle, a British spotter plane flew over. We knew then that someone had reported hearing shooting and the British were out to investigate. Very soon after the plane flew over, the RIC from Finglas Station were searching for us. We managed to avoid them on this occasion. Later still, while we were holding night exercises between the hours of 2 a.m. and 4 a.m., in conjunction with "H" Company around the area known as King James Castle, we discovered that the RIC were hiding in a wooded area nearby known as the "Glen." They were armed with carbines. The weapons we had were no match for high velocity rifles, so we beat a hasty retreat escaping across Glasnevin Cemetery. The RIC were such a nuisance in that area that it was decided to curtail their activities; so their barracks was burned to the ground.

Meetings were also held in the Tara Hall Gloucester Street and the Foresters Hall in Parnell Square. We commandeered the Fowler Hall from the Masonic Lodge and were amazed to discover whom their members were when we looked through their files. There were quite a number of refugees from the North and we housed them in this hall. We seized food, clothing, and cigarettes that was destined for Belfast and distributed it to these people. We sometimes needed extra help to move the goods and called on the Northern men to help. This they did reluctantly and on occasion we had to order them to do it. The food, etc. was after all, for their use. It was ironic that most of them joined the Free State Army during the Civil War.

Following all this training, I was selected to attend an NCO course, which took place in the Banba Hall in Buckingham Street. Soon afterwards, I became a Section Commander. A section consisted of twenty-five men. Sean Hegarty, the man in charge of the course was later to become a high-ranking officer in the Free State Army. We were now ready for action but nothing happened and when I asked our officer why we were not doing what we had been trained for, he told me to mind my own business. I reported this to the Company Commander and soon afterwards, the lieutenant was relieved of his command. He claimed to have a weak heart. He hated me for what I'd done and told me so in no uncertain terms.

We carried out our first ambush under Captain Corri shortly afterwards. The Black and Tans regularly drove up and down Bolton Street, and on this particular occasion we laid in wait for them. As the leading armoured car approached, I walked into the road, trying at the same time to control my nerves. The car slowed down and as it did I drew my pistol, and shot the driver through the observation slot. At the same moment, the rest of the section ran into the Street hurling hand grenades. There was pandemonium and in the confusion we all got clear with no casualties.

Early in 1920, at 2:30 in the morning, the Wiltshire Regiment raided the house where I was staying and I was arrested on suspicion of being a member of the IRA. They marched me through the streets, pushing and shoving and shouting obscenities, until we reached the Royal (later Collin's) Barracks where I was lodged in the Guardroom. While there, I received a visit from a Captain Jim Jones who lived near to my parent's house in Dominick Street. He said he was sorry that I had been arrested and that he would see to it that my parents were informed of my whereabouts. I had great respect for the Captain, who had earned his rank the hard way. He had served in the trenches during the World War. He was kind enough to leave me some newspapers to read.

Following an IRA action, the Wiltshire's ran amok one night and pulled me from my cell into a small compound at the rear of the guardroom where they proceeded to punch and kick me. When I retaliated, they felled me with a rifle butt. Dragging me to my feet, they stood me against the wall and cocked the firing action of the rifles. Just as I thought the end had come, the guard commander rushed in with some other men and disarmed them. I was bleeding badly from the wound on my cheek that had been opened when they kicked me. I was also bleeding profusely from the nose but received no treatment for these injuries until the following morning, when I was taken to see the Medical Officer. I was then asked to identify the culprits, which I did but I never heard if any action had been taken against them. On returning to my cell, I found that the new guard commander was very civil and I had no further trouble.

A week or so later, a covered truck pulled up outside the guardroom. I was handcuffed and placed in the back where I found myself in the company of two other men. It turned out that one of them was none other than Martin O'Sullivan, the manager of the Queens Theatre, and the other was a Mr. Fleming who lived in Drumcondra. We were warned that if we made any attempt to escape we would be shot. An armoured car escorted the truck as we were taken to Mountjoy Goal. After being relieved of all of my belongings, I was locked up in cell number

33. This was located on landing 3 of "C" wing. My cellmate was Mr. Walton, the owner of the Walton music store in the city. The Governor of the prison at that time was a Major Munro.

Kevin Barry was held in "D" wing. Kevin was just eighteen years of age and a medical student. He had been involved in a raid on a British Army patrol that had arrived at a bakery in Church Street to collect the bread for their barracks. There was a problem with the raid and he was unfortunately taken prisoner. He was tried and despite his plea to be shot like a soldier, he was sentenced to death by hanging. I will never forget the day of his execution. Feelings were running very high as we attended Mass, which was celebrated by a Father Waters. We were incensed at the idea, not only that one so young should die. Much more so, because they refused his request that he should die a soldier's death. There were extra security precautions in place that day as the authorities anticipated trouble. I was told to report to the prison doctor and the warder began pushing me along for no reason, so I turned and punched him. I was promptly paraded before the governor and awarded fourteen days in solitary confinement on a diet of bread and water. The solitary cells were located in the basement of the building and were known as "The Dungeons." The prison authorities were puzzled by the fact that I looked healthier after solitary than I did before. What they didn't know of course was that my comrades were smuggling food out of the dining hall. They would then put it into a tin can and using a long piece of string they would lower the can out of the window until it reached the outside of my cell window. I would then reach out my hand and pull the tin inside and eat the contents.

On returning to "C" wing, they told me that my new CO was Commandant Rory O'Moore of the 5th Cycling Corps 3rd Battalion. There was a sombre mood in the whole prison following the execution of Kevin Barry, and the mood was sadder with the news that the son of Peader Doyle, one of our inmate colleagues had been killed in the Dublin Mountains while trying to avoid arrest. This was often a convenient way of covering up a cold-blooded murder. Commandant Tom Barry in Cork had taken decisive counter-measures to this sort of behaviour in his area, resulting in the British being more careful about murdering prisoners. All it did was to strengthen our resolve to carry on the fight to the finish, regardless of the consequences. The commanding officer decided that we should start a hunger strike. The word went out to friends and family outside and before long a very large crowd gathered outside of the prison, saying rosaries, singing hymns and waving handkerchiefs. This escalated into a general strike in Dublin and it took a battalion of troops and two tanks to disperse them.

Maurice and Joe Twomey of the Tallaght Battalion were dump keepers. In other words, they held a store of arms and ammunition in secret, ready for use by the IRA. They informed the CO of its location, who decided that it could be put to good use by those still free. So he drew up a map and told me that as I was only held on suspicion of being in the IRA, I should agree to have my fingerprints and photo taken, which would allow me to be released. The British had begun to release the hunger strikers anyway due to the pressure being exerted by those on general strike in the city. They were obviously concerned that a full-scale uprising was likely to occur if something wasn't done to relieve the pressure. It would be useful to note that I was incarcerated merely on suspicion. I had not been tried in a court of law. Not that we recognised British Law anyway. I informed the governor that I was willing to have my fingerprints and photo taken. It was done and I was duly released. The map was in my sock as I walked out of the prison a happy man, thinking of a reunion with my family. I delivered the map to Commandant Paddy Houlihan the Battalion CO, together with a note from Commandant O'Moore, explaining the reason for my release. Commandant Houlihan saw to it that the information reached its final destination. The boys in Tallaght would not go short of the things they needed to carry on the fight.

I was soon back in action. I took part in ambushes in Bolton Street, Frederick Street and Capel Street. Many of the families living locally had a son or a husband serving in the British Army and they didn't take too kindly to what we were up to, particularly those living in Henrietta Street. They would hang out of their windows and shout obscenities at us as we passed by. We were obliged to issue them with a warning about the consequences of informing. That seemed to bring them to their senses and the name-calling stopped.

Two fellows were relieved of their shotguns in a bar in Lower Dominick Street. They had been out hunting and decided to call in to the pub for a pint. I just happened to be there with Mick O'Brien, one of my comrades in arms who lived on Phibsborough Road, and we relieved them of their weapons. The stupidity of some people never ceases to amaze me. The two guns were sent to the Galway Battalion. We also raided a company in Upper Dorset Street named Puller Phibbs Ltd. They were making equipment for use by the Black and Tans. These were, as everyone knows by now, a bunch of criminals sent over by Mr. Churchill to teach us manners. They had Carte Blanche as far as their activities were concerned and they didn't discriminate between man, woman, or child when it came to murder. We burned everything in sight. We also executed an informer in Ballybough who had been the cause of a number of deaths among the volunteers.

Although we felt that we were holding our own against superior odds, there was, nevertheless, great jubilation as a *Truce* was declared. The British were willing to talk. In the meantime, the 1st Battalion took over Hoey's Fields in Mulhuddart and set up camp. We were armed with Lee Enfield Rifles, as well as our personal handguns. Michael Collins and Richard Mulcahy paid us a visit one afternoon. They complimented us on our efficiency with the Lewis Machine Gun. Most IRA units went into training camps following the Truce. Those on holiday or unemployed spent all of their time there. Training was programmed for 7 a.m. (5 a.m. at weekends) and generally went on until 7 p.m. Macready, the British General, complained that advantage was taken of the truce to transform a "disorganised rabble" into a "well-disciplined, well-organised, and well-armed force." The days were long gone when we only had a .22 rifle to practice with. We were now a well-armed, fully trained force, ready to do whatever was required of us. About 100,000 volunteers were on the rolls at the time, some of them had seen active service in France. In addition, many new recruits ("trucileers") now flocked in from hitherto inactive brigades. They were keen for immediate action. Referring to their previous inactivity, Collins's caustic comment was that they had arrears to make up.

This was just another reason why the author's father refused to attend commemoration parades. Indeed it is still noticeable even today at the Arbour Hill commemoration parades, that father's and grandfather's medals are worn that denote membership of the IRA. Those who were in action have a *bar* attached to the ribbon. Those who weren't have no bar. Most of the medals worn at the parade are conspicuous by the absence of a bar.

CHAPTER TWO

FATHER AGAINST SON, BROTHER AGAINST BROTHER

T
hen the greatest tragedy to ever afflict our nation happened. The delegation sent to London headed by Michael Collins to negotiate with the British had signed a Treaty with the British Government. This was against the wishes of Eamon DeValera, the President of the Republic, resulting in a split that effectively left us with two armies. We now had what was to become known as the "Free State Army" and the Irish Republican Army, the latter being the legitimate army of the State, as far as we were concerned. Irishmen in 1921 were now doing the Crown's dirty work for them by killing each other. Brother took up arms against brother, and father against son. Families were divided by a bitterness that would last for generations.

The signing of the Treaty brought to the surface deep-seated differences in Sinn Féin. The Dáil narrowly ratified the Treaty by sixty-four votes to fifty-seven. The debate divided the country and split the army. DeValera pledged that the army would remain loyal to the government and subject to the Dáil. His rhetoric however, was open to different interpretation. The majority of GHQ officers complied with the IRB orders to support the Treaty. The First and Second Southern Divisions under Lynch and O'Malley rejected it.

On January 14th 1922, a provisional government was brought into being to administer the twenty-six counties, before the coming into existence of the Irish Free State on December sixth 1922. This divided the flow of authority, in effect neutering the nominal Dáil. Moreover, the British evacuation had left in its wake a state of chaos: no regular police force; no system of justice; no security; trade and commerce at a standstill; a divided country; a split army.

I got married in 1922 to my best friend's sister. Jim Miller and I had grown up together and his sister Catherine or "Ciss" as she was known, was as committed to the Republican cause as I was. Many a time, she carried my pistol tucked under her dress as we walked through British Army patrols. They were gentlemen in that they didn't search ladies, unlike their Black and Tan counterparts. I was now assigned to the guard in Battalion Headquarters that was located at 44 Parnell Square (now known as Kevin Barry Hall). I was paid the princely sum of £2.10.0. It may not seem much but it was enough to scrape by on. When the split happened, Jim, my brother-in-law and life-long friend joined the Free State Army. He was now the enemy.

I had been married just a few short months when at 11:30 at night there was a knock on my front door. It was Jack Bird, one of the HQ guards who had been sent by the Battalion CO to get me. I took my .45 automatic pistol from under my pillow and reported to HQ, where I found our men on stand-to. Some of the Battalion had taken over the Four Courts building and a raid by the Free Stater's was expected. We set out to gain the freedom of all of Ireland, and we were intent on seeing our dream fulfilled whatever the cost. I helped our weapons instructor, Lieutenant Jim Kelly to load the Lewis Gun in readiness. When we finished we had a cup of tea, and around dawn we heard the first artillery shells being fired at the Four Courts.

Lieutenant Kelly took me with him on a patrol along Parnell Street. We carried the Lewis Gun but didn't encounter anyone and returned to HQ. Sometime later, several lorry loads of Free State troops arrived in the square and began to attack our men in the Fowler Hall in Cavandish Row, on the far side of Parnell Square. They didn't seem to know about us until we opened fire with the Lewis Machine Gun. That soon drove them off. As the day wore on, we came under fire from a house in Lower

Dominick Street. Some of our lads were wounded, including Lieutenant Kelly. I managed to locate exactly where the firing was coming from; and Harry Bodie and myself crept round to the house and got inside without being seen. We slowly made our way up the stairs until we were outside the door of the room where the enemy was located. We called out to them to surrender or we would toss grenades into the room. After a few tense moments, the door slowly opened, we rushed inside to find six of them with their hands held high. On our way back to HQ, we met Commandant Houlihan and Captain Leddy of "A" Company. They were very surprised to see us with six prisoners and their weapons. Then a Crossley Tender appeared and we were forced to take cover behind a lorry that had been knocked out earlier. I spotted another Free Stater and chased him into a shop in Parnell Street where he threw down his rifle and surrendered. I took him back to HQ along with the others.

Captain Bill Oman of "C" company decided to put a column together to try to get to the Four Courts where the men needed help urgently. We all had confession and began the perilous journey to try to relieve our comrades. On the way, we came under heavy fire and Volunteer Markey fell mortally wounded outside of Todd Burn's shop in Henry Street. The fire was so intense that we could go no further and we had to abandon the attempt. We then made our way back to HQ once again. On our return, I got word that my company was fighting in O'Connell Street. I asked permission of the Battalion CO to join them. He gave it, emphasizing that it was at my own risk. I eventually met up with my CO, Captain Garland who was delighted to see me. The fighting grew more and more intense over the next week, but we kept at it, snatching a few minutes sleep when we could.

During a lull in the fighting I got bored, and I decided to leave my mark for future generations to see, so I took careful aim with my rifle and fired a shot at one of the angels at the base of the O'Connell Monument, hitting her in the right breast. Then, to my surprise, I received a visit from my wife and her friend Kathleen Eastwood. How they managed to find me I still don't know today. Anyway, they informed me that my brother-in-law

Jim was with a group of Free Stater's in Clarkes (Bridgemans) Tobacco Shop on the corner of Parnell Street and O'Connell Street and they had run out of ammunition. Captain Garland asked for a volunteer to take a message across O'Connell Street to General HQ in the Imperial Hotel (Clery's Store). I took the message and though the firing was heavy, I managed to reach the Hotel without incident. I presented the message to Cathal Brugha who was accompanied by the Countess Markievicz and several other senior officers. Clarkes garrison was captured and I got permission to return to my unit. There was no facility for holding prisoners, so the usual practice was to disarm them and send them on their way. I ran like blazes with my coat tails flying out behind me and when I reached the safety of the buildings on the other side of the street, I found that my coattail had been shredded by machine-gun fire. I must be mad, I thought to myself as I thanked the good Lord for His protection.

Artillery shells began to fall around us. The gunners seemed to be aiming to hit the hotel where the leaders were located and not having much success. The *Staters* had set up a machine-gun on top of Nelson's Pillar and it was causing us a lot of trouble. These were the ones who tried to get me earlier, I thought. So I sought my CO's permission and climbed out onto the roof of the Edinburgh Insurance Company, opposite the Pillar. They hadn't spotted me and I soon knocked the machine gun and its crew out of action. While I was on the roof, I noticed there was a machine-gun firing from a top floor rear window in Moore Street. I took careful aim and fired. The machine-gunner staggered forward and fell out of the window into the yard below. Years later, I discovered that his brother was one of my neighbours on Mulroy Road in Cabra West.

Then an armoured car arrived on the scene but our lads managed to force it back. Realising that this was only temporary and that the *Staters* would soon pick up the courage to attack us again, we decided to break through the wall of the Insurance Company into the next building. We got through so quickly that it was decided to break through all of the walls in the buildings in between until we reached the Edinburgh Hotel that was just up the Street. It meant that we could keep under cover from fire and from view. There were still a number of guests in the hotel and when we broke through the wall, the look on their faces was priceless. They were all packed and ready to leave and awaiting safe conduct from the St. John Ambulance Brigade. Captain Garland gathered us together for a quick meeting. He suggested that we leave our weapons and escape whatever way we could. One of the guests offered me a soft hat and a bag to carry and when the ambulance men arrived to escort the guests out of the hotel under a white flag, Christy Garrett, (who had also borrowed a coat and hat) and myself, joined those leaving.

We walked out right under the noses of the enemy who were outside the hotel. The ambulance escorted us all as far as the Rotunda Hospital where we shook hands with the guests, returned the borrowed hats and bags, and made our way down Parnell Street. On the way, a young Free State soldier stopped and questioned us. I had left my rifle but held on to my handgun. I put my hand in my pocket and fingered the trigger in case of trouble. But accepting our explanation for being there, he let us go. We fully expected him to have second thoughts and come after us. So we walked as quickly as we could without arousing suspicion and we turned into Parnell Square out of his sight and took to our heels. Christy survived the war and we were later to become neighbours in Mulroy Road. I'm sure that if the man whose brother had been killed had known who was living in the same road with him, there would've been hell to pay.

One week later, I was spotted in Bolton Street by a Captain Joe McConville, an ex-officer of "E" Company who was now with the Free State Army. He had me arrested and taken to the King's Inn, where I was held prisoner for a short while before being taken to Wellington (Griffith) Barracks, where I was interrogated by a Lieutenant Liam Murphy. He was a former member of the Fianna Scouts. His first words on seeing me were, "What Company of the *Irregulars* do you belong to?"

"They weren't irregulars when you were a member," was my reply. "You know me very well!" Just then a Captain Frank Bolster approached me and invited me to join them. There was a promise of rank and rewards if I did. "I can't make a decision like that as a prisoner," I said. "Put me outside the barrack gates and let me decide as a free man."

"That's too much to ask," he said, and had me escorted to the gymnasium where I found a number of my comrades were also being held. I noticed over the next few days that a number of those guarding us were none other than the Northern refugees that we had fed, not so long before. How ironic, I thought.

I discovered also that my brother-in-law Jim Miller was serving in that barracks. He let my wife know what had happened to me and smuggled out several letters to her. He didn't forget that he was treated fairly by our side when he was taken prisoner. We at least had remained friends and didn't let our political differences come between us, an unusual occurrence for the time. My shoes were in a very bad state and he took them to be mended. But on the evening of that very day, we were told to get ready to move. It was 11:30 p.m. when we were loaded onto trucks and taken to Kingsbridge (Heuston) Railway Station. There was no information given as to where we were been taken. It was disappointing to learn that my pal and brother-in-law Jim had joined the Free State Army, but I was utterly astonished to discover that one of the armed guards accompanying us was none other than my uncle Jim Sheridan. He was my father's brother and I had been named after him. This was the tragedy of civil war; families were torn apart and some never recovered from the trauma. I'm delighted to say that we remained friends after the fighting had stopped.

We had been sleeping on mattresses on the floor of the gym, and when the guards lifted them they found parts of Free State uniforms hidden underneath. Jim and other friends had been helping us with a planned escape. There was hell to pay and a Captain Cullen, who was wearing civilian attire, was one of what we called "The Murder Gang" threatened to shoot me there and then. Other uniformed officers restrained him. I was forced to hide under one of the carriage seats however, as he sought me out on the train. I was to discover later that this gangster became Aide-de-Camp to President W. Cosgrave.

The train stopped at Portlaoise Station and we were handcuffed and herded like cattle through the streets in the pouring rain to Maryborough Prison. I was still without shoes and marched to the prison in my stocking feet. Once inside the gaol we were searched and assigned to cells in pairs. My cellmate was Christy McEvoy who had worked as a clerk in the Southern Railways Office in Inchicore in Dublin. He knew my father very well, who also worked there as a coachbuilder.

Next morning, they let us out of our cells into the exercise yard where we discovered that there were a number of IRA lads from Kerry who had been sent there some weeks previous. We decided that we would cause as much disruption as possible. I got hold of a block of wood from the Tailor's Shop and used it to lever the cell door off its hinges. Everyone else followed suit and before long we had every cell door off and leaned them against the wall. It drove the "Screws" mad. We later used the doors to build an altar on which the priest could say Mass. We also started a tunnel and in order to get rid of the clay, etc. we had a mock pillow fight and saw to it that the stuffing was emptied out of the pillows, and was then replaced with sand. We disposed of it later when we had more time. It mostly went into the drains. The lads from Kerry were a great help and really enjoyed what we were doing. The tunnel was finished and lots were drawn as to who would be first out. My number didn't come up but a Doctor Gough was among those whose name was drawn. He got out but was later recaptured. On his way back to prison in the truck he attempted to escape and was gunned down. He died from his wounds. Some nights we would leave a candle burning in an empty cell. The screws would shout for it to be extinguished. When that didn't happen, they would put a burst of gunfire into the cell only to discover that it was unoccupied.

I still had no shoes and I was paraded before the prison governor. To my utter astonishment, he turned out to be none other than Joe Twomey who had been with me in Mountjoy Gaol in 1920. He gave me a pair of army boots and questioned me about my activities during the present conflict. I swore to him that I had had no part in it, particularly since I had been married a short time before. He then offered to release me if I gave him my word of honour that I would not engage in any military action in future. Next day, Peter Cullen, the well-known boxer and I were given tickets for the train to Dublin and set free. We hitched a lift on a railway lorry from Kingsbridge Station to Arran Street, where Peter's wife had a fish stall outside of the Corporation Market. She rushed into his arms when she saw him, and after much hugging and kissing insisted that we all retire to Hara's Pub where she poured glass after glass of whiskey into us.

Having had no food at all so far that day I quickly found myself well inebriated. Peter's wife ordered a taxi, paid the driver, and sent me home. As I got out of the taxi, I noticed that Ciss was standing outside our house chatting with my mother and some other friends. Nobody recognised me until I was right up beside them, as I had grown a beard and moustache. Once they did, there were great shouts of celebration. My wife threw her arms around me, followed by my mother and all who were there. I almost fell over and they thought that I was weak from being in prison, until my wife smelled my breath. I explained what had happened and she just laughed. People stopped me to shake my hand and clapped me on the back. It was a great feeling. It was also great to be home and in the arms of my lovely wife again.

Some weeks later, I was ordered to present myself at a court-martial. Captain Garland and Lieutenant Sean Merrigan questioned me at length about the reason for my release from prison. They were entirely satisfied with my answers and I was exonerated of any wrongdoing and returned to active service.

I was soon up to my old tricks again. An order had been issued to seize all British trucks. Captain Garland and I captured one in Watling Street near to Guinness's Brewery and we took it back to Headquarters in Parnell Square. Later on Jimmy Poynton, Leo Farrell, and I seized an ambulance in Kenilworth Square in Rathmines. There was a running fight with a local doctor outside whose premises the ambulance was parked. He was a well-known British sympathiser and he was armed, so we shot him dead. We took two Webley revolvers away from the ambulance crew and drove the vehicle back to our HQ where it was painted in different colours.

The "Staters" continued to raid my house on a regular basis but I managed to evade them. I was the "Dump" keeper for E&F Companies. They searched high and low for weapons but they never discovered them. If they had, they would've found rifles, handguns and a good supply of grenades. It wasn't unusual to have a flat truck call to my parent's house at 61 Upper Dominick Street with signed authorisation to collect weapons, etc. for other needy units. Generally, the supply went to the West of Ireland where the lads were very active. I usually stayed with Mrs. Ormsby, an aunt of mine when I was on the run. On one occasion, I had just left the house having been tipped off to an impending raid and a Captain Stephen Murphy told my wife and mother that I was listed for execution when they caught up with me. The manager of Monaghan's Pawn Shop in Lower Dominick Street was a Mr. Murray and he proved to be a trusted friend. He stored parcels of arms for us.

In 1923, Frank Aitken issued a ceasefire order. All IRA units were to lay down their arms. We had lost. The Free State Army, together with the help of the British, had won the day. Michael Collins was dead. He had been killed in an ambush in Beal Na mBláth in his own home, County of Cork. Many more were dead on both sides and all for nothing, as far as I was concerned. Families had been wrecked; leaving a legacy of bitterness that would last for generations. I was not sorry that the fighting was finally over. But I deeply regretted not having achieved the one thing we set out to do. Our country was still not "Free."

A new political party called Fianna Fáil was founded by Éamon De Valera and in 1932, I became a member soon after its formation, and was a member of the Erskine Childers Cumann. When the party contested the elections, I acted as Personating Officer for Sean T. O'Kelly who had played a major role in the War. He was later to rise to the highest office in the land, that of President of Ireland. The voting station just happened to be in St. Mary's, my old school. I was very active in the party, lending it my full support. Mr. Kelly made a solemn promise to me that he would see to it that I got my old job back. I had been dismissed from the Department of Post and Telegraphs during the Civil War. That promise was never kept. I was to discover to my utter disgust that politicians promise much and deliver little. I wouldn't have minded so much if I had approached him but I hadn't. I never asked for anything except to be treated fairly.

The government founded a "Volunteer Force" in 1934 and I became a member of the Dublin/ E. Wicklow Regiment 1st Field Company Supply and Transport. We paraded in what is now known as Clancy Barracks, weeknights, and Sundays and fired our weapons courses in Gormanstown Camp in County Meath. The camp is still occupied today. They later transferred me to the 5th Engineers Company in Portabello (now Cathal Brugha) Barracks. It was here I met Vivian De Valera (Dev's son), and Matty Feehan, along with several others who formed the nucleus of the 26th Battalion.

I found myself out of work in 1942 and contacted Bill Corri, my old Company Commander, and asked him if it were possible for me to transfer to the regular army. When it was discovered that I had ten children, I was refused. So much for serving my country! Many of my old comrades found themselves in the same predicament and bemoaned the fact that ex-members of the IRA were being discriminated against where job opportunities were concerned. The jobs in government departments seemed to be monopolised by Free Staters.

I thought long and hard about my situation and desperate to support my family, I decided to join the British Army. A World War was in progress and the British were not interested in whether I was ex-IRA or what. All they were concerned about was whether I could do the job. Many of my old comrades were amazed that I should've even considered joining. But they later accepted that I had little choice. Indeed, more than a few of them followed suit. My only concern was to feed my family. After training, I was posted to the Royal Pioneer Corps and served in North Africa, Sicily, and Italy.

Following demobilisation in 1946, I was offered a job with a company in Leicestershire. The company offered to find me a house; I returned home and asked my wife to come back to England with me to get the house set up for the family. The older family members would look after the younger ones until things were ready for them in England. We got as far as the Boat Train at Westland Row Station and just before the train pulled out, my daughters began to cry. That set my wife off and finding the trauma of parting too much to bear, she got off the train, saying she couldn't leave the children. That was the end of what I thought was the beginning of a new life for all of us. So I got off the train, too, and went home with her." Here ends my father's personal account.

CHAPTER THREE

MY EARLY YEARS

The human memory is a wonderful thing. After spending seventy years on this earth, I can still remember snatches from the time I lived with my family on St. Jarlath Road in what is still called "Old Cabra" on the north side of Dublin. I was born on the twelfth of October 1938 in the Rotunda Hospital, Parnell Street, just off the top of O'Connell Street. My mother told me much of what I know now about those years, as I got older. She told me for example, that Éamon De Valera's son was the consultant obstetrician, and he asked her what name she had chosen for me. She replied that she hadn't yet decided, whereupon he suggested that she call me after his father. Being a Republican and an ardent admirer of "Dev," she decided to do just that.

I can recall sitting on the curb-side near the number twelve bus stop, which was close to the traffic island that is there now with the shrine to "Our Lady" on it. My father was late and had missed the bus. One of our neighbours, who normally sat beside him on their way home from work, told me this and offered to bring me home. I wasn't having any of his stories and refused to budge.

He called in to my mother on his way home to tell her about my father, and where she could find me. She almost had a heart attack. There were so many children in the house; she hadn't noticed that I was missing, especially as she had a new baby to care for. She quickly despatched one of my sisters to get me. A short time later, she arrived at the bus stop and dragged me kicking and screaming all the way home. There was no consoling me by all accounts, as my mother tried to explain why my father was late and that he'd be home soon. One might be forgiven for thinking that my behaviour was that of an only child. But, I had been born into a large working class family of twelve children and I was ninth in line. That's not quite accurate actually. While there were twelve of us in the family, the eldest was a half brother. My father had a relationship with another woman. He fathered a child who was three months older than my eldest sister. Why my mother didn't throw him out, I'll never know. Far from doing that… she took the child in when he was six years of age after his mother abandoned him. He was treated as a brother by all of us; this, despite our knowing that something wasn't quite right when it came to birthday time for him and my sister Alice. He told me the whole story just before he died at eighty-three years of age.

My mother, like many women of her day, actually had twenty-three pregnancies. She lost at least two children in the four years that separated my older brother and myself. She certainly earned her sainthood. My sister Olive was born eleven months after me, and she was now the baby of the family. We were what became known as "Irish twins." So there's no explaining why my father took to me in the way that he did. We were great friends all through my life. He spent more time talking to me about things in general and his army service in particular, than any of my brothers and sisters. I hero-worshipped him anyway, and he obviously appreciated that. I think that the gap in years between my brother Jim and myself allowed my father to spend more time with me as a baby than he did with any of the rest of my brothers. Because of this, I became so attached to him that he couldn't go anywhere without me following him. If he wanted to slip out for a pint or just leave the house on his own for any reason, he would leave his coat upstairs and tell me he was just going up to get something from the bedroom. He would then throw his jacket out of the bedroom window, come down again and tell me he had to get some coal for the fire from the outside coal-shed. He would then collect his coat from the garden and run down the road. I got wise to his tactics after a short while and I would insist on going outside with him.

So, he then took to bringing me up to bed, he would lie down beside me and twirl my hair, which I loved, and it would put me to sleep. I got used to that also and more times than not, my father would fall asleep instead. I got a terrible time from my siblings over this when my mother and father would reminisce about it, among other things as we sat 'round the fire, years later.

I became known as "Daddy's Blue-eyed Boy," and I was subjected to some terrible verbal abuse. There was worse to follow at school. I became introverted and shy as a result, and I would blush terribly in the company of strangers, particularly women.

As I stated earlier, my father had been a member of "E" company 1st Battalion Old IRA, during the War of Independence. He stayed with the Republicans during the Civil War and kept his handgun fully loaded in an air-vent in his bedroom. As the family numbers increased, he and my mother moved into a smaller room (forgetting the gun) and gave up the larger one to my sisters. Alice, the eldest was searching around one morning and found the gun. She pointed it at May, another sister and said, "Stick em up," she pulled the trigger and the gun went off with a tremendous roar. When the screaming stopped, it was found that the bullet had penetrated the bedpost just inches from my other sister's head. My mother went ballistic and insisted that my father get rid of the gun. He took it with him next morning and threw it into the river Liffey.

My godmother, Mrs. Alice Swords, lived across the road from our house. She looked after me most of the time, so my mother said. It always amused her that my godmother used me like the Artful Dodger in Charles Dickens's *Oliver Twist* to steal vegetables from Reid's shop on the Cabra Road. The footpath outside of the shop was very wide indeed (it now has a Service Road cut out of it) and Mr. Reid used to get his staff to display the fruit and vegetables on raised boxes on the footpath. It looked like a carpet to all intents and purposes. Mrs. Swords would park my pram right up against the side of the display. It was just the right height for me to reach out my hand and lift whatever goods were nearest. She would then come out of the shop with her bag of messages in hand and put it into the pram covering whatever I had taken. Whatever it was, my mother told me later that I was the best-fed kid for miles around. I wonder if that's why I still love vegetables today, and have most of my own teeth and hair. The earliest photo of me certainly bears out what my mother said. I have a belly on me like an old beer drinker.

I don't have any memory of leaving Cabra. But I do remember that the next place we lived in was not nearly as nice. It seems that my father was out of work, perhaps due to a strike, and as there was no dole in those days, he had to find some way of earning money to keep the wolf from the door. These were desperate times and service to the nation counted for nothing when it came to men of his ilk looking for a job. Many of the employers were British or Protestant anyway, so there was no hope of them employing an ex-IRA man. This included his ex-employer in the Marble Trade. The newspapers at the time carried job advertisements that stated, "No Catholics need apply." He was prepared to do anything and spent many long hours seeking some sort of employment.

The Second World War had broken out and like many Irish men before him, he joined the British Army. This didn't sit well with his old comrades, who were of the group of die-hards that had not accepted the *Treaty* with Britain. His only interest was feeding his family and paying the household bills, and since they weren't offering financial help or employment, he felt he had no choice but to do what he was doing. After his basic training, he was posted to North Africa and was involved in the Desert Campaign with the 8th Army. He went on to Sicily and Italy after that. My eldest brother Paddy and my sister May left around this time to work in England. Paddy went to London and May worked in a cotton mill in Oldham, Lancashire.

During his time in North Africa, my mother received a telegram from the British War Office stating that he was missing in action, presumed killed. She, naturally, was in a hell of a state; she could not see how she could keep up with the rent on the house and feed a large brood. So she handed back the keys and

moved into rooms in a tenement house in Bolton Street. The house stood on the site where the extension to Bolton Street College of Technology now stands. I'm not sure if the rent was in arrears anyway, but I do know that my father had been on strike for thirteen weeks at one stage without any strike pay, and this would certainly account for the dilemma my mother found herself in. No one has ever said this, though it seems logical to me. Dublin Corporation had a reputation as one of the most egregious landlords in the city. They didn't hesitate to evict defaulting tenants even from the filthy tenements that they owned, and she wouldn't have wanted the embarrassment of being evicted. People of that era were so private about things like that. They would've been ashamed to admit to anyone that they were in financial trouble.

That strike was a blessing in disguise for me, though. My father got some odd jobs to do for a doctor who lived in Ballsbridge, before he joined the British Army. He had a son who was about my age and the doctor gave my father some of his son's cast-off clothing. At one stage, I went around dressed in a full naval captain's uniform, complete with cap. My brother Jim used to go nuts when my sister Rosaleen would tell him that he went to school dressed as a Japanese General.

Six weeks after we moved, another telegram arrived announcing that they found him and he was on a hospital ship heading for Tripoli. I learned much later in life that he went to help a pal who had been hit and as he bent down to pick him up, a shell landed beside them, blowing him and his pal quite a distance into the desert. His unit moved on and a following unit found him. His pal had been blown to smithereens. When they found my father, he was bleeding from every orifice and it was touch and go as to whether he would survive. My mother was, needless to remark, overjoyed. I was too young at that time to appreciate the significance of it all.

However, I wasn't too young to remember being called by my brother Jim one day and him saying, "Look... look," as he pointed to the sky. What I witnessed is still as clear in my mind today as if it had just happened. There were two planes, one chasing the other, with its guns blazing away. I later learned that it was a Spitfire chasing a German bomber. I believe that the bomber crashed into the sea near Howth.

My mother told me that I accused my uncle, James Byrne of being responsible for my father going away in the first place. All the family called him Jamesie. He had lost a leg in the First World War, while serving in France with the Royal Dublin Fusiliers. He was wounded on the Somme in July 1916. He had helped my father with filling in the forms for joining up. My father had brought me along to 61 Upper Dominic Street where the Byrnes, among others of our family lived, including my Grandparents and I witnessed what went on between them. It was an old tenement, and various relations completely occupied it.

The Campbell's lived on the ground floor, the Byrnes on the first floor, then the Ryan's on the second floor and finally my father's parents on the top floor front. All of these were closely related, i.e., brothers and sisters, cousins and aunts, with their respective wives, husbands and children. It still puzzles me even today as to why my grandfather, who had a good job as a coach-builder with the Great Southern Railways, lived in a tenement.

Jamesie was quite a character and liked his pint of stout. The British Medical people had issued him with two wooden legs. One of these was a spare. So he pawned it for drink money. I wonder if my uncle is the same man that Timmy "Duckegg" Kirwan speaks of in his account of tenement life, when he says that he witnessed a man pawning his wooden leg so as to have money to buy drink. It is such an unusual story, that I feel it most likely was Jamsie. His wife used to hide the other leg to prevent him from going to the pub. When she wouldn't tell him where it was, he would hop outside, hold on to the iron railings that surrounded the basement of the old house to get his balance right, before hopping across the Road to Levy's Pub that was almost directly opposite. She would then have to bring him his leg so that he could get home again.

I had been born into a house with electricity, running water, a bath and toilet and gardens front and back. How my father managed to secure a house in what at that time would have been on the outskirts of the city I will reveal later. The tenements were something strange and frightening to me. The only lighting was by gas and this I found fascinating. I can remember seeing the "Lamplighter" doing the rounds on his bike and lighting up Mountjoy Street as he went from lamp-post to lamp-post. Years later, I would come to appreciate the song entitled, "The Old Lamplighter." There was no lighting on the stairs in the house, and it was an eerie experience to have to walk up those stairs at night. It had a unique pungent odour that would immediately assault your nostrils as soon as you opened the hall door. The walls were painted with what was commonly known as "Red Raddle." This was a strong mixture of lime and water with a colour added. It not only served to colour the walls, it also kept some of the vermin at bay, and it was very difficult to remove if you got it on your clothes.

My mother told the family that two maids had burned to death in the upper rooms in Dominick Street. Fires were not uncommon in these dilapidated old Georgian houses. My younger brother Bill swears that he saw the spectres of both of these ladies. But he firmly believes that they watched over him and kept him safe from the other ghosts that occupied the place. Because of the dark, and the likelihood of seeing something you didn't bargain for, we would open the hall-door wide; then, using the available light from the street, try to reach the top floor before it closed. He held the record for getting there before the door slammed shut.

In those days, people were obsessed with Ghosts, Spirits, and the "Banshee." The Banshee is an Irish word that translates into English as "fairy woman." She is reputed to follow the old Irish families and forewarn them of an impending death. She is said to be a very old woman with long grey hair and grizzled features. Those people who claim to have seen her, state that she would sit on a window-sill or a nearby wall, close to the chosen family. She would wail and comb her hair as a warning.

Death would visit that family very soon afterwards. Alternatively, a picture would fall off the wall in the family home. The nail would still be there and the picture wire would be intact. This was another sign. I heard so many of these stories growing up, that I became frightened of the dark. A cold sweat would break out on my forehead and back as I walked passed certain dark alleyways or entered a dark hallway. Was it due to the fact, I wonder, that I was more attuned to the spirit world as a child than I am now? On a very odd occasion, I do get that eerie feeling in certain places, and I know when my family or close friends are in trouble. I am prompted to pick up a phone and call to see them when this happens. The dark doesn't frighten me anymore. I out-grew that fear before I reached adolescence. In fact, I cannot sleep properly unless the room is dark. I came to realise, as I grew older that "Spirits" cannot hurt us. Except the ones you find in a bottle.

People used to entertain each other with ghost stories in those days. A good story-teller could keep a group enthralled for a whole evening. I remember on one winter's evening, listening to one of the "bigger boys" telling a group of us gathered under a lamppost in Cabra West about the film he had just been to see.

He told the story right from start of the film to the end. He was so good at it that we felt as though we had actually seen the film ourselves.

Although I do not place any credence in the stories about the Banshee, I cannot deny that on the night before my mother died, I heard what I thought was a dog howling. I was an officer in the Reserve Defence Forces at the time. I was on duty in Griffith Barracks (the same barracks where my father had been held prisoner, all those years ago) when I heard the awful mournful howling. I asked a colleague if he could hear it. He gave me a very puzzled look and said that he couldn't hear anything. Next day, I had word that my mother had passed away.

It amazes me when I think of what the people endured while living in these rat-infested tenements. The unbearable stench, the single toilet, in the yard, one water tap and the "slop" bucket for nighttime use, which someone discreetly emptied next morning ,or not so discreetly in some cases. It was not uncommon to find human excreta scattered about the yards. I can testify of this, for as young as I was, I can still remember this awful scene. Although, for some reason I don't know of, there was a second tap and sink outside of the Ryan's door on the third floor landing in No. 61. The death toll in these horrible places from diphtheria, tuberculosis, scarlet fever, and typhoid, etc. was at unbelievably high levels, particularly among the children.

Because of the filth lying about the yard, Mrs. Campbell would tie the ends of her washed bed-sheets across two lines hammock style, so that they didn't trail on the ground and pick up dirt. One lazy "get," (the word "get" is peculiar to Dublin people, while "git" is used in England,) who lived in the top floor back room, emptied his bucket out of the window. This practice was not at all uncommon. The contents included "brown trout" (excrement) and it landed in the sheets. While this may bring a laugh, it explains nevertheless, the mentality of some who lived in the tenements. It is hardly surprising then, that human excrement was littering the ground.

I cannot understand why my mother would move into such an awful place as Bolton Street. I can only assume that she fell

31

into arrears with the rent and had to leave our house in Cabra. My father had already left home to join the British Army. Economic reasons forced him to take the pragmatic approach, like many other Irishmen before him. She must have been in a desperate situation, especially when she received the telegram informing her that he was missing in action. It wasn't long before the younger ones in the family contracted "scabies" (which was endemic in the tenements). People used to blame returning soldiers for this. That might have been true after the Great War, when men had numerous diseases in the trenches, and returned home crawling with lice, etc. But it was not the case in this instance; particularly as the war was still in progress, and the men were still serving at the front.

The cure for scabies was quite radical. We first went to the South Dublin Union. This had been a workhouse that had been converted into a hospital for the poor people of Dublin. I can still remember arriving outside of the gates in an ambulance. The high walls and locked entrance were frightening to see, and we felt as though we would never see our mother again. Once there, we were assessed and stripped of all our clothing. They then shaved our heads and sent us to the "Iveagh Baths," off High Street, where we got into a bath of very hot water and left to soak. Next, the nurses took us out, dried off, and painted us from head to toe with an ointment that burned like hell. Then they gave us a gown to wear that promptly stuck to the ointment, making life even more uncomfortable, before we returned to the hospital. This treatment was repeated a number of times in the succeeding days. I loathed the porridge that they gave us for breakfast. It was really thick, and there was no sugar to sweeten it or milk to thin it down. Occasionally they gave me a boiled egg. That was a real treat. But they flatly refused to serve this every day, when I asked.

While most tenement people were happy to move out to the new housing estates, it took some time before the tenement ethos moved out of the people. There were some who just couldn't set-tle in areas such as Cabra West, and returned to live in a tene-ment. Cabra is approximately four miles from the city centre yet there were those who felt that this was too far away from what they had become accustomed to, and they just couldn't take it. I do remember one family in particular whose mother died shortly after moving to Cabra West, blaming her death on the move and vowing to go back to "town" as soon as they could.

Professor Aalen of Trinity College states, with regret, that much of what's been learned about tenement life has been filtered through the minds of outsiders looking in. He explains also that only through oral history can we reliably capture the life experiences of tenement folk. Since the tenements continued on into the late forties and to some extent, dare I say it, into the fifties, I trust that the experiences related here will help in some small way to fill the gap. For we, as a family, continued to visit our relatives in Dominick Street and Bolton Street.

When visiting my grandmother I noticed, as evening fell, that she would turn a tap on the wall at the side of the mantelpiece, above which projected a swan-neck shaped piece of pipe with a white globe, called a mantle, on the end of it. She held a lighted match to this and it lit the gas flowing into the globe, giving light. The globe was very delicate and if one wasn't careful when lighting it, one could easily damage it and it would have to be replaced. When lit, its area of cover was very limited and there were dark shadows in the corners of the room. This, together with the light from the fire lent an air of mystique to the surroundings. On the one hand, it was warm and homely, and on the other, it felt ghostly. Only the spirits of the dead could live in the dark recesses of the shadows, and if you looked hard enough, you could see the misty form of those spirits beckoning to you. On more than one occasion, I felt the hair rise on the back of my neck and a quick shiver would run down my spine causing me to shudder. "Has someone just walked over your grave?" my grandma would ask as she touched my hair smiling benevolently.

"N... no grandma," I would lie, putting on a brave face, averting my eyes, not wanting to get the reputation of a scaredy-cat.

Most of the tenants used buckets (mentioned above) for urinating into after dark. Perhaps it was because of the lack of light on the stairs. But I believe that it had more to do with their reluctance to go all the way down to the yard in the cold of the night. So they left the bucket on the landing. One night when I was with my father visiting my grandmother, I asked to go to the bathroom! "Sure use the bucket," said my grandmother. I refused and so my father took me down the stairs in his arms to the toilet in the back yard. The dark didn't mask the obnoxious smell and I refused to enter the cubicle. My father felt compelled to take me home to Cabra. Weeks later, when my mother was visiting, my grandmother told of my behavior, and asked how the little "Duke" was. My mother used that name for me from then on.

My family tried its level best to keep the yard and the toilet clean. But there was no way of controlling entry to the house or its surrounds, because the hall door could not be locked. Vagabonds could enter during the hours of darkness and they weren't too fussy about where they defecated. Many of the tenement dwellers were sympathetic to the homeless (and there were lots) and allowed them to sleep on the landings and in the hallways at night. It at least gave them shelter from the elements. But it did nothing for the general hygiene, as it increased the occupancy of the house dramatically at night. Another good reason for using the bucket! This did not help the situation were the toilets were concerned. There was no agreed roster for cleaning the toilet either, and when it got blocked no one wanted to put it right. So it overflowed, and it would remain like that until someone finally gave in and unblocked it. All of this added to the risk of infection and this, coupled with the rampant malnutrition, resulted in a very high death rate.

The Campbell's who lived on the ground floor of Number 61 were related to my maternal grand- mother. Johnny, the father, was a Belfast man and he had an accent that was a typical town centre rasping type. He missed nothing during the day because the door to his room was always open and he would sit there watching everyone who came and went. My father didn't like him and only tolerated him because he was a Catholic. Many years later I learned why. My grandparents were not married, and Johnny Campbell had made the mistake of referring to my father and his sister as bastards. The use of that word by anyone in those days, whether true or not, was suicidal. Had he been a younger man, my father would have beaten the living daylights out of him. But he did warn him that he ran the risk of severe sanctions if he ever repeated what he had said. So we kids were told to ignore him, and not to go into his room, visiting. His wife was a lovely woman. Her name was Byrne, and she was warm and friendly, and always smiling. This was a common feature of tenement dwellers. Despite the desperate plight they found themselves in, there was always a smile and great humour. Perhaps this is where "Dublin Wit" was born.

Later in life I informed my father that I was going to research the family tree. He told me that I would discover certain information that would be best kept to myself. When I asked him to tell me what this was, as it might just save me save me unnecessary hours of work, he refused. I was to discover much later, that we certainly had a cupboard full of skeletons. It turned out that my grandmother had been married to the foreman of a brewery in Chapelizod, in County Dublin. He was violent and beat her regularly. She left him after he threw pepper in her face, before giving her a good hiding. Her eyes suffered badly as a result of this attack. Beating women was a common occurrence in those days also. The drunken thugs, whom they had the misfortune to marry, treated women appallingly. I cannot think of a more cowardly act than a man doing what this one did.

I was listening to a friend of mine delivering a lecture at a meeting recently and he stated, "The only time a man ought to raise his hand to a woman or a child should be to bless them." How profound this statement is.

She met my grandfather, a gentle man, who treated her like a lady. He also looked the part and presented a very elegant figure in his bowler hat. It was the custom in those days for tradesmen and professionals to wear a bowler hat. This distinguished them from the labourer, who wore a flat cap. They fell in love and set up home together, despite the fact that she was considerably older than he. The implications of this are enormous, when you think about it. No one pays any attention to unmarried couples living together these days. But imagine how it must have been for them in the early part of the 20th century, particularly as my grandfather sang with the choir in Halston Street chapel, and this would have brought him into close contact with the clergy.

My father grew up a tough man as a result of his "illegitimacy" to give it the legal term that was used until recently. It was a bit like the song "*A boy named Sue*" sung by that great Country & Western singer, Johnny Cash. On more than a few occasions it was as the song goes, "the mud and the blood and the beer," as he defended his and his father's honour. His father was a coachbuilder, as mentioned earlier, and worked for the Great Southern Railways. He was also a very talented man with a wonderful singing voice. He won the gold medal at the Feis Ceol in 1900 (the year my father was born). I learned in later years that he had performed during the interval at the Abbey Theatre. He also sang on the same show as Count John McCormack, the renowned Irish Tenor, who had the title "Count" conferred on him by the Pope as a reward for singing at the Eucharistic Congress, which was held in Dublin in 1932. My grandfather was a Baritone, so there would've been no conflict with the "great man." The Rotunda, which was originally the lecture hall of the maternity hospital, had been converted into a theatre in those days, and he performed there also. I can just about recall being at a show in the Rotunda with my parents. Afterwards, we called into Larry Sherby's Fish & Chip Shop in Lower Dominick Street on our way home. Larry's was a very popular shop and had booths where the customer could sit and enjoy the delicious fare that he produced.

The theatre was one of the treats that the tenement people looked forward to. They were to be found in what was commonly known as the "Gods." This was the highest gallery, at the back of the theatre. My father decided to go the whole hog and bought seats for my mother and him in the stalls, which are the front of the house and on the ground floor. My mother had borrowed a large, wide-brimmed hat from a friend and she felt that she really looked the part of the moneyed lady. Friends in the "Gods" spotted her and began to shout down at her. When my mother tried to ignore them, they began throwing things at her. She was mortified at the time, but she could laugh at it years later.

Tenement life was the cause of my paternal grandfather's death, through cardiac failure brought on by influenza, at the age of fifty-nine. This was not uncommon in the damp draughty conditions in which he lived. He managed to last a bit longer than my mother's father however, who died as a result of tuberculosis, which was rampant among tenement dwellers. Billy Miller was a young sailor. At thirty-six years of age, he spent the last days of his short life in the hospital at the Pigeon House in Ringsend. It is said that Billy was a protestant, and that he came from a fairly well-off family. He met my grandmother, who was catholic, and they fell in love. His family, in a fit of pique, refused to attend their wedding. On the birth of their first child, so it is told, they offered to pay for the children's education and see to it that they wanted for nothing as they grew up, if he would raise them in the protestant faith. He refused and they had no further dealings with him until he lay dying. They made it known that they wanted him buried in Mount Jerome, a protestant cemetery. He wasn't having any of that, so he changed his religion and became a Catholic. He was a very good-living man by all accounts, and despite his protestant beliefs, would insist that the children attend confession on Saturday evening. They then had to come straight home afterwards, and they would not be allowed outside of the door until Sunday morning to attend Mass and receive Communion.

The Byrne's were related to my mother's mother. A little woman called, "The Nan Byrne" occupied one of the rooms. She read fortunes and had clients come to her from all over the city. Many of these were women, who travelled across town from the wealthy suburbs. I remember her very well. She had a Harpsichord in her room and she would let us kids play it whenever we came to visit her. She would ask Jim and me to go over the road to the Model Stores and get her supply of snuff. She let us sample it one day. We sneezed for ages afterwards and it cured us of asking again.

She was great fun and taught me the rhyme, "Holly and Ivy went to fair. Holly brought Ivy home by the hair. Holly and Ivy went for a glass. Holly brought Ivy home by the arse." Another one went as follows, "A ch ch chee cauliflower sittin' on the grass, up came a bumble bee and stung her on the a ch ch chee." My mother roared laughing when I repeated them for her, but told me not to say it to my father, as he might get annoyed. He was very strait-laced in many ways, which puzzled me, considering what I was to discover later in life about my brother Paddy. My father had an affair after he had married my mother and Paddy was the result. In my whole life I never heard my father swear or use bad language of any description. He wouldn't tolerate it under his roof and as a result, none of the family ever used foul language within our home. Nor, for that matter, did I ever hear him argue with my mother or raise a hand to any of us. He was unique among the men of his day. When he gave an order, you just carried it out and there was no dispute.

My Aunt Molly and Uncle Sean were my grandmother's children by her husband. Molly used to look after us like an old mother hen. She would inspect our heads for "Nits," and make sure that we were kept free of infestation. Sean was a quiet man and kept very much to himself. He worked for a potato merchant called Lambe Brothers. They had their yard in Mountjoy Street, just across from the house where they lived. Molly always insisted on being called Gaffney, her father's name, despite the hard life that she had with him. After our family moved to England in the fifties, she became a patient in Portrane Hospital, her condition as a result of depression. On hearing this, my parents returned from England to visit her with the intention of taking her back with them. She refused and no amount of persuasion would change her mind. I accompanied my parents on that visit. It was heartbreaking to witness the mental decline she was suffering. She was surrounded by some seriously ill people, and a nurse explained that she ought not to be there. But try as we might, she just would not agree to go to England. We went away frustrated and feeling powerless by her refusal. Not many months later, we were back there again, this time to remove her remains to Glasnevin Cemetery. My uncle Sean had left the house in Upper Dominick Street and seemed to disappear without trace. Before he left, he disposed of all of the family records that were kept in a chest at the end of my grandparent's bed. My eldest brother Paddy, finally found him in the Iveagh Hostel, off High Street where he died, to the best of my knowledge. Here was an example of the effects of the break-up of a closely-knit family. While my aunt and uncle had the rest of us around them, they were fine. But once the companionship and protection of the family was removed, physical and mental deterioration set in, finally resulting in death.

The Ryan's were my mother's sister Peggy, who was married to Michael Ryan. He had been a Sergeant Major in the Free State Army. He was in charge of the Detention Centre on the Curragh Camp in County Kildare and allowed a prisoner to escape. An Army court-martial demoted him to Corporal and he never got over it. His army buddies knew him as "Cushy File." He was also quite a man for the ladies, so my aunt Peggy told me, and he didn't care too much about who knew. That included her. He had the gall to bring one or two home with him, so she said. When he retired from the army, he worked as a labourer for a construction company. There was no health and safety organisation in those days, and on a very windy day he was blown off the scaffolding surrounding the "Bus Árus" (Central Bus Station). He fell several floors and cracked his skull, suffering a stroke shortly afterwards, that left his face disfigured. Safety nets were installed following his accident.

The company gave him a couple of hundred pounds and promised him a job for life if he kept it out of court. He agreed and they quickly found a way of getting rid of him anyway. He proceeded to drink all the money. My aunt didn't get to see one penny of it. That's how it was in the "Good old days." Women were the property of their husbands. If my memory serves me correctly, they were no more than "chattel" according to the law, and they were treated as such. No one interfered between man and wife, no matter what the circumstances. If the woman went home to her parents, she was told to go back to her husband.

"You've made your bed, now you lie in it," she'd be told. Or, if she went to the priest and told him that she was denying her husband his "Conjugal Rights" because of his bad behaviour, she was refused absolution for her sins. Things have changed for the better, I am pleased to say.

One night, my aunt Peggy woke to find that the floor was on fire. Embers fell out of the grate, rolled across the hearth and set light to the tinder-dry floorboards. She woke "Mikie" and told him to get out of bed and get some water to put the fire out. He, in a half daze from sleep and too much booze, jumped out of the bed and stood on the burning floorboards. Letting out an expletive, he ran out onto the landing where their tap and sink were. When he didn't reappear, my aunt called out to him asking what the delay was, as the fire was getting worse. "Eff that," he yelled, "I burned me effen foot and I'm cooling it off." He had his foot in the sink with the cold water running on it. She had to jump over the fire and get a pot, fill it with water while he complained that he needed it for his foot, rush back into the room and douse the flames. On another occasion, he complained to her about the "Hoppers" (fleas) that were in the bed. These were nasty little things that were brown in colour and sucked your blood when they bit. The more they sucked, the fatter they got. She said that everybody had them and she had killed some earlier. "Is that right," said he, "well, there's a few thousand at the funeral then and they're all wearing hobnail boots." He was quite the comic and his favourite song was, "The Ragman's Ball," which he sang at weddings and funerals.

Funerals could be more fun than weddings. There was a wake being held in one of the rooms. I'm not sure if it was when the Nan Byrne died. Anyway, the booze flowed freely; throughout the evening more and more people arrived to pay their respects. Pretty soon the room was full, so they moved the coffin into the corner to create more space. Someone had the bright idea to put the lid on the coffin and used it as a bar. It was done and a jolly good singsong got under way.

On another occasion at a different wake, the corpse was laid out on the bed and my grandmother tied a piece of twine around the deceased person's foot and looped it over the lower bar on the iron bedstead. As the evening wore on and the visitors got more and more inebriated, she pulled the string. The leg of the corpse rose and the crowd, on seeing this, made a mad dash to get out of the room. One of the women broke her arm when she got jammed in the doorway by others rushing to get past her. Weddings and funerals attracted gatecrashers; smart-alecks looking for free drink and entertainment. This often resulted in a "ruggy-up," (fight) and that proved to be even more entertaining. At one wedding, there were so many guests jammed into the room where the breakfast was being held that the floor collapsed and descended like a lift, and everybody wound up in the cellar.

After recovering from his injuries, my father arrived back home on leave from the British army. Seeing the conditions under which we were living, he went to visit an old IRA friend who worked in the housing department of Dublin Corporation. They arranged for us to move to the new scheme of houses in Cabra West. Now you know how we got the house in Old Cabra in the first place. Well, what are friends for?

Charles Darwin is quoted as saying, "A class will exist in the crowded poor districts, indifferent to insalubrities, indifferent to their surroundings, and sunk in ignorance. Even when change means improvement this class abhors it... ...they prefer the old insanitary rookeries to the modern comforts of block dwellings."

This may be true of some, but it would be unjust to generalise. All of the people who moved to Cabra were from the slums of Dublin. The vast majority of them were glad to be rid of the filthy hovels that they had been forced to live in through economic circumstances. They appreciated their new homes and set about improving the surroundings by cultivating their gardens, etc. I doubt if Mr. Darwin had studied the situation in Dublin. It seems as though he was referring to the tower blocks in London. That being so, perhaps it would have served all concerned better if he had understood that the people were fearful of being herded into vast ghettos. With so many living in close proximity to each other, the conditions would rapidly deteriorate to the same level, or worse, than what had been left behind. The Ballymun project is a clear representation of what I mean.

Bolton Street still holds certain fond memories for me, although I never realised until I read in a book by Kevin Kearns that it was famous for its brothels. During our time there, the Nazi's bombed the North Strand. It was claimed later by them that it was a mistake. But that fooled nobody. Everyone thought that they were aiming for Amiens Street (now Connolly) Railway Station, where the trains ran north to Belfast, and the bombs overshot the intended target. Although I was only three years of age, I remember being taken to the air-raid shelter that stood in Kings Inns Street, close to our house. The shelter reeked of urine and excrement. Those who had nowhere else to relieve themselves used it as a toilet. I could see the beam of the searchlights as they scanned the sky, looking for the offending airplanes.

I had fun playing with my pal Sheamie Towel, who lived at the top of the house. We had been born on the same day in 1938, in the same hospital and almost at the same time, so my mother said. We would put the sweeping brush between our legs to simulate a horse, and race off like cowboys, round the corner into Kings Inns Street and shout at the women in Williams & Woods factory where my two sisters, Alice and Rosaleen now worked. I would shout at the workers "Hey that shook yeh, and the brown bread run ya!" We would hit the trail quick, whooping as we went, and shoot a few red Indians on the way home.

There was the time also, when workmen were resurfacing the road and laying tar. I noticed that every so often, a woman or a man would appear with a child, and one of the workmen would lift the child, and hold him or her over the hot tank. I got a hell of a fright thinking that they were burning the children. I called my mother and in shock pointed to what was happening across the street. "Ah! Don't worry," she said soothingly, "they're only trying to cure them of the whooping cough." Whooping cough was yet another disease in the tenements, and it was believed that breathing the fumes from hot tar would cure it.

So wherever there was road works, there would be a queue of people with their children waiting their turn to have them treated.

I remember also going to McLaughlin's shop on the corner of King's Inns Street, just across from our house. My mother had asked me to get a stone of potatoes. I had no bag and Mrs. Mac, who ran the shop, put the spuds into a newspaper for me. I struggled as I made my way out of the shop holding the parcel, cradled in my arms. I had my arms so high that the paper blocked my view and I forgot about the steel lamppost on the corner of the footpath. I walked into it and fell, spilling the potatoes all over the footpath. The people who came to help me were tut-tutting about the unkind mother who would send someone so young on such an errand. I was not more than four years of age at this stage. What would they know? One thing's for sure… we kids from large families learned to stand on our own two feet at a very early age. My mother was the kindest and most loving woman you could meet. She was humble and meek, and has earned her sainthood as already mentioned.

One thing she wasn't however was a seamstress. Someone gave her a length of cloth one day and she decided that she would make me a pair of pants. She wrapped the cloth around me, marked the end and cut the piece. She then joined the ends together like a skirt and stitched it. Next she found the middle of the piece and hand-stitched the back and front together for about three or four inches. This formed the openings through which I put my legs. In no time the stitching came undone in the middle and I was left wearing a skirt. At my age, I couldn't have cared less. The problem was, when I sat down on the front step, my credentials were exposed for all to see because I had no underpants.

CHAPTER FOUR

THE WEST

The day was cold and wet as I held onto the side of the pram that my mother was pushing up the hill and across the bridge, leading from Old Cabra into "The West." The pram was laden with whatever she could carry to help us settle into our new house on Mulroy Road. My father would follow on, the next morning, with the remainder of our stuff on a hand-cart. In those days you could hire a handcart from a company in Granby Lane, at the back of Dominicks Street chapel. This was the very lane in which the Venerable Matt Talbot collapsed on his way to Mass one morning. The handcart was still being used in the 1950's.

Matt was born in 1868, one of a family of twelve children. He began his working life in a wine store at age twelve. He developed a craving for drink at a very young age. For fourteen years, he was a hopeless alcoholic, spending every penny he had on drink. One morning in 1884, his companions refused to loan him money to buy drink and this seemed to bring him to his senses. He swore off it, took the "Pledge," and began a life of prayer and fasting. He overcame illiteracy and studied… mainly religious books.

Thanks to the help he received from a Monsignor Hickey from Holy Cross College, he won out in the end. He spent the rest of his short life helping others, especially those similarly afflicted. On his way to early Mass in Dominicks Street Church, he collapsed and died. When he was taken to the hospital the doctors discovered that he had wrapped chains so tightly around his body that they had cut into his flesh. His remains are now in a tomb in "Our Lady of Lourdes" chapel in Sean McDermot Street. The Pope declared him "Venerable" in 1975.

The excitement of the new house was wonderful. My mother had brought a double mattress and some bedclothes, so that we could stay the night. There was no way she was going to leave our new home and risk the possibility of someone moving in to it while she was gone. She lit the fire and wonder of wonders… it heated the water. There was a boiler at the back of the fire with a gap above and below it to allow the flames from the fire to embrace it and heat the water contained therein. This then drove the cold water ahead of it until it circled back and ended with a full tank of hot water in the bathroom and hot water for washing the dishes. She had loved her house in Old Cabra, but this was something new and special. Although, to say the least, she found it awkward that we could only have two lights on together at any one time. It took some years before the houses in the area were re-wired so that this situation could be rectified.

We sat by the fire and with moistened eyes, she would recount the happy days in Old Cabra. She particularly loved the idea of having a "Parlour," so that she could lock the door and have a room set aside for visitors. My father, she said, would sit in there on Sunday after he returned from Mass and read his newspaper. We didn't have a parlour in our new house, but we had three bedrooms, as opposed to the two we had previously. More rooms but less privacy. Although she had sold much of her furniture in Old Cabra, she managed to replace it when we moved to Cabra West. So, unlike some families, we had our house furnished to a large extent. We even had a piano. We had a man call occasionally to tune the piano. He looked as if he had led a hard life. His face always reminded me of autumn leaves. It was cracked and a very deep brown. He would sit at the piano and sing a song he must've made up himself. It was called, "The war is over, the war is over," and we'd all fall around the place laughing, when he sang it at the top of his voice. My brother and sister in England were sending money home, and my two sisters who worked in Williams & Woods Ltd. were also contributing. So things began to look up for us financially. We still used the "eiderdown with the sleeves" (overcoat), especially in the wintertime. We also slept four and five to a bed so the heat of other bodies helped.

Tom, an older brother, who would've been about sixteen years of age, and Dick who was fourteen, started work in Murdoch's Ltd. where they manufactured Bird's Custard. The factory premises were just off Parnell Square, near to the Plaza Cinema. They used to come home like snowmen from the white dust of the custard powder. Tom was made foreman, and after a disagreement with Dick one day, he sacked him. It seems that Dick had farted, and Tom decided that this wasn't allowed where they were preparing foodstuff. My mother used to crack up laughing at this, whenever she thought about it in later years. So things began to look up for us financially.

Next morning, I went exploring my new surroundings. The footpaths were still not completed and there were mounds of earth in the gardens. It was an adventure playground for a young boy. I also discovered that Jimmy next door was the same age as myself, and like us, his family had just moved in. We became close friends then and although we treaded different paths after leaving school, we are still friends today.

Soon my father was gone again, leaving my mother pregnant with my sister Kathleen, the last of the eleven surviving children. My mother was forty years of age by now. He reported back to his unit and was off to the war once more. I pestered my mother to ask my father in her letters to have him write to me. He did so eventually and I carried it with me for years before I was old enough to read. So I would ask any visitors to our house to read it to me. Then one day it just disappeared. I never did find out what happened to it.

It was now time to start my education, and I was taken to Christ the King school by my older brother Gerard. He would have been eleven or twelve years of age at this stage. I had been born in October 1938 and this was now September 1943. It was just before my fifth birthday. My teacher, Mrs. O'Brien looked the part of the "School Marm." She wore spectacles, had a long face and her hair was done up in a bun at the back of her head.

She looked fierce, used the cane liberally, and simply terrorised us poor kids. I had a habit of saying "Ah J..." or "Jaynee..." whenever I heard a sad story. She almost had a fit when she heard me, claiming that I was taking the Lord's name in vain. I couldn't understand why she was fussing so much. Blasphemy was the last thing on my mind. But I soon got out of the habit, thereby saving myself a severe beating. She taught us the alphabet and eventually I was able to write my own name.

"You'll be proud of that one day," she said to me as she inspected my work. She was right, I am proud of it and all that goes with it. An English friend asked me to explain why I used two "N's" in my name. It had piqued his curiosity. "My English name is Edward," I began, "and this is what is recorded on my birth certificate, despite the fact that my parents wanted to call me Éamonn in the first place." This was not allowed under the law at that time. We were still under British Rule. The Taoiseach used the name Éamonn and spelled it with two "N's." As the schools were doing what they could to reinstate the Irish language, they converted the student's names into our native tongue. Later on Mr. De Valera dropped one "N" and the teacher adjusted my name accordingly. Later still, she told me that he was now using two "M's" in the middle and she was going to change it again. But even at that young age I decided enough is enough, and reverted to using the name that I had been given in the first place. The original way of spelling it was, I was told by a fluent Irish speaker friend from the West of Ireland, Éadhmon and pronounced Yammon. My friend, who is a Professor of Engineering, looked totally baffled and reckoned that I should get a Degree just for being able to explain all of this.

My teacher also taught music and I will never know how I came to love it the way that I do. I've always felt that people without music have no soul. She beat the hell out of those who couldn't sing "Fe" in tune. Anyone who knows music will understand why this is difficult, because it's the sharp note between "Fa and Sol." If you don't have a musical ear you're in real trouble. I got it reasonably quickly. But some of the others kids suffered mercilessly.

We were treated terribly by all adults, especially those in authority. I remember my teacher asking one day if anybody knew where Father O'Callaghan the parish priest lived. My hand shot up, along with another boy and she gave us a note to take round to his house on Charleville Road. This would be a handy hour or so off. So we took our time strolling along and enjoying the sunshine. The house was a Georgian type, with granite steps leading up to the front door. The basement was usually used to accommodate domestic staff. Just as we got there, a lorry load of firewood arrived. They were all loose and the driver was complaining to the priest that he hadn't the time to carry them in by himself. So the priest told us to give him a hand. We laboured all the rest of the day, and when we had finished he didn't have the decency to give us a penny for our troubles. Next day, we got into trouble with the teacher because she wouldn't believe what we were doing all afternoon. She told us that she would check with the priest and if we were telling lies, we'd better watch out.

My mother told my father about this and he was furious. When he was out of work years before, the same priest asked him to repair an arm that had fallen off the very large crucifix that hung over the side altar in the church. He knew that my father was an experienced marble worker and that he was on strike. Some days after the job was finished, an envelope arrived at our door addressed to my father. It bore the parish logo and my father tore it open with excitement, fully expecting a reasonable sum of money for his labours. Especially as he knew that the priest owned racehorses and had a stud farm down the country. To his dismay, he discovered that all it contained was a sixpenny piece and a holy picture. He was so disgusted; he sent the envelope and the contents back to the priest with a note, saying that he obviously needed the money more. The crucifix is still there and the joint is as undetectable today as it was when the job was finished.

My father used to carve headstones at home to keep the money coming in. On one particular occasion, he had left the headstone that he was working on standing in the bath. My sister Alice sneaked downstairs during the night to get something to eat from the larder in the kitchen. As she entered the kitchen, her attention fell on a light that was coming from the bathroom. The door was open and the moon was shining on the white marble. Just then a cat howled. Alice, thinking there was a ghost in the room, screamed and charged up the stairs, waking the whole house. My mother and father were not amused just then, but saw the funny side of it next morning. It cured Alice of her craving for food in the middle of the night.

The best memory I have of my time in this school is the six weeks that the teachers were on strike. There are a couple of other memories that I would prefer to forget however, but since this book is going to be a "Warts and all" treatise I will include them. I was a bright kid and got on well with the teacher. She used to let me take the attendance figures to the Head Teacher, every morning. One morning during the winter it was very cold. I didn't have an overcoat, none of us did. I wore a thin jacket and short trousers. My teeth were chattering as I waited for the school doors to open. When they did, I rushed in hoping to warm myself on the radiator in the classroom. But the teacher was there and I had to sit down at my desk. By this time, I was beginning to contract a cold and my nose began to run. By the time I reached the head's room, I was suffering and trying my best not to sniffle. I was second in-line as a sneeze began to well up in me. Try as I might, I could not stop it. I had no handkerchief and tissues were unheard of. Then suddenly, it happened. I sneezed, and as I did a length of snot flew through the air and landed right beside the large book into which she was recording the figures. The boy in front of me moved away as she finished with him, and as she reached for the book that I had in my hand she noticed the gleaming snot.

"Did you do that?" she screamed, her face contorting as though she was about to be sick.

"No mam," said I sheepishly.

"He did," said the "fecker" behind me; delighted that squealing on somebody had made his day.

"Get out of my sight," she ordered, with a look that would have turned me to dust on the spot if she'd had the power, "and don't come back here again." Not only had I been exposed as a dirty little liar, I was now going to have to tell my teacher that I was not allowed to take the figures to the head anymore and explain why. I felt very ashamed for ages afterwards, especially when the teacher didn't show any sympathy to my plight.

On another occasion, I had stomach cramps and asked the teacher if I could go out to the toilet. She refused, saying that I could go when she had finished the lesson. The cramps got so bad that I couldn't hold off any longer, and I soiled my pants. Because the pants were short and I wasn't wearing underpants, (nobody did in those days) the contents of my stomach rolled down my leg when I stood up to tell her I was in trouble. "Get out," she yelled and hurried me out of the door. I stood outside in the corridor crying loudly.

One of the other teachers heard me and came out of her room. "What's the matter," she said in a way that a mother would speak to her baby. As she walked towards me, she saw what the trouble was and quickly disappeared. My brother came after class as usual to bring me home. He reluctantly walked beside me as the other kids poked fun at me while I walked like a cowboy... you know... bow-legged. That horrible experience lives with me still.

The teachers shouted at us, used the leather frequently, and ridiculed us on a regular basis. As a result of this and the punishment received regarding the learning of the music scale, I cannot sight-read music today. This, despite the fact that I have sung in choirs all of my life, since seven years of age. I also tried learning the piano, but when it came to practicing the scales I was told by my siblings to cut out the noise. My piano teacher got annoyed when I showed up not having done my homework and this, in turn, upset me. Finally, it got too much for me and I gave up.

Physical as well as psychological punishment was the norm at all schools. Some were worse than others. It is sad to note that psychological punishment was a feature of home life also.

My brother Gerard was attending the primary school in the same complex as myself. There were three schools in all that formed three sides of a square with the church forming the fourth side. One side was for senior boys, one was for junior and senior girls, and the other side was for junior (infant) boys. He was so severely beaten by his teacher when he was thirteen years of age that he could barely walk. My father, had just been discharged from the British Army after completing his service in 1946, and decided to visit the school next day. The classroom doors had a glass panel in it and my father could be seen as he knocked. The teacher opened, smiling and asked with a questioning look "Can I help you, Mister…?"

"Sheridan," my father replied, as he punched him on the chin. The teacher reeled backwards and collapsed in a heap on the floor. "Touch one hair of my son's head in future and I will put you into hospital for a very long time," he said. The kids cheered and the teacher learned an object lesson… "Don't mess with the Sheridans,"

Normally parents didn't interfere in this way, and if you came home crying you'd be told, "You must have deserved it." But my brother was in such a bad way, my father made an exception in this case. There were no legal proceedings taken. The teacher didn't have a leg to stand on… to use a pun. And no one in those days bothered the law with that sort of stuff in any event, especially when they knew that they were in the wrong.

There were dinners available at the school for a penny per day, a facility that was unusual for the time. I tried it once, but didn't like the fatty stew they served. I was terribly shy in any event and I didn't like the idea of eating with so many other people present. So I preferred to go home for a cup of tea and a "cut" of bread.

On my way back to school one day, there was a heck of a crash that came from the railway that divided the two Cabras. I peered over the parapet of the bridge to discover that two trains had crashed into each other. There was a real mess and people were frantically shouting for help as a driver and fireman were trapped in their battered cab. I learned later that the fireman on one of the trains was thrown out of the cab onto the line and the engine fell over, crushing him beneath, and killing him. I was traumatised by the news, but there was no such thing as counselling in those days. You just had to get on with it. So I pushed it to the back of my mind and, "got on with my life."

CHAPTER FIVE

ST. FINBARR'S

At seven years of age and just before I left Christ the King school to attend St. Finbarr's in Cabra West, I made my First Communion. The year was 1946, and my father was back home from the war and was looking for work. My mother was in hospital, recovering from another miscarriage, and it was left to my eldest sister Alice, to get me dressed and take me to the church. She would've been nineteen years of age then. All went well and Alice took me around to visit our relations. She was courting a very nice chap named Frank Curtis. He was a motor mechanic and he worked in Crawford's Garage, which was in Harcourt Street at that time. We went to visit his family in Fontenoy Street. His parents were really nice people and treated me to a lovely tea. On one occasion, Frank was spotted heading in the direction of our house by one of the family. My mother wasn't expecting him and immediately began in a panic, trying to tidy up before he arrived. Willie (Bill) was about to have his tea, but was told by my mother that he would have to wait, because Frank Curtis was on the way and would arrive at any moment. "F... Frank Curtis," said Willie, "I want my tea." My father almost collapsed with a heart attack when he heard what Willie had said. He didn't allow bad language under our roof. Only the timely arrival of Frank saved him from a good hiding. I really liked Frank, and loved it when he'd sit me in a chair next to him, pretend it was a car and teach me how to drive.

Somehow, my mother had got the money together to buy me a whole new outfit for the Communion Ceremony. It felt really great to be wearing my own fresh new clothes. Although my pleasure was short lived as my new clothes were pawned the following Monday. The men at the time would refer to their suits as "Indigo suits…" in-they-go on Monday, and out-they-come on Friday. All of those we visited gave me money and I was naturally delighted. I had never had so much in my hand before. Again, my joy was cut short, because my sister told me next day that she would have to borrow all of it to get food for the house. I asked her when would I get it back and she replied, "Tomorrow, when I see me Da." That was the last I saw of it. I gave her a terrible time for years afterwards. As far as I was concerned she had stolen it.

My pal Jimmy had attended the Dominican Convent Schools on Ratoath Road in Cabra West. I wasn't aware that there was a school there until it was too late. Considering the fact that the Nuns had purchased the old Segrave mansion in 1819 in order to set up a school, it wasn't as though they had just moved into the neighbourhood. It simply proves how naïve I was, or perhaps more to the point, how little my parents knew of its existence. The Seagrave family have a long and interesting association with Cabra West. They were loyal Catholics who had a difficult time during the invasion of Oliver Cromwell and his "Band of Butchers."

The Dominican Sisters had originally been invited to set up in Ireland by none other than the son of "Strongbow" and his wife "Aoife." Her father, Dermot McMurragh had given Aoife in marriage to the Earl of Pembroke as a reward for his help in securing the High Kingship of Ireland. They had originally occupied the Channel Row Convent in Brunswick Street. This was later to become the Chapel Ward of the Richmond Hospital. It became known for its excellent standard of music and during the Christmas celebrations of 1746, the Adeste Fideles was first sung there. They carried on their love for music and I had the pleasure of performing in the Convent Hall in Cabra with the choir from St. Finbarr's, after we won the Feis Ceol in 1950.

I had tried to switch over to the convent schools so that I could be with my pal Jimmy, but the Nuns turned me down. The students there were given a big breakfast when they made their first communion.

The nuns took on the education of deaf girls in 1846. Two of their number received their training in Caen France and on their return to Dublin, set up St. Gabriel's school for deaf girls. It was one of the deaf girls, in later years, that reported Dickie Rock for taking a drink of water before receiving his First Communion, and he was made to wait until the following week. We poor souls at Christ the King got nothing. But then Father O'Callaghan, the parish priest, was not known for his generosity.

The summer holidays seemed to fly by that year, and it was time to register at St. Finbarr's. My brothers Richard (Dick) and Gerry had been away on holiday for a week to the "Sunshine Home" in Balbriggin, Co. Dublin. The St. Vincent De Paul Society ran it. My other brothers, Jim, Willie (Bill), and myself got hobnail boots provided by the same people. We were delighted to have decent footwear for the coming winter. Only the most under-privileged families received attention by the Society. We had great fun learning the songs that they had learned while they were away. And we were enthralled as they told us about the campfires and the adventures they enjoyed while they were there. They frightened us with the tales they heard of Lord Norbury. They called him the "Hanging Judge," who it was said condemned hundreds to the gallows on a whim. He lived at the junction of Fassaugh Avenue and Ratoath Road. His ghost was seen on horseback, clattering along Ratoath Road late at night, so the story goes. We were regaled with many a story about the infamous Lord Norbury as we grew up. It was he who presided at the trial of the patriot Robert Emmet and imposed the awful sentence of "Hanged, Drawn, and Quartered."

I remember one winter's evening, as we sat round the fire, my mother told us of the ghosts that haunted the streets of Cabra. There was a storm blowing outside and the rain was lashing against the windows. The lights were off in the sitting room and the fire threw weird shadows on the walls. She had just reached the climax of the story about the "Headless Horseman," when the hall door burst open, with the weatherboard making a terrible clatter. The weatherboard was a shaped piece of timber that was on hinges and was attached to the bottom of the hall door. It dropped down when the door was closed and acted as a way of casting off water when it rained. There was pandemonium as we kids grabbed my mother for safety. It was one of my elder brothers returning home after an evening out. The wind had caught the door and whipped it out of his hands, causing the sitting-room door to fly open at the same time. I think my mother got as big a fright as the rest of us.

The year was 1946; my father had returned from the war, bringing with him a supply of "Iron Rations," we had chocolate for the first time. It was so hard that my brothers had to spend ages shaving pieces off with a knife so that we could experience the joy of its taste. He also brought some souvenirs. One German prisoner of war gave him a replica of a Junkers 88 dive-bomber (Stuka) that he had made out of bone. It was a lovely piece of craftsmanship. Another prisoner, (an Italian Doctor) gave him his ring because he had helped him in some way. He had also noticed the rosary beads hanging around my father's neck and informed my father that he was a catholic, too. So the enemies soon became friends. The ring was made of steel and it had a Garnet set into it. Not worth anything in monetary terms but my father always wore it in remembrance of that man. It seems that all gold trinkets had been sought by Mussolini during the war to help finance the campaigns. A replacement steel ring was given in return for a gold one. He got along well with the Italian prisoners, most of whom didn't want to be at war in the first place. Some of the Germans were a different story however. The Africa Corps proved not to be as invincible as their propaganda and they didn't like being prisoners of the British. One of them spat the water that my father had given him back into his face. My father kicked his legs from under him and put a burst of machine-gun fire through his shoulder. A German officer who had witnessed the incident walked over and kicked the Nazi on the ground calling him a swine. He then interceded with my father's CO, telling him that the other guy deserved what he got. Nothing further was said and no action was taken.

Enrolment time for St. Finbarr's soon came around and I found myself standing in line next to my pal Jimmy as we waited to have our details taken. We were delighted to be assigned to the same class. "What's your name," I was asked when I reached the top of the queue. The voice belonged to the Head Master, a Mister McCarthy. It was gruff and unfriendly, but it was typical of those who found themselves in positions of authority. I handed him my Baptismal Certificate as I gave him my name. He demanded my father's details, and asked if I had any relations in the school. I confirmed that my brother Jim was already a student, and that my younger brother Bill (Willie) would be looking for a place in a couple of years. He was two years younger than me, having been born in 1940. He often joked later in life that he was a "Grudge" baby. When people asked what he meant, he said that our father was in North Africa when he was born, so someone had it in for him. On checking the records, I was able to assure him that our father didn't join up until 1942, so his parentage was intact.

"Was your father in the army," the head master asked.

"He was, Sir," I said. His attitude became somewhat softer then, which puzzled me. I related all of what had happened to my father later at home and he informed me that he had also punched him because of his violent behaviour towards my brother Dick, when he was attending St. Joseph's School in Dorset Street. I wish to emphasise here that parents generally did not interfere when their children were being disciplined at school. My father was no exception to this rule. However, there was a limit beyond which masters, teachers, or anyone else was not allowed to go. These men had crossed that line and paid the price.

The very first day at St. Finbarr's I was standing in a line with my classmates out in the schoolyard waiting to go to class. I got a tap on the shoulder and turned around to find myself facing a taller boy with a menacing look on his face. "I'm Patsy Flynn (not his real name) and I'm the boss of this class."

"Not anymore you're not," I replied punching him hard. From there on in, we were the best of pals. Survival was what it was all about and if you showed any sign of weakness you were in trouble. Shy I might have been, but scared… not on your life.

That was certainly the case where those punishing my two brothers were concerned. My father never interfered, for example, when I came home after school one day with my hands bruised. Mr. Lewis, our master, didn't show up and the class was getting a little boisterous as we waited to see what would happen. The boy who sat next to me slid across the seat and pushed me onto the floor. I sat there laughing and was about to get up when the door flew open and in walked the "Head Master."

"Come out here you," he hissed through clenched teeth and squinting eyes. In fear and trepidation, I picked myself up and went forward. "Hold out your hand," he said as he raised the cane high above his head. I did, and it came swishing through the air and made contact. The pain was excruciating. The second one hit the heel of my hand and my wrist, leaving a nasty bruise running approximately four inches up my arm. After the third one, he told me to hold out my other hand. Three more were delivered to this one. "Now, that'll teach you to act the funny man in future," he said, looking into my face. I stared straight back into his eyes showing my pain but refusing to cry. Medical people have told me on more than one occasion that my pain threshold today is very high, which doesn't surprise me one little bit. The punishment administered could be with the cane, or as some of the teachers used… a leather strap. The strap was about twelve inches long and it was shaped at one end to facilitate the handgrip. The other end was rounded and overall it was quarter of an inch thick. Some of the lads said that there were metal discs inserted between the layers of leather to give it added weight. We regarded this as the soft option, as it was an inch wide and so the area of contact was wider and therefore less painful.

Our master only used the strap when he ran out of bamboo canes, and that wasn't very often. When he did, he would send one of the boys out to buy a supply. The nearest stockist was a hardware shop on the Cabra Road. As this shop was quite a distance away, it meant that whoever was sent on the errand would have a nice break from class. So there was a choice to be made; volunteer to go and risk the ire of the rest of the class, or try to avoid being picked and miss out on a welcome break. Whoever was chosen to go was warned by the lads to slit the bottom of the cane with a blade and suck the juice out of it. This dried up the cane fairly quickly and it didn't hurt so much when it made contact. I'm delighted to report that I managed to avoid being chosen. The sound of the cane swishing through the air was frightening in itself, and the master would do this constantly as he walked around the class. Punishment was a feature of life at the time, but "big boys" didn't cry. It could be inflicted for being late, wrong spellings, bad writing, and no homework, or just for smiling at the wrong time.

So I went in constant fear of punishment that might or might not come at home, as well as at school. The punishment at home was psychological rather than physical, and was perpetrated in the main by my siblings. There will be more about this later. It was hardly surprising that I was diagnosed with a duodenal ulcer at the tender age of fourteen. Difficult though this might have been for me, the fear was compounded by the sight of one of my neighbours after his father had punished him. He was tied to the bars at the end of his bed and lashed by his father with a leather belt. He used the end with the buckle on it, and it left ugly welts all over him. Thankfully for my neighbour, his father left home for England shortly after that, and never returned. He, the father, had served in the British Army during the war and it had brutalised him.

I began to settle in at my new school. It was still fresh and bright, having been opened in 1943. As we walked to class from the schoolyard, the first two boys in line were assigned to stand at the corners so that the rest of the boys would not rub against the paintwork. This was repeated whenever we came to a corner until we were into our classroom. The boys assigned would join the end of the line as the last ones past by. A bell was rung at the end of each period to let the teachers know when to change to the next lesson. I was chosen for this task and was nicknamed "Benbo" by the master. My friends continued to use this name for years after we left school. Things had obviously changed radically by the time my friend Martin Coffey began to attend, since he found the school in a dilapidated state.

Christmas was approaching fast and there was much to do. We had to buy our new books and this proved to be a struggle, but my mother managed to get the money together. We could've had them free if our parents were willing to apply. It would have meant that they would be subjected to a "Means Test." This was an extremely invasive inquiry into the family and its finances. The books were then stamped in purple ink stating that they were "Free." No one wanted to be seen to have this stigma, though some had no choice. I don't ever remember any of the boys who could afford to buy the books slagging off those who couldn't afford to buy them. My guess is that we were all aware that it wasn't long before that we were hungry and scratching for a crust. There's always the exception to the rule however, and Barty, one of my classmates fell into that category. He was a real problem, and was constantly causing disruption in the class. The master sent for his mother, and when she arrived in the class-room we couldn't believe what we were seeing. She was dressed in a beautiful coat with a fox-fur collar, and her jewellery was so much as to be obscene. In contrast to this, her son was dressed like a tramp. The poor guy; I felt so sorry for him that I invited him to our house thereafter. He loved my mother who, in the typical fashion of the tenement dweller, would take in a "stray" and feed them, and this she did often. Perhaps it accounted for the fact that our funds were constantly in short supply.

At the end of the day, we were marched out to the schoolyard where there were crates of milk in half-pint bottles, and trays of sandwiches. We were given a bottle and a sandwich each; we were expected to eat and drink these there and then. For some of the boys, it was the only food they got to end the day. Some gathered unwanted sandwiches to take home. On Wednesdays, we were given a currant bun and on Fridays we got jam in our sandwich. Nobody gave these away. On the other days, we got either cheese or corned beef. Not many liked these, so they were passed on to the kids who were collecting for home. It was quite a trial drinking freezing cold milk in wintertime or in the rain, so many of the boys would pour their milk onto the ground. There was severe punishment for anyone caught doing this, and the guys found all sorts of ingenious ways of spilling their milk. The ground looked so white at times, the schoolyard often looked like it was covered in snow.

Our "Master," a Mr. Lewis, was generally a nice man. Although, if he knew I was using that word today, he would be very upset. "Nice is not a nice word," he used to say. Christmas was almost upon us and the master decided he would offer prizes to us for getting certain tasks right that he would set us. Before he started however, he discovered that he hadn't any change. So he sent me around the classrooms to ask the other teachers if they could change a shilling into pennies. There were twelve pennies in a shilling. After trying a few, I was successful with a teacher whose name I didn't know but who had a small square moustache. When I got back to the classroom I was asked who had given me the change. "I don't know his name, Sir," I said, "but everybody calls him Hitler."

"Wha, what!" he stuttered, trying to stifle a laugh, "That was Mr. Maguire and don't ever let me hear you call him that again." I couldn't understand what he was fussing about.

A friend named Dickie Rock mentioned that his parents showed great affection for each other. His father constantly told his mother that she was a wonderful woman.

My parents, on the other hand, never displayed any obvious outward signs of affection for each other. While he called her by a pet name (Cis), I only ever heard her call him by his first name (Jim) once in my whole life. They never held hands or referred to each other in the way that a friend's father did when he got home from work and called out, "Hi, Sweetheart."

What a lovely example to set the children. I remember my mother telling my father with some embarrassment, I might add, that she noticed the couple who lived opposite our house kissed every morning on the doorstep before he left for work. On another occasion, they were at a party in a neighbour's house and the wife of the host grabbed her husband, and told him that she loved every bone in his body. She found both incidents highly amusing and more than a little embarrassing. My mother would've loved to have him buy her a bunch of flowers, but men were not to be seen carrying such items. It might be construed as "sissy." In later years, we heard of Englishmen pushing prams and regarded them as oddities.

There were never any hugs once I had passed the baby stage, and I'm not sure that there were any when I was a baby, anyway. I don't blame my mother. She would hardly have had the time with having another baby so soon after me. I do believe however, that we are all products of our parent's example and teaching. So I grew up never showing my emotions publicly. I love my wife and children dearly, and I've always made an effort to hug and kiss my wife in front of our children. Yet, it's only in recent times that I have managed to bring myself to hug my children and they are all adults now anyway. There is perhaps a reason for this, apart from my upbringing, which I'll discuss later. But I do hug and kiss my grandchildren. I am aware however of the paranoia surrounding this today, because of the stories regarding child abuse. Despite this, I am not going to allow the offences of others stop me from showing affection toward my children's children. So I hope that I am making up for the lost years, at least in some small way. After all this time, I still do not show my true feelings. Sure, I've cried... but never in public or in front of my family.

Just like my friend Dickie's parents, however, mine never had arguments that I know of. My father never raised his hand or his voice in anger to my mother. I never witnessed my father being emotional over anything. And while there was no obvious show of affection, I assumed that they loved each other, because they went everywhere together. Then there were all of us children! We weren't found under a cabbage plant in the back garden, like my mother used to say when I asked. I remember many years later, during the great debate about contraception, asking my mother why she didn't limit the size of her family. She answered me by saying, "If I had done that, you would not be here today." She might not have had much in the way of formal education but she had the wisdom of a sage.

The parish priest, Fr. Valentine Burke, who was the school manager, decided to form a choir and sent a boy around the classes seeking recruits. My teacher taught music, and on hearing me sing in class decided that I had a reasonable voice and sent me along. It was to be the beginning of many happy and satisfying hours in the years ahead. One of the boys who later rose to stardom and is still performing today was Dickie Rock. I have always had the greatest admiration for him and the effort he put into his performances. I took my wife to see his show for my birthday on October 12th, 2007. He gave a non-stop two-hour performance that would have put many a younger performer to shame. He, like myself, was a boy soprano.

We prepared immediately to sing at the first Mass on Christmas Day. This was to start at 6:00 a.m. and we were then to sing at the High Mass at noon. I still look back with great fondness to that first wonderful Christmas. My mother stayed up all night preparing the turkey, the ham, and the pudding. My father kept her company and they shared a sherry or two. At 5 a.m., my father got me out of bed and after I had a wash and some breakfast, my mother gave me my new clothes to put on. The cold crisp feel of my new shirt was thrilling and it was lovely to walk up our road on that frosty morning when all was dark and still. The moonlight glistened on the frost and it looked every bit the Christmas card scene, as we made our way towards the lights of the chapel that was situated at the top of our road. The chapel, which was erected in 1944, was a temporary building situated on Dunmanus Road, which runs across the top of Mulroy Road.

Made of corrugated iron, it was known to us all as the "Tin" chapel. It had a special odour of wood and polish when you walked in through the doors and the heat made it feel very homely. I made my confirmation there in 1950. It was built in the shape of a cross and the organ and choir was situated in the right arm of it. The choir had practiced hard and we sounded as though we had been together for years. A Mr. McElroy, who was blind, played the organ. He got to know every one of the boys by name just from the sound of their voice. It used to amaze us when we spoke to him that he would immediately recognise us.

There is nothing like sacred music to set the tone for a holy Christmas. I still play it over the holiday, even now. After Mass,

I rushed to get home to see what Santa had brought. All I ever asked for was watercolour paints. They came in a flat tin box and the colours were about one quarter of an inch square and about one eighth of an inch thick. They didn't last very long but they brought me great happiness for the time that I had them. A brush was included in the box. Its quality was poor but it served me well and was adequate for my purposes. There was also at that time, a small shooting set made of stiff cardboard. It showed the highwayman Dick Turpin on horseback, and there was a wire gun with a wooden pellet that was used to shoot him with. If you hit it right he would tumble off his horse. It's probably not surprising that I like to paint today, and that I was a crack shot during my service in the armed forces.

CHAPTER SIX

BETTER TIMES

My brother Paddy (who was one of the skeletons in my father's cupboard) had returned from London, and was now working in the Water Department of Dublin Corporation.

He was actually a half-brother. There was only five months difference in age between him and Alice, my eldest sister. He had joined our family when he was six years of age, after his mother decided that she could no longer afford to keep him. He was known to the family as "The Bull," and my mother treated him as though we were all adopted and he was her only genuine son. He was demanding, and overbearing, and got his way in everything.

Paddy played football with Shelbourne Football Club, and boxed for Corinthians Boxing Club with considerable success. He became a very close friend of Liam Whelan, who went on to play for Manchester United. Liam lost his life in the Munich Air Disaster when the plane came down shortly after take-off, following the semi-final of the European Cup in 1958. Liam was a good-living lad and was heard to say just before the plane crashed, "If this is the end, then I'm ready for it." As I write this, I am conscious of the fact that it is fifty years exactly since that awful tragedy. The twenty-eight people who died included players, club officials and journalists. The team was known as the "Busby Babes," after their manager Matt Busby. He actually survived the crash, and went on to win the European Cup. Eventually, the Queen of England knighted him. There's a clock outside the grounds at Old Trafford in Manchester, which never moves passed the time of 3:04, the time of the crash on February 6th. May their souls rest in peace.

Paddy was the only one of us boys who had his own bed. He used to hang his socks along the top headboard so it looked like a clothesline. The spring in the base was so worn it hung down like a hammock. Shortly after his return from England, he met my father in town after work on Saturday at lunchtime. They were both walking down Moore Street, intending to call into a pub near the Henry Street end. As they sat down with pints of Guinness in hand, Paddy laid a turkey on the table. "Where did you get that?" asked my father.

"It jumped off a stall when we were coming down the street, and it wouldn't go home," replied Paddy smiling broadly.

"Put it away quick, before someone sees it and realises what you've done," said my father with a widening grin. He was a good-living man, but this was considered "fair game," particularly as times were so difficult financially. On another occasion my mother was short of cash and she decided to sell a spare single bed that was cluttering up a bedroom. Paddy volunteered to take it to a second-hand furniture dealer close to where our grandparents lived. The "Long Lane" was full of dealers (mainly Jews) of one sort or another. All of them operated out of what were originally the stables at the bottom of the gardens of the big houses. Nowadays, they are referred to as "Mews." He called into the first one and showed him the bed. A price was agreed, and the dealer told Paddy to leave it outside in the lane. That was too good an invitation to miss. Paddy promptly took it to the next dealer further down the lane and sold it a second time. My mother was delighted when he told her what he'd done. Robbing dealers who happened to be Jews wasn't considered a sin. They also operated as moneylenders and had a bad reputation among the poor of Dublin. So it was all right to "diddle" them.

My father was whitewashing the ceilings in all the rooms and left a basin containing some whitewash in the boy's room one evening, intending to finish off the next day. My brother Bill woke during the night and got out of bed. Paddy had not long gone to bed and was still awake and asked him why he was up.

Bill said that he needed to go to the toilet. Paddy thought that he meant that he wanted to pass water and told him to do it in the basin that was in the corner of the room and thought nothing more of it.

Next morning my mother was tidying the room and making the beds when she noticed what she thought was the cloth that my father had been using to wipe small splashes. "Will you look at where your father has left the cloth," she remarked to one of my sisters as she reached to pick it up. Suddenly she let out a yell as she picked up what, in fact, was a "turd." My younger brother had defecated in the basin and my mother had the result dripping through her fingers. She got over the worst of her nausea by the time the evening meal came about, and everybody was laughing their heads off when my mother told us what had happened.

On another occasion, Bill was sneaking down the stairs very late one night, intent on raiding the larder for something to eat. One of the small panes of glass in the top of our hall door had been broken and as he got almost half-way down the stairs, the wind blew the curtain on the door. As it did so, a cat yowled and Bill hearing and seeing this, let out an unmerciful roar. My mother and father were out of bed like a shot, and ran to see what was happening. As they ran down the stairs, they met Bill running up shouting, "The woollen ban is after me." He was white as a sheet and shaking like a leaf. No one has ever made sense of what he was saying. But it cured him of any further night manoeuvres.

My sister May had come home from Lancashire and was working in the finishing section of Irish Carton Printers, Ltd. She also had a lovely singing voice and had the honour to perform on the radio in a programme called "Workers Playtime," that was broadcast from the factory canteen. She turned down an offer of a career in the music world, preferring to return home. She is the only other person in the family besides me to have obtained her Primary School Certificate. She was also a proficient Irish speaker and had won her Gold Fainne (Ring). This is worn on the lapel of a suit jacket, so that others of like mind can converse with the wearer.

My father was working in the security section at the cigarette manufacturer, John Player & Sons, Ltd. In those days before we all got sophisticated, his job was known as "Watchman." It was quite a responsible job however, and the police issued him with a revolver when he was on night duty, because of the danger of thieves raiding the place. The British Legion had helped him to secure this job. We may criticise the British for many things, but credit must be given them for looking after the welfare of their ex-servicemen and women. They also provided free medical treatment for ex-service people and their families through their hospital in Foxrock.

My father had now been home almost two years, and the winter of 1947 came at us with a vengeance. There were three to four inches of snow on the ground and the air was raw with frost. Fuel couldn't be had anywhere; and when it was available, it wouldn't burn because it was wet turf. My mother went walking with a pram, accompanied by some of the other women who lived nearby. They were desperate to find a supply of coal. They got as far as Phibsborough, close to Dalymount Park, when they came upon a man delivering a lorry load of coal to a house there. They pleaded with him to sell them just one bag split between them, but he refused. Just then Alfie Byrne, the ex-Lord Mayor of Dublin arrived on the scene. He demanded that the coalman sell a bag of coal to the women. By this time, the occupant of the house where the coal was being delivered opened his hall door and came out. He refused to allow the coalman to part with the one bag that the women sought. Alfie swore that he would go to the newspapers, and have them publish the names of the coal company and the tenant of the house. They relented finally, and the bag was shared among the women. Alfie Byrne became a Champion of the poor long before this and has since taken his place among the great historic figures of his era.

He dressed like a dandy with a pin striped suit, bowler hat and bow tie. He also had a white-waxed moustache and wore spats. Whenever he ran for election, the poor saw to it that their champion was returned every time. Such was his popularity that he was Lord Mayor of Dublin for eight years in the 1930s. We kids used to follow him around when he visited an area and sing at the top of our voices, "Vote for Alfie… vote for Alfie… vote for Alfie, number one."

An appropriate memorial ought to be erected to him outside of the Mansion House in Dawson Street. Perhaps the figure could be seen to hold the hand of some of the Dublin characters like "Bang-Bang" and "Johnny Forty-Coats." Bang-Bang was a poor shell-shocked victim of the First World War. He would ride on the platform of a bus with a key in his hand and shout, "Bang… bang," at pedestrians and cars as he went. His voice was so loud that he frightened the life out of me one day as a bus passed by. Johnny Forty-Coats was homeless, and wore as many coats as he could to keep himself warm in the cold of the winter.

The winter was long and hard that year, and people were saying that it was in memory of the million or so people who perished in the "Famine." The men who lived on our road were also looking for fuel, and approached the parish priest, asking if they could have his permission to cut down a tree on church property and divide it among those in need. He refused and they made an approach to the Nuns, who allowed them to cut down a tree on convent property, much to the annoyance of the priest. The Phoenix Park was very close to Cabra West and it was being used as a storage area for coal. It was so difficult to get supplies during the war years that the Government had built up some reserves of fuel. The only convenient place to store it was the 1,760 odd acres of the park. The coal was banked up at either side of the roads leading onto the "fifteen acres." This is the area that is now set aside for football today. I remember the poles that were inserted into the stacks to allow air to circulate, in order to avoid spontaneous combustion. It was a prime area for raids and though it was guarded pretty well, some of the local inhabitants of Cabra and its surrounds managed to successfully procure a supply. The same applied to the railway sidings near Broom-bridge. Trains would off-load coal and turf there and many was the time I saw local lads climbing over the parapet of the bridge with a shopping bag full of coal. Trucks from McHenry's fuel merchants would load up there also. As they trundled along

Bannow Road with their diesel engines whining and trying hard to build up some speed, local lads would jump onto the rear tailgate and climb onto the load. While they threw sods of turf onto the road, other friends would pick them up and put them in bags ready to take home.

Money was also in very short supply that year. I don't know why, but we were as badly off as everybody else. We couldn't afford meat for the Christmas dinner, so the President of Ireland donated a deer or two for slaughter. The President didn't know it at the time, but the local men were sure that he wouldn't mind. Some of them had stalked the herd in the Phoenix Park and killed enough to feed the needy in our immediate area. We got a shank and I always boast to my friends that I got a taste for the high life and fine food at a very early age. While my parents were out of the house one day, my older brothers forced me to go to the shops for a bottle of milk. My hands were so cold when I got home that I cried with the pain when the heat was returning to them. This was a symptom of frostbite, but I was told to shut up and behave myself.

I was nine years of age in 1947 and it was very difficult to keep warm. When my socks wore through at the heel, I used to pull them at the toe and turn the material under. It was most uncomfortable and up until my father taught me how to darn, it had to do. During that year, the schoolmaster was out sick, and the class was split up and sent around other classrooms. About a dozen of us were sent to one particular class. I can't remember the teachers name but he wasn't a bit pleased with having us, and insisted that we stand against the wall down one side of the classroom. Whatever I'd eaten that morning didn't agree with me and I was absolutely full of wind. Try as I might, I just couldn't hold on to it any longer. Had I been allowed to sit I might have been able to ease it out without anyone knowing. I pressed my backside against the wall and tried to ease it out that way. It sounded like someone had discharged a shotgun. I immediately turned to the boy standing next to me with a disgusted look on my face and told him to behave. The teacher went mad and ordered the boy out of the room. He protested that it wasn't him but to no avail. I prayed very hard that I could hold on for the rest of our stay in this class otherwise I would've been severely punished. Thankfully, I managed to hold off on any further discharge until I got outside at lunchtime. I ran home and quickly paid a visit to the toilet. Having cleared whatever it was that was causing me discomfort, I had a better afternoon. The boy who'd been thrown out of the room had gone home and there was no further problem with him. "It's an ill wind, etc."

The Republic wasn't declared until 1949, and every Sunday the newspaper sellers would walk around the estate shouting, "Get your Press or Indo, Despatch, Chronicle or Empire News." The only surviving newspaper today is the "Indo" or Irish Independent. A family named Bowler, who lived in number three on our road, sold newspapers. Almost opposite them in number six was the Keanes. One morning as I walked down the front path to our house, I looked to my left on hearing a voice and saw one of the girls running down the path leading from her house. Her mother was calling her to come back and she ran through the gate and on to the edge of the footpath. Her momentum carried her forward as she tried to stop, just as the milkman came around the corner. He was driving a horse-drawn two-wheeled cart that looked like a chariot. It had two large steel-rimmed wheels. His horse had spooked and he was struggling to get control of it. He had almost succeeded when the girl who had been running, tripped and fell under the wheel. If I live to be a hundred, I will never forget the result. Blood spurted like a fountain; it was everywhere as kids screamed and vomited. Her mother was frantic and the poor milkman was inconsolable. He picked the child up in his arms and with the blood soaking his clothes took her to the Mater Hospital, approximately two miles away. Unfortunately, she was dead on arrival and the whole of the neighbourhood went into mourning. The train crash suddenly came to mind again, although it was nothing like the awful thing that I'd just witnessed. But again, I pushed it to the back of mind, and within days it was as if it never happened.

My brother Dick was now working at Raleigh Industries, Ltd., assembling bicycles and Gerard worked for Birmingham

Small Arms, Ltd. (BSA), in Baggot Street doing a similar job. So there was a reasonable amount of money coming in to the house again. Our prosperity having returned, it began to show with the number of bicycles outside our door. Jim had also gotten a job in the Raleigh through my brother Dick; and my father had gotten Tom a job in the stores department of John Player & Sons, Ltd. We ought to have been very well off and yet money always seemed to be scarce. Having had the experience of raising a family myself however, I have some understanding of the amount of food consumed by growing lads. This coupled with clothing the family; schoolbooks and all of the other things that go into keeping a family reasonably happy can soon drain the financial resources, especially when a man's full wages for the week was only £7.10.0.

The next big event was to prepare for confirmation into the Catholic Church. I was twelve years of age by now. We were all marched down to the chapel for Confession every Friday. There was at that time, a priest who was affectionately known as "Flash Kavanagh." He could say Mass in twelve minutes flat, and the chapel was crowded for half ten Mass every Sunday. He was no different when it came to confession, and as I knelt down in the confession box on one visit from school, the hatch flew back with a bang. It startled me and in my confusion I hesitated while I gathered my thoughts together. "B... bless me father, for I have sinned, I... I..."

"Get out," he shouted, "and come back when you can remember your sins."

I left the box all red faced and trying to avoid the looks from my schoolmates who were waiting their turn. They had a good giggle at my embarrassment. *F...youse*, I thought. Now I have something to tell him when I go back. We kids were so innocent that we had to make up things to tell the priest in confession anyway. Because we were poor didn't mean that we were uncouth. It wasn't usual to hear kids using bad language at the time, unlike today. One of the reasons, perhaps, is that any adult within earshot was entitled to chastise you, and there would be no question of lawsuits or anything of that nature.

The preparation for the important event of confirmation involved learning the Catechism by heart. I think that there were over one hundred questions relating to our religion in it, and we had to know them all. We learned the "Parables" also, but we never studied the Bible. Ours was a handy religion. All we needed to know, the priest or the schoolmaster told us. Learning of all subjects was by rote anyway, and none of us understood what the heck we were saying half of the time. One or two of the boys were rejected, and their parents came up to the school to plead their case. They got no joy, despite them having bought their sons new clothes, etc. I vividly remember how upset these poor people were and how their pleadings were to no avail. We kids could be a hurtful lot at times when we "slagged off" our peers, but I really felt sorry for these poor souls, as did the rest of the class.

It also instilled a terrible fear in me, particularly when we were told that the Bishop himself would ask a question of every second boy when we were at the altar rails. The master had told us that we'd be thrown out of the church on the day, if we failed to answer correctly. Fear was the constant throughout my schooling, though we managed to have a laugh from time to time. I remember on one occasion being at a retreat in the old "tin" chapel, and the missionary conducting the service announced that we would say one decade of the Rosary. I put my hand in my pocket, knowing that my rosary beads were broken, and extracted just one decade. I showed it to the lads around me and we all began to giggle uncontrollably. The missioner was a sour faced Jesuit, and if he had heard us, we were in danger of dire consequences. Each time we looked at each other, we got worse. Our faces were as red as beetroot and it looked as though we were about to explode. Thankfully, the decade was finished very fast, and the retreat was over. We hastily got out of the chapel and fell into each other's arms laughing loudly. On the morning of the ceremony, my mother asked my father to give me a good wash. He stood me in the bath and used a nailbrush to get the dirt out of my knees. All the kids wore short trousers then and all of us, without exception, had dirt ingrained in our knees. This was from playing football and other games on grass and no amount of ordinary washing would shift it. Knees would also be scarred from cuts obtained when we played football and other games on the road. The scars were like trophies.

Playing football on the road was hazardous in another way. The Gardaí carried out raids on a regular basis. But most of us escaped because we could outrun an adult with no problem. We also knew the layout of the land and we would disappear down the side of certain houses and through the back garden and out onto the road at the back. They would also sneak up on us on dark evenings as we played cards under the light of a lamppost. On one occasion two garda corralled us in with their bicycles. I managed to push between the opening where their front wheels met and took off like a hare. There was no five bob fine for me in court on that occasion. They had little to do with their time. People may have been poor but they were generally law abiding. One night, when the lads were playing cards for money my pal Jimmy got dressed up in a police uniform that belonged to the sister of John Doyle, another of our neighbours. Sheila, his sister, was acting in a concert and had brought the uniform home for safekeeping. Jimmy came flying down the road on a bicycle. When the boys saw him they scattered fast, leaving all of the money behind. He fell around the place laughing and they swore at him for an hour afterwards, threatening him with all sorts.

Punishing us for playing games was just another form of oppression, as far as I am concerned. Families were hard pressed enough without taking them before a judge for such minor offences, if offences they were. However, it didn't match the punishment that was meted out to those poor lads who were taken to court for "mitching" or missing school. One of my classmates was sent to Artane Reform School for six years at age twelve. He didn't like school and he was taken to court for non-attendance. He was so traumatised by this experience that he neglected his health, and died all too early as a result of excessive drinking.

One great moment of satisfaction that we had was when the "big fellas" (older boys), were playing football at the crossroads of Carnlough and Kilkernan Roads. One of the lads spotted two plainclothes police approaching fast, and he shouted a warning. Another of the lads placed the ball as if he was about to take a penalty. He ran back a few paces and rushing forward made contact with the ball. It flew like it had been discharged from a gun and caught one of the cops flat on his face. He went down and the other one rushed to help him. As he did so the road was cleared as if by magic. The boys lived off this for years afterwards. If we had a player like that on our national team now, he would be worth a fortune. Because the police were big countrymen, usually from County Kerry, we came to hate all country people, known to Dubliners as "Culshies," with a passion. It was as if war had been declared, whenever Dublin played any of the country teams at Gaelic Football.

CHAPTER SEVEN

THE WINNING BEGINS

The school choir was entered for the Father Matthew Feis in 1950, our confirmation year. It was exciting to be backstage, just watching the contestants in the various disciplines practising. While we were in the wings, waiting our turn to go on stage, one young lad was so wrapped up in rehearsing his violin solo he actually walked onto the stage. The judges laughed and the audience applauded. Realising at that moment where he was, he made a quick exit, his face red as a beetroot. We sang our piece and listened intently as the judge's spokesman gave their assessment. We were the last choir of the day and remained on stage to hear his comments. When he mentioned that we were a little bit quick in cutting off the end of sentences, I thought, "Well, that's that."

But then he followed up with the comment, "Apart from that, the interpretation was perfect and so the first prize goes to… St. Finbarr's Boys Choir." We screamed with delight and jumped around the stage like buck rabbits. It was exactly fifty years since my grandfather had won his gold medal. This was a special day for me, in more ways than one. Father Burke found it difficult to contain himself. He even shed tears. We were feted by all and sundry at school and in Cabra West generally. He arranged to take us all out to Howth Harbour for the day and have a slap-up lunch. We sang on the bus going out, we sang on the harbour wall while we were there, and we sang all the way home again. My father was extremely proud of the win and boasted to family and friends alike. This, of course singled me out for further criticism among certain of my siblings. The label

76

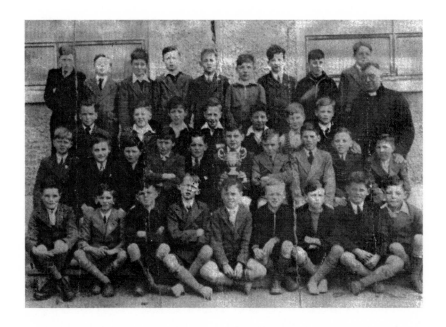

now was "Big Head." But one of the great moments of my life then was when my aunt Molly presented me with my grandfather's tuning fork. It is something I still treasure today.

The slagging at home got even worse when later that same year, I won a plaque at school for my knowledge on the Mass. A thousand boys attended the school. We were crammed in sixty to a class. The competition was open to all. It was split into two sections. The first part was an essay on a religious subject. I can't remember what the subject was. I think it had to do with the death of Jesus on the cross. The idea was that the winner from each class would then compete in an oral competition that was to be held on stage in the school hall. Bernard Moore, a friend of mine, won the essay in our class hands down. Bernard was brilliant at essay writing and should have gone on to be a journalist. On the day of the contest however, he was out of school with a heavy cold. The master asked the class whom they thought should represent them and they chose me. The contestants gathered on stage at twelve and one by one, people were eliminated until there was just two left... myself and another boy.

We battled on to one o'clock with both of us neck and neck. If one missed an answer, the other did likewise. When the other answered a question the opponent matched it. Dinnertime had arrived and people were getting restless, so it was decided by the judges to toss a coin for first prize. I won and to the resounding cheers of my classmates, I carried my plaque home. Back at school in the afternoon, the master asked why I had chosen the plaque and not the prayer book that had been on view. The winner was allowed first choice of the prizes. "Because the plaque had been specially blessed by Pope Pious XII," I answered. He was highly impressed and made sure that Father Burke was informed of the success of one of his choirboys. He needn't have worried; Father Burke was there in the hall to see for himself. The following week Bernard's father visited our teacher, claiming that the first prize rightfully belonged to his son. He was quite put out when he was told by the master to take a hike.

This was to be a landmark year for me and I was beginning to realise that I was as good as the next fellow. My confidence was growing steadily, although it would be a while yet before I could look a person in the eye and challenge what they had to say.

The mother of Billy Ellis, a friend who lived in number twenty-three on our road, asked me if I would be interested in joining the St. John Ambulance Brigade. I said I would and a week later, Billy and myself, accompanied by his mother, presented ourselves at the headquarters of the City of Dublin Ambulance Division in Great Strand Street. We were welcomed with open arms and had our details entered in the book. After a few weeks Billy dropped out. So I asked Jimmy Johnston my friend and next door neighbour, and Alec Jackson, a friend who lived opposite my house if they would care to join. They came the very next meeting night and signed on. We served together for the next six years.

After our training, we were examined in our knowledge and proficiency and awarded our Junior Certificate in First Aid. And after buying our uniforms, we then carried out duties in company of a senior man, at Croke Park Gaelic Football Grounds every Sunday afternoon that matches were played. I also did duty at the Spring Show in the Royal Dublin Society ground

in Ballsbridge. My Divisional Officer complimented me on my discretion when treating a lady who had fallen and had cut both of her knees. I was the only person on the stand when she arrived to seek treatment. I invited her to sit on a chair at the back of the stand, and asked her to remove her stockings. As she took the chair, I turned my back and stood in front of her, shielding her from anyone who might be walking in the aisle. She was so impressed with this that she went and sought out my senior officer and gave a glowing report of my actions. Well, my mother always referred to me as a gentleman. The credit is hers... she raised me.

Being in uniform and taking orders was never a problem. My father had always insisted that we children address all adults as either "Sir" or "Mam." He ran the house like a barracks. There was a notice on the bathroom wall saying, "Cleanliness is next to Godliness; now clean the bath after you." If I wanted sixpence to go to the Plaza Cinema on Saturday, I had to wash down all the paintwork in the house. I also had to clean the toilet and he inspected my work before I was paid. The "Brigade" members were lovely people, all of whom were serving at their own expense with one ideal… treating those who were injured or sick. There was quite a representation from the "Protestant Community."

Perhaps the best known of these were the "Overend" sisters. They were what my mother-in-law would refer to as, "The remains of auld Decency." They drove a Silver Ghost Rolls Royce and were a privilege to know. There was a strong British influence in the Brigade also, and I remember that we were invited to view a film at Headquarters of the Coronation of Queen Elizabeth 2nd in 1952. I have to admit that I attended. But it was more out of fascination with the magnificent uniforms than anything else. I still feel the same today and like to watch the "Trooping of the Colour," etc.

My knowledge of anatomy and the circulation of the blood were helped considerably by my proficiency in Latin, and the method of teaching that I was experiencing at school. If the reader doubts my recall of the very early years of my life, let me assure you that what I have written is an accurate account. As an example, I quote here the opening page of the First Aid Manual that I learned at the age of twelve…

"A knowledge of first aid enables trained persons to render such immediate assistance in cases of accident and/or sudden illness as will help in Preserving Life, Promoting Recovery and Preventing Aggravation of the injury or condition until such time as Medical Aid is available."

I can still name the bones and the arteries of the body in Latin, and also remember the circulation of the blood. With the smallest amount of encouragement, I would have completed my secondary education and who knows what would've happened after that. A medical doctor delivered a lecture on the contents of the abdomen when I was doing my Senior Certificate Course. I would have been just sixteen years of age then. Before he began, he asked if anyone in the audience knew any of the organs he was about to speak on. I raised my hand and he looked at my young face with a degree of scepticism and asked me which one I was familiar with. "All of them," I replied.

"Well go ahead and name them," he smiled.

"Stomach, Pancreas, Spleen, Kidneys, Liver, Large and Small Intestines, and the Bladder," I replied.

He was incredulous and couldn't speak for a moment or two. When he regained his composure, he congratulated me and admitted that he would have had difficulty in recalling all of them himself. All of this worked wonders on my shyness and I began to become more confident. The blushing had also all but disappeared.

On one occasion, I was about to leave home to carry out a duty when my mother asked if I had time to go to the shops for her. "Of course I had," I told her and headed off to the butchers to get the meat she wanted for the dinner.

As I entered the shop, a guy around my own age looked at my short trousers and sneered, "Cover yer knees, yer over seven,"

"Cover yer face, yer a livin' disgrace," I immediately retorted. The butcher behind the counter and a woman customer burst into laughter, and she complimented me on my uniform and my wit.

At age fourteen, I entered a first aid competition and won a trophy that had never been won by a cadet since its inception in 1946. There was great jubilation in the division. I had my photo taken for publication by one of the officers who was a photographer with the Irish Press. I arrived home with the silver cup, to the great delight of my parents. The cup was a perpetual trophy and I also had a gold and silver medal to keep. I still have it and the plaque I won at school. There is one thing that I shall ever be grateful for and it came with the training that I received. It is the ability to remain calm in crisis situations and to become the "Master of Inactivity" when dealing with people involved in accidents. For example… get people to boil water and make tea, etc., to keep them occupied while you deal with the real crisis. There was a song going around at that time entitled, "*Why does everybody call me big head,*" and certain of my brothers and sisters would sing this to me.

This knocked my confidence back somewhat, and I kept quiet at home, trying not to draw attention to myself. When one of my uncles who produced variety shows tried to get me to perform on stage, I refused. This came about when the schoolmaster was out sick one day and the class was divided out among other teachers. I was sent to "Hitler's" room and he asked if any of us was in the famous school choir. I held up my hand. "Right," he said, "let's hear you sing." I sang a popular song of the time called "Liberty Belle." The class applauded and we were then told to keep quiet for the rest of the day.

One of his pupils was a lad called Maloney, whose father used to collect slop for pig-feed and whose family performed regularly on the school hall in shows produced by my uncle. His mother played the fiddle while she danced an Irish Jig and his three sisters sang in harmony and sounded just like the "Andrews Sisters," an American group that was popular at that time. He came over to me afterwards and told me that he thought my voice was good and would I not think of performing on stage. I would have loved to, but I was being hounded at home and I didn't want to be the focus of any further jeering, etc. I was already getting a hard time from some of my family because I had played the part of a girl in a show at the school, not long before. I loved acting and musicals were my favourite. So I refused, but he spoke to the producer, not knowing at that time that he was related to me. My uncle then appeared at our house one evening and my father sent for me. The choir was also performing during the interval at the current show that depicted the life of St. Francis Xaviour. So I stood there in front of my father and him. "I was watching you during the interval of the show and you weren't singing," he said,

"I was, Sir," I answered, looking at the floor.

"No, you weren't," he said, "Sure, you can't sing."

"You're right, Sir," I said, blushing like a beacon and biting my lip.

"Ah! Go on, sing something for us," he said.

I refused and was told by my father that I was useless and to get out. That put paid to any notions I might have had to follow a career on the stage. If only they had known the damage they were inflicting, I'm sure that they would've seen things differently. I guess it's difficult to be positive when you've been downtrodden all your life anyway. Yet, some parents were encouraging their children, like Dickie Rock and Bill Cullen, the author of *Penny Apples* and *Golden Apples* fame. To me, that is the difference between us. They went on to be successful, doing what they loved to do best.

I went on to do a job that I didn't particularly like, but managed to be successful at. Do I sound bitter? Well… I'm not and I never have been. It was just such a waste, I feel, as I look back. Why this should be, puzzles me even today, because my father used to talk with pride about his father's contribution to the music of the day. My whole family were terrific singers and not at all bad looking, if I might say. But the encouragement wasn't there and the Irish music scene was denied talent that would have given some of the performers of today a run for their money.

It was around this time that I witnessed my father in action. He ran the darts and rings club in the local public house. It was situated on Fassaugh Avenue, a short walk from where we lived. He brought my mother with him and having bought her a drink, he left her in the lounge while he went into the bar to get a competition under way. When he went back to the lounge, my mother wasn't there. A friend informed him that one of our neighbours had passed some insulting remark to my mother. She got upset and went home. I was there when he arrived back at our house and asked her what the guy had said. She didn't want to tell him, but he insisted. I followed him down the road and stood at the guy's gate while my father knocked on his hall door. It opened and I saw my father's arm shoot forward and connect with the fellow's chin. That's the only punch that was thrown. The guy was out cold. Just then the paper seller from across the road who had seen what happened, ran over, and vaulted the railings into the other guy's front garden. His intention was to attack my father. He was met with one of those punches I had just seen my father deliver to the guy who was lying in his hallway. The second fellow went down like a sack of potatoes. Again the message went out, loud and clear: "Don't mess with the Sheridans."

CHAPTER EIGHT

THE GAMES PEOPLE PLAY

We had a season for the different games we played. In the summer, we played cricket during the daylight hours. When we got tired of that we'd get our hoops out. These were old bicycle wheels with the spokes removed and we'd drive them along with a stick. We could perform all sorts of sharp turns and make them spin, etc. Then came the trolleys. These were made up of two or three pieces of plank nailed together with an axle back and front onto which were attached four ball bearings for wheels. A hole was drilled through the front axle and through the cart itself. A long bolt was passed through the holes and a nut was screwed to the top so as to secure the axle and to allow it to be moved. We would then tie a piece of thin rope or strong twine either side of the front axle, so that we could steer it. Then a coin was tossed to see who got to ride on it first and who would push.

On one occasion, I was delighted with myself for having won the toss and as we rolled down the footpath at great speed and turned the corner at the end of the road I ran into another cart coming in the opposite direction. I shot forward and as I did, a splinter of wood tore an "L" shaped gash in my new flannel trousers that my mother had just bought me. I tried to stitch the rip but only made it worse. Eventually, I had to tell my mother. She whacked my behind good and hard and put a patch on the hole. Next, there was skipping, and this was all the more enjoyable if the rope was a long one. So two or more of us could skip at the same time.

Alternatively, we would get a "Cut" of bread and a bottle of water from our mother and head off to the open-air swimming pool or "Baths," as they were more commonly known, for the whole day. The baths were located about halfway between Cabra West and Finglas. Finglas was only a village at that time. The vast housing estate was built much later, which was just as well because there was hardly room to move in the pool as it was. The weather always seemed to be fine in those days and you could smell the chlorine in the air from quite a distance down the road. It's a wonder we weren't all blinded with the amount they used to put in the water. All of us went round with red-rimmed eyes, looking like vampires following our visits to the pool. We used our shirts to dry off with and we would then lay them on the grass to dry in the sun. Once, I remember an older guy from our road tried to molest a couple of us. We told him where to go and threatened to tell our fathers. He soon got the message, although I heard some time later that he had been charged with molesting other boys. He had to clear out of the area after that. It reminded me of a story my father told me about a paedophile that was found guilty by a Republican Court during the "Troubles." His sentence was a bullet in the scrotum and that's what he got. This latest guy was luckier than that, but only because his family moved him out of the area good and quick.

Sometimes we would swim in the "Silver Spoon" and dive off the "Broken Arch." The silver spoon was a section of the river Tolka, and it flowed past the swimming pool. Its water was used to fill the baths and when the baths were emptied, the water was returned to the Tolka. The broken arch was an old bridge that had collapsed. The girls weren't allowed swim in the baths, they had to use the river; and we would stay with them for their safety and comfort. There was never any risk of molestation to the girls. We stayed around in case they got into difficulties in the water. Though I do remember getting an eyeful on one occasion, when one of the older girls got changed behind a bush. She was screened from the crowd at the swimming pool and she didn't notice me and my companions sitting in the long grass on the hill behind her. That was the first time I'd seen bare breasts, but I quickly put any inappropriate thoughts out of my head. At least I think I did. At other times, we swam in the canal. But often there would be a dead dog floating in it, so we tended to avoid swimming there. We would enjoy watching the older lads diving off the bridge though. It was here one evening that Barty Wiley, one of my schoolmates, decided to make a name for himself. He was the boy that I took home to my mother after seeing his mother and how he was treated. No one was sure if he wanted to commit suicide. He stood on the parapet of the bridge fully clothed, shouted "I'm Barty Wiley," and threw himself into the canal. I never heard of him after that. Some said that he was in a mental hospital. I hope he's well and that he got to live a full and happy life.

There was a quarry at the end of Broombridge Road where we would go to play in the wrecked cars that were dumped there. Someone had the bright idea of using the detached bonnet lid of a car as a sleigh. So three or four of us would sit on the bonnet lid and ease our way over the edge one of the hills surrounding the dump. We would then take off at breakneck speed into the valley below. The thrill of it was just fantastic to us kids. On another occasion, I actually fished the quarry for perch and roach, and caught some. I fried them up when I got home, but found that there was very little meat on them. They were also full of little bones that drove me nuts trying not to swallow them. Some of the older lads used to thrill us by diving off the high banks of the quarry into the dark green waters below. None of us younger ones ever attempted to swim in the quarry, because we had been told that an older lad had drowned there and it was weeks before they found his body. Some claimed that the quarry was bottomless and that was enough to scare us off.

During the winter months after it got dark, we would play "Kick-the can." This involved a person being chosen to hide their face and allow the rest of the players to hide. He/she would try to find those who were hiding while protecting the can, which was located in the middle of the road. It could happen that most of those in hiding were caught and they would get released by one of the last people in hiding by running out and kicking the can. This meant that the person guarding the can would have to start all over again. If all were caught, then a new person was chosen, usually the first one to be caught. Relievio was a similar game except it was played without a can. Those who were caught would have to stand in a line along the railings outside one of our houses. Someone would have to run past the line between the person guarding it and the prisoners, thus affecting a release or "Relievio."

Then there was my favourite, called "Catch-a-girl-kiss-a-girl." This one hardly needs further explanation. It soon fell out of favour with me however, when I caught one particular girl and after I had kissed her, she complained that I had hurt her sore lip. On checking, I saw that she had a scab the size of a halfpenny. This coupled with the fact that the husband of one of my sisters saw what I was at and made fun of me. While we played this game and others such as skipping and swinging on the lamppost with the girls, it was really very innocent fun. There was no question of sex involved. Sex education didn't exist in any shape or form. What we did know we got from the older guys and that was so ridiculous as to be laughable. For example, we were told that the way to check a girl was "clean" if we found ourselves in a sexual situation was to hold a penny up to her vagina and if it turned green, keep away from her! Or squeeze the juice from an orange skin into her and if she complained of pain and especially if it made her jump… keep away. We thought that a baby was delivered through the navel. Not once during my years of service with the Ambulance Brigade was the anatomy of a female discussed. The ignorance in which we were kept in this regard was nothing short of criminal. When a couple of the older girls who lived locally got pregnant, their names were whispered behind people's hands. In one case, the girl was not seen outside of her house for the full-term of her pregnancy. The other was sent over to relatives in England. We are still exporting our problem in this regard today; although this time, it's to terminate the pregnancy.

The "Grand National" was another favourite, although it didn't please the neighbours. It involved us all starting in one of the back gardens and racing through as many gardens as we could, while jumping the wire fences that divided them. On one occasion, the male occupier of a house saw us from his bedroom and got so excited that he threw a pillow at us. We all disappeared, roaring laughing.

The older guys, my brothers included, played "Handball." My brothers Dick and Gerry became well known on the circuit.

Another game involved peeing into an empty can, then using the shadow cast by the lamppost at night to run a piece of dark wool across the footpath. The string would then be tied to the can, and it would be placed on the inside slope of the wall that surrounded the gardens of the houses on the corner of the road. The capping on top of the wall was pyramid shaped. We would lie quietly in a garden opposite and wait for someone to walk between the lamppost and the wall. This would then cause the can to be pulled over the wall and onto the passer-by. I only ever did this once. I didn't think it was funny, especially after the can landed in the hat of one old lady. She was carrying it in her hand at the time and she was naturally upset when it got filled with pee.

The older guys then started to wrap excrement in parcel form and leave it on the footpath for someone to find. My mother arrived home one dark evening and placed a parcel on the kitchen table, asking my father to open it. She watched expectantly as he cut the string and opened the paper. "Oh! Sweet J...," my mother cried, almost vomiting as she saw the contents. My father got rid of it very quickly, swearing to put manners on whoever was responsible. There were limits beyond which people shouldn't go and that rotten trick was way beyond the line.

When the weather turned frosty, we would get an old sack, dip it in a drain to get it wet and then beat the ground with it. There were very few cars in those days so we did this on the road, usually for the distance between two lampposts (approx. 25 yards). Once the wet ground had frozen, we used it as a slide to skate on. We would run a short distance and with one foot in front of the other slide along to the end. Many happy hours were passed in this way, and it kept us all fit as fiddles. At Halloween, some of the older guys would buy fireworks, and it wasn't unusual for them to put a lighted banger through the letterbox of a house where someone lived who they didn't like. But this didn't happen very often, I'm delighted to say. While we were doing this, we had to keep an eye out for the police or the priest. It was legal to buy fireworks when I was a kid. I remember them being banned following an incident in a shop, when someone threw a lighted one into the stock on the shelves. A magnificent display followed, with fireworks going in all directions. Soon afterwards a law was passed, banning them entirely. Not to be outdone, when Halloween came around again we would spit on the carbide from an old car battery, this would cause it to fizzle and discharge a gas. Then we would put a tin can over it, which had previously had a nail driven through the top to make a hole. We would then hold our thumb on the hole for a minute or so to let the gas build up. As we took our thumb away we would hold a lighted match to the hole. It would set the gas off with a great bang as the can took off into the air like a rocket.

There were other great games we played apart from football. During the summer, we would use white chalk to draw cricket stumps on the concrete lamppost, and use a hurley stick for a bat and a tennis ball to bowl with. In order to avoid any disputes, we would wet the ball, so that it left a mark on the concrete where it had struck. The chalk we used sometimes came via the school. Any small pieces the teachers threw in the bin were rescued; and sometimes it came from broken statues. Every home had a statue of "The Sacred Heart" (Jesus), or "The Virgin Mary." These conveniently got knocked over and broken and they were the best for getting the thick lines we needed. The priests would've been horrified. They poked their nose into every aspect of our lives. Not only were we threatened with hellfire and damnation for our sinful ways, they used to hunt us off the road and into our houses, shouting at us to do our homework or "ecker" as we called it. Ecker was a shortened version of exercise. I always did mine as soon as I got home, but that cut no ice with them, anyway.

They would patrol the streets at weekends, checking to see if any of the men were playing pitch and toss. One of the favourite gathering places for the men who played was beside the Turf Depot, on the hill opposite the playground. This was a game were two or more pennies were lined up on what was known as a "feck" and thrown into the air. The clergy, in place of the other Anglo-Saxon four-letter word, encouraged the use of the word "feck," as it wasn't considered to be a swear-word. The players would have placed bets on whether the pennies would land showing heads or tails. A lot of money could change hands at times, and sometimes a loser would get annoyed and a fight or "ruggy up" would start. That would attract all of us kids, cheering and shouting, which in turn would attract the attention of their wives who would be screaming for them to stop. This was one game that needed the intervention of the priests and or the police, because some of the men lost money that ought to have been going to feed the family. On one occasion, one of the men told Father Kavanagh that if he weren't wearing the collar he'd beat the living daylights out of him. The priest promptly took the collar off and invited him to try. His companion, Fr. O'Brien, intervened and prevented the fight taking from place. Before long the word was all over the parish, and Father Kavanagh became something of a folk hero.

We also played "jackstones," which involved using five small smooth stones and throwing them into the air and catching them on the back of your hand. That was the first move. The next involved throwing the stones onto the ground; then while holding one on the back of the hand, the player would throw this in the air and while it was in flight, pick one of the others off the ground, finally catch the falling one on the back of the hand again. There were other more complicated moves as the game progressed. Not only did it pass the time, it improved our dexterity and it was really enjoyable.

Some of the girls would organise a concert and we would be charged a penny in to the performance. As money was in very limited supply, we didn't attend many shows. We had our own little gangs and I remember one occasion when I was asked to join the Murphy gang. I was taken around the house to the back garden where they held the initiation rite. The sun was high in the sky (it always seemed to shine for the whole of our school holidays); I was told that if I wanted to be a member, I would have to drop my trousers and sit on an upturned cast-iron bath. I did and it was so hot I jumped sky high, much to the amusement of all those present.

My pal Jimmy decided to form his own gang and a meeting was arranged in the wooden garden shed that his father had built in their back garden. My younger brother Willie wanted to join but we refused, telling him that he was too young. While our gang members were sitting in the shed, having our first meeting, we noticed smoke coming from under the door. Then suddenly there were flames and we quickly evacuated. When we got out-side, Willie was stood there. When we asked him what he was doing, he told us that if he couldn't be a member of the gang he was going to burn our clubhouse down. He had piled old papers and anything else that would burn outside of the door before setting it alight. We abandoned the idea after that.

We were always looking for ways to earn the price of the pic-tures. So Jimmy and I decided that we would make Mr. Maloney the slop (pig-feed) collector an offer. We would collect all the slop on the road and save him calling to every house if he would pay us sixpence each. It was four pence into the Plaza cinema and we'd have tuppence to spend on sweets. It was agreed, but we'd only get paid if Mr. Maloney was satisfied with the weight of the sack of waste. All went well for a while, until he started to demand more weight. We decided to give it to him by adding tealeaves and grass, and hide it by mixing it through the slop. It seemed to work well for a week or two until he discovered what we were up to. He chased us all over the road claiming that we had sickened his pigs with our mixture.

We needed a new idea and sat down to discuss our next move. We bought sugar in thick brown paper bags in those days. Because our family was so large, my mother would discard more empty bags in a shorter time that Jimmy's mother. So, I soon got my hands on one. "What do we do now?" asked Jimmy. I took a handful of dry clay out of the garden and began to rub it between my hands until it was very fine. He helped as I explained that we would fill the bag with clay, reseal it, and sell it to his mother telling her that it was surplus to my mother's requirements. He thought it was a brilliant idea and we did the deal. His mother gave us the money and we headed off to the Cabra Grand Cinema where there was a favourite cowboy film playing. We had plenty left over for a feast of sweets and enjoyed a wonderful afternoon show. When we got home, Jimmy's mother was gunning for him. She had opened the bag and without looking at what it contained poured it into the sugar bowl. I could hear the wallops through the kitchen wall as she administered his punishment. She had told my mother also. But my mother thought it so funny that she just gave me a verbal warning. Poor Jimmy, a true friend always.

CHAPTER NINE

THE REAL GANGS

O n Sunday afternoons, my pals and I would walk out the Cappagh Road, at the top of Fassaugh Avenue. When the fruit was in season, we would pick blackberries, damsons, plums, sloes and crab apples, which grew in abundance along the sides of the road. There were lots of fruit farms in North Dublin at that time, and some seeds were no doubt carried on the wind and germinated in the hedgerows and ditches along the roadsides. We would then wend our way through Cappagh Village and on to Finglas Village and back along the Finglas Road on our way home. Other times we would walk out towards Blanchardstown and the Dunsink Observatory.

One evening as we got near to Blanchardstown, a gang challenged us to a fight. There were six of us and about fourteen of them. Jimmy picked two and started sparring. We had been carving our initials on the trees with a hunting knife that belonged to Georgie Heffernan, one of our gang. He had his bike with him and we dispatched him to get help. I had the knife in my hand, as I was the last one to use it before the others arrived, looking for trouble. One of them spotted it as I drew it from its sheath. "I'll take the rest of yeh," I said, waving the knife. As soon as they spotted it, they took off like hares running down the road. Dusk was upon us as we made our way back home satisfied with ourselves. We met Georgie on his way back to us. When we asked him what happened to the help he had gone for, he told us that he met a Garda on the way who ignored his plea for help and issued him with a ticket for having no light on his bike. We all roared laughing… except Georgie, he didn't see the humour in it.

94

I mentioned earlier the Murphy gang and Jimmy's gang. These were a harmless little kid's way of "Herding," I suppose. But there were more sinister elements about. My first cousin Billy Miller was at a dance in the church hall in Santry. He was dancing with a girl that he had just met when he got a tap on the shoulder. The guy said, "You're dancing with my girlfriend. Leave her alone." My cousin apologised, explaining that he didn't know this and was about to walk away, when the girl told Billy that she wasn't that guy's girl. She explained that the guy, whose name was Billy Kelly, had the hots for her and was pestering her, in fact. So my cousin, being a gentleman, told him to get lost. When he left the dancehall at the end of the night, Kelly and a gang of his friends attacked Billy. He was left for dead by the side of the road. The girl called an ambulance and my cousin was taken to hospital. After he had recovered and returned home, he discovered that his attackers were in fact a gang from Cabra West. Their leader had styled himself on the American Wild West murderer "Billy the Kid."

Our area had become known generally as "The Wild West" and was reported in the newspapers as such. A meeting was held in our house between my uncle Jim (Billy's father), his eldest brother Michael, my father, and my eldest brother Paddy. A strategy for dealing with the gang was agreed on. The local police superintendent was ex-Old IRA and a friend of my father. He was asked to keep his men away from the area on a particular night, the reason having been explained to him. He agreed and the plan was put into action. The gang used to hang around outside of Marcella's, the local chip shop on Fassaugh Avenue. That's where all but Kelly, who happened to be somewhere else that night, met my family. They were beaten to a pulp and warned that any threat to our family in future would result in much more severe consequences. A few weeks later, my eldest brother was walking by the chip shop late in the evening when he recognised Kelly. He went over to him, picked him up by his throat, and flung him through the chip shop window. The gang ran off, leaving Kelly behind, no doubt remembering their recent encounter. The message had gone out again… "Don't mess with the Sheridans."

My eldest brother Paddy told me that many years later, he met Kelly in London. He used to sing in the local pub and had a very good voice, too. But one evening he was acting the tough guy with a Londoner and he was slashed with a razor. He received over one hundred stitches to the wound on his face.

Journalists have a lot to answer for, in my opinion. This mobster had his story in the Sunday Newspaper and he was portrayed as some sort of folk hero. He told of how one evening, after breaking into a house, the couple returned home unexpectedly. He was forced to hide under the bed because his escape route was cut off. There he lay until the couple went to sleep. He then left, taking with him what little they had of value. No mention was ever made of the beating he and his gang had suffered at the hands of my family. Neither did the newspaper make any reference to the fact that he was robbing poor working-class families.

Sometime later, my pal Jimmy and I were walking by the shops at the top of Fassaugh Avenue when a gang came running at us from out of a laneway, by the side of the shops. Eight guys confronted us and they were looking for trouble. Jimmy recognised one of them as Billy Kelly's brother and told me. "Do you know who I am, Kelly?" I asked.

"No… who are you," he said with a sneer.

"I'm one of the Sheridans," I replied, raising my eyebrows.

"Ah, hold on lads," he said, pushing his friends away from us. "We don't want any trouble with that family." And as quick as they had appeared, they were gone.

We found ourselves in a similar situation on another occasion, and one of the gang was the brother of a guy who was courting one of my sisters. That was enough to get us out of trouble, especially when I warned him of the consequences of picking on a Sheridan. A short while later we met the leader of this gang, walking past the shops on his own. We invited him up the lane beside the shops, where he could have a go at whichever one he chose. He declined, swearing that it wasn't him who had been with the gang. We knew better, and we gave him a going over anyway. As far as we were concerned, another coward had been dealt with.

During the "Teddy Boy," era it was common for gangs then to have a bicycle chain hidden under the lapels of the drape jacket that they wore, or a knuckleduster would be carried in the jacket pocket. This would be used on anyone that they had a disagreement with. A posse of men was formed and very soon teddy boys were being found with shaven heads, lying in gardens with their drainpipe trousers slashed. Not all teddy boys were troublemakers, I would hasten to add. Most of them were ordinary decent lads who simply wore the fashion of the Rock and Roll bands. I knew a few of them and they never caused any problems.

One of the great advantages of having a large family was the reluctance of others to pick a fight, especially if they knew that your family would fight back. Much has been written about the "animal gangs" that plagued Dublin in the Tenement era. The newspapers had branded them with the name because their behaviour was no better than that of animals. They used a variety of weapons; the worst of these was perhaps, the cap with razor blades inserted into the peak. It was vicious and in many ways the lino or hobby knife is the modern equivalent. One policeman called "Lugs Brannigan," took these gangs to task. He was a police-boxing champion by all accounts and he had no fear. He didn't hesitate to use his skill as a boxer to put manners on anyone who stepped out of line. It wasn't long before the gangs were no more to be seen, terrorising the people. Today unfortunately, the weapon of choice is the gun, and there is very little that anyone can do when confronted with such a weapon. One thing I can say with certainty is… those who roam in gangs and use weaponry of any description are cowards. They always were and always will be.

—⟡—

I sat and passed the Department of Education examination for Primary School children. I was just approaching my fourteenth birthday. There was no compulsion on anyone to sit the nine subjects and many of the students didn't bother. While I felt that I had done reasonably well, waiting for the results was traumatic. In the meantime, I set about writing letters of application to the three main employers of the day. These were the Electricity Supply Board, Guinness, and Coras Iompair Eireann (CIE) or the Transport Authority. I also sat an examination for a scholarship of two years free training in the local Technical School. My written work was excellent and the final hurdle was an oral Irish test.

I entered the room where the test was to take place and was greeted by a Mister Finnachta. We conversed in Irish for a while before he handed me a book and asked me to read from it. One of the problems with trying to learn the native language was a change in the spelling of words. For example, I was taught to use dots and strokes over certain letters to denote the meaning. The book I was given to read didn't have these and the "H" was used in place of the "dot." I struggled and the examiner started to badger me. This exacerbated the problem, and for the next twenty minutes I argued with him through the medium of Irish but to no avail… he failed me. I remember today what I said to him in closing… "Nuair a astrín an litriú astrín an focal," (When the spelling changes, the word changes.) Mr. Lewis, my schoolmaster, went nuts when he heard that I'd failed and went to see the examiner to get him to change his mind, without success.

I thought that I was a total failure, until I received the results of the State examination. The head master sent for my father and asked him to bring me along to the school. I had no idea what this was all about and approached the school, anticipating trouble. However, when we got there, Mr. McCarthy, the head teacher, showed my father my marks for the exam. Of the nine subjects, none was below 88 percent. This was an outstanding result, the head master said, and it would be a terrible waste of talent if my father didn't send me on to secondary school. He was given the name of a school, together with the name of the Principal and encouraged to make contact as soon as possible. A week or so later, I was taken by my father to meet Brother Barry, the principal at St. Mary's Christian Brother's School in

Mary's Place off Dorset Street. It was just up the Road from my favourite cinema, the Plaza.

I was interviewed and told by Brother Barry that I would have to undergo an entrance examination. This was arranged for the following day; and in the year 1952, I sat down at a desk at the back of a classroom to read the first of the questions on the exam paper. When I finished, I handed the completed paper to back and Brother Barry told me to stay where I was while he checked it. He was back within thirty minutes, asking me where I had learned my maths. Once again, I thought I was in trouble and I was prepared for a rejection. When I told him that I had done my primary schooling at St. Finbarr's, he expressed surprise and told me that my maths were in advance of what was being taught in First Year Secondary. My exam results, he said, were excellent and he would be delighted to have me in his school. Our conversation, I should add was totally through the Irish language. The school's policy was to teach all subjects in Irish and Latin. English was only spoken when it was being done as a subject. That section of the test was in the spelling that I was used to, and it presented no problem for me. To be fair to Mr. Finnachta, other students from my school had passed the exam for technical school. So the problem was mine. I don't know why I failed the exam for "Tech" and passed a much harder one for Secondary School. It was just one of those days, I think.

Brother Barry brought me to a classroom and introduced me to a colleague who was teaching the scholarship class. This class was composed of students who had undergone an examination similar to the one I had just completed, and having passed it, they were granted free secondary education. I was asked to bring in my Baptismal Certificate and I complied with this request within a few days. A week or so later, I was standing in the head brother's office once again. He regretfully announced that he was being forced to remove me from the class I was in, because I was a month older than the qualifying age. He was outraged that the Department of Education, which granted the scholarships, would not be flexible enough to allow me to stay.

Consequently, I was taken out of that class; and because of the results of my entrance examination, he put me in with the second year students, explaining that I was too advanced for first year.

Scoil Mhuire, or St. Mary's to give it its English name, was where my father attended when he started school first. The building was very old and the desks reminded me of the film I saw entitled *Tom Brown's Schooldays*. It was set in the early part of the nineteenth century. They were long enough to seat twelve boys, side by side. There was a sloping timber front and the seat was timber also. The desk had no back to it, so when we sat down we simply stepped over the rigid seat. We had to sit upright at all times and the only chance of a bit of comfort was when we leaned forward to write, so that our chest would rest against the front section. But I liked the place. At around midday every day, there was a lovely aroma of freshly baked bread from the bakery next door. Loud gurgles and roars could be heard coming from empty stomachs, all around the room. We had a sports day every Thursday, when we would meet up in the Phoenix Park to play either Hurling or Gaelic Football. Because of this, we then had to attend school on Saturday mornings.

Homework took three hours every night. One of the tasks was to translate Latin to Irish and vice versa. Latin didn't present too much of a problem for me, since I was used to singing it in the church choir. One day in class however, Brother Barry asked me a question and I hesitated before answering. He hit me on the top of my head with the window pole and told me not to hesitate… just answer. The discipline was even more rigid than I had experienced at primary school. On another occasion, I had not completed my English homework and the master called me out to the front of the class. He was a small fat man with a comb-over of red hair that was oiled to keep it in position. The pupils called him "greasy chips."

"Hold out your hand," he said, while baring his teeth. This was a common trait with teachers in those days. It exemplified the hatred that they had in their hearts for those in their charge and the viciousness with which they delivered their punishment. He picked up a twelve-inch wooden ruler and I thought to myself, "This is nothing; I've been used to getting hit with a bamboo cane." I soon found out that the bamboo would've been the better option. He told me to bend my fingers so that my hand was half closed. Then he took a swipe from the length of his outstretched arm, catching the ends of my fingernails. My hair stood on end as the pain shot up to my brain. He smiled... I looked him in the eye and didn't show any tears. No way was I going to let this clown see me crying. Can you imagine that happening today? He'd be hauled into court and be sued for everything he owned.

Brother Barry sent for my father and explained all of what had happened, regarding the scholarship class, and told him that he would be liable for the fees. My father realised that finding the fees would stretch the family finances to the breaking point. So he approached the Irish Pensions Board, from whom he had been granted a small pension in recognition of his IRA service, and asked if he could surrender this for a lump sum. They refused his request and he then made the same request to the British Pensions Board, from whom he also had a pension, with the same result. He contacted Brother Barry and informed him of his situation. Brother Barry then contacted Mr. McCarthy, my previous Head Teacher, and he in turn contacted Father Burke, our Parish Priest and the choirmaster. Father Burke called to see my father and offered to provide the necessary finance for my schooling. My father turned this down. He was too proud to accept charity from the priest, and I was taken out of school. I overheard him speaking to one of my older brothers about this situation, and my brother told him that he, for one, would not contribute any money from his hard earned wages to keep me in school. The year was 1953... it was time now to get a job.

CHAPTER TEN

JOB HUNTING... SUCCESS

My sister May was working in the finishing department of Irish Carton Printers, Ltd., and she tried to get me apprenticed to the print section. But printing was a "closed shop" and apprenticeships were kept exclusively for the families of those already qualified. So, there was no hope for me there. I had written to the three main employers previously but there was no reply to my letters. So there was nothing for it but to check the classified advertisements and try my luck there. I travelled all over the city searching for work in all sorts of places.

On one occasion, I attended an interview with a company that turned out to be the forerunner of the employment consultancies that proliferate in the landscape today. They wanted me to pay them to find me a job, and what they offered me was one at five shillings a week. I overheard one of the interviewers tell the other that I couldn't talk and that's all he felt that I was worth. He was right, to some extent at least; I was so shy that my head was bowed when I spoke to people, and these two totally intimidated me, anyway.

Eventually a man who ran a small bakery in Ballsbridge hired me. I became an apprentice confectioner on the princely sum of five shillings a week. That just about paid my bus fare from Cabra. But it was work and he was kind enough to give me a bicycle so that I wouldn't have to spend my money on bus fares. Pretty soon I was spreading the jam on the sponge base and rolling this into a "Swiss roll." The base was about three feet long and I cut this into twelve-inch lengths when I had rolled it. At lunchtime, his mother would bring me a cooked lunch on a tray and I would sit in the bakery and enjoy that. He was having the place extended and one wall of the bakery was missing. The workmen were not allowed to work during bakery hours. The weather was cold and unless I was working right up beside the oven, I was freezing. I remember complaining about this to my father one evening at home when my brother, Tom asked jokingly, was I making "Rock Buns." These were similar to scones but they were made to resemble a piece of rock. They were hardened on the outside with melted sugar and they were quite tough to bite into. He was inferring that I was working with stone, hence the cold. The rest of the family got a good laugh out of that.

Then a friend of his offered me a job in Eason's the stationers. I was told that there were great possibilities for progression here. What I got was a messenger bike with a very large basket set into the front of it. I would then take basketfuls of papers and magazines across from the stores off Gardiner Street to the shop in O'Connell Street. The front of the bike was so heavy that it was difficult to keep it on the road. One day when I pulled hard on the brakes to avoid someone who had stepped in front of me, the bike stood on its front end, dumping me unceremoniously over the handlebars and onto the road. I got no sympathy from my boss when I eventually got back to the job. All he was concerned about was that I delivered everything intact.

Thankfully, a letter from the Electricity Board arrived soon afterwards at my home, inviting me to attend an interview. I passed the test that was set by the interview board and I was informed that I would be hired, subject to my passing the medical examination. This of course meant that I had to resign from Eason's, much to the annoyance of my brother Tom, whose friend had gotten me the job in the first place.

All went well with the medical exam, and I received a letter confirming my position as a messenger with a weekly wage of £1.17.6p. This was fifteen shillings more than I had been paid at Eason's and I thought I was really well off. It was a long way from the five shillings I got as an apprentice. My unopened wage packet was handed to my mother every week, and she returned five shillings to me for pocket money. Now I could go the cinema without having to ask for money. Independence was just great. Life was looking good.

I was assigned to the "Adrema" or addressing section, where I spent most of my time sitting at a table, inserting bills into envelopes for the consumers. I was given time off to report to Clery's Store in O'Connell Street to be measured for a uniform. From there, I went to O'Callaghan's Outfitters in Dame Street to be measured for a raincoat. The uniform was bottle green with a stiff high collar, on which the letters E.S.B. where embroidered in gold thread. It also included a cap with a black patent leather peak over which was the E.S.B. in gold. It really looked very smart, and the first day that I wore it on my way to work, everybody I passed stopped to look. I found this very embarrassing and quickly took to leaving my tunic and cap at work and travelling in my uniform trousers and civilian jacket. The head office of the Board was in Fitzwilliam Street. It's still there, except that when I started work, the original Georgian houses still stood. They were all inter-connected and you could walk the full length of the street on a rainy day without getting wet. The original "Adams" fireplaces were still in place and on the whole it was a very pleasant atmosphere in which to work. Unfortunately, the Board were granted permission to redevelop the street in the 60s and these wonderful houses were lost forever. Part of the agreement with the demolition company appears to have been that they could salvage anything from the houses they thought of value. No one realised apparently, the value of the fireplaces and the demolition company made a fortune on them alone. Thankfully, a successful campaign was started following the demolition to prevent any further desecration of our architectural heritage. Many felt that the Board should've been forced to build in the original style. What replaced the Georgian structure is an eyesore.

The staff structure in the Board was pyramidal; with the chairman at the top, and layers of departmental heads and supervisors layered, all the way to the bottom where us messengers operated. I had three bosses, for example. There was my departmental head, Mr. Tony O'Toole, who was very nice. Then there was Larry O'Neill, the Head Porter. He was a good man, also. We had to report to Larry first thing in the morning, where he witnessed our signing the attendance book. This book was taken away at five minutes past 8:30 a.m., the time we were due at work. Lastly, there was an obnoxious little Nazi, a Mr. C… who, I was told, had fallen afoul of the system and was relegated from a high position, and put in charge of all messengers. It was he whom we applied to for leave (holidays), and for replacement uniforms. He also disciplined us when we stepped out of line. We had an unofficial boss also. He was a labourer named Tommy Flynn and he kept an eye on us from time to time. He always insisted that we call him mister. He played football for Shamrock Rovers and received a badly broken leg during a game. It ended his football career. He was a really nice guy.

The head porter was always complimenting us for our excellent timekeeping. He didn't realise that there was an incentive to get in very early in the mornings. The buildings opposite were let out in flats, and a young lady who didn't bother to draw her curtains occupied one of them. This may have been because she thought the offices opposite her were not occupied before nine. Or she was an exhibitionist. At any rate, she rose at eight, naked, and she then proceeded to go through an exercise routine before having her shower. The lads crowded round the window of an office on the top floor and had a first class view of the proceedings. Some "Holy Joe" among the boys got to hear what was going on and reported it to Larry, who was scandalised. Needless to remark, the viewing had to end forthwith. This really upset Pascal W… who played with his penis so much that he had a hole worn in the crotch of his uniform trousers. I was always wary of him when he was around. It's probably as well that he didn't work in the addressing section, otherwise he would've gone blind looking at "Blondie," the cleaner. She always wore low-cut dresses, and the sight of her breasts was very distracting as she bent over in front of us. She came on duty at five, after the adult clerks had left for the evening. We had to stay on until five-thirty, so we got a private showing every evening. There would've been hell to pay if it had been known among the seniors that she was flaunting her charms in front of us juniors. No one reported her. Well why would we? We all enjoyed the show. She liked me and asked at one stage if I would accompany her daughter to a dance, as she needed a partner. I agreed, but it was obvious that she didn't like me from the start. I think I was a little too innocent for her. I didn't drink or smoke, and I wasn't interested in getting involved sexually, so that was the first and last date that we had.

Generally, life was good in the Board. I made good friends and enjoyed working there. More importantly, I began to lose some of the shyness. Oh, I still blushed at times and the older women used to love that. But it was happening less and less and I thanked God for it. We played football in the lunch-hour. Or if the weather was bad, we played chess or draughts, etc. Or we'd have fun with playing around with the names of the departmental heads. We laughed long and loud at the idea that the manager of the women's section was a Miss U. Ryan. On one occasion someone brought in a whoopee cushion. We had great fun with this. One day, when returning from lunch, a few of us were walking along the corridor behind some of the female staff. I had the cushion up the back of my tunic and as we turned into a very narrow corridor, I pressed my back against the wall. There was a loud fart, and pandemonium broke out as the guys tried to get passed each other before the women saw who was behind them.

I mentioned earlier that I had won a trophy for First Aid with the St. John Ambulance Brigade. It turned out that one of the examining officers on that night was a senior clerk with the Electricity Board. The day after the competition, I was walking along a corridor having delivered a letter, when I came face to face with the examiner. "Are you the cadet from last night?" he asked, with a look of astonishment on his face.

"I am, Sir," I replied.

"I hope nobody finds out you're working here," he said as he walked on.

I don't know why he was so concerned. I thought, surely he didn't think his reputation was in jeopardy or that he would be accused of favouritism. I don't think he even congratulated me on my win; he was so concerned about his good name. His brother Des, it turned out, worked in the same department as myself. By some strange quirk, they both had the same Christian names.

It was around this time that my mother collapsed at home and was taken into hospital. After several tests, it was discovered that she was diabetic and she was in a coma. Her health was at serious risk and the medical people told my father that the prognosis wasn't good. My mother was made of tougher stuff, and she recovered after a couple of weeks. However, she was obliged to inject herself with insulin every day for the rest of her life. My father suggested to the doctors, when it was made known that the injections would be a permanent feature, that as a first-aid person, I might be trained to administer them. The medical staff pointed out that this would tie me to my mother for the rest of my life and it would be in her own interest to look after this herself. This she did and there was only one occasion when she was feeling unwell that I gave her the injection. She was grateful to me and I was proud to be able to help.

One of my workmates lived in Cabra, and we became friends. His mother would often invite me to tea and it was here that I first learned how to cope with side plates and a full set of eating utensils. They were a lovely family. His father worked for a car dealership in Pembroke Street, not far from the ESB offices in Fitzwilliam Street and we used to call round every once in a while to see the new model cars and sit in them. Our friendship wasn't to last, however. I had borrowed my father's bicycle as per usual and called down to his house. We had planned to cycle out to Dunsink, which is a fair distance up the country lane running towards Blanchardstown in west county Dublin. His mother informed me when I got to his house, that his father had gotten two tickets for an international soccer match, and that he had gone to the game with him. As I cycled away, I happened to meet Rosaleen, his girlfriend. She had her bike with her and asked me what I was doing. I explained what we had planned and what had happened regarding the football match. She said that she was at a loose end, and asked if we might both go for a spin. I didn't see any harm in this and agreed. So we headed off to Dunsink as per the original plan, and enjoyed a visit to an old graveyard while we were there, before returning home. It was getting late and as my pal still hadn't returned from the match, I said goodnight to Rose and headed home.

A few days later, he accused me of trying to steal his girl-friend. I tried to assure him that I had no interest in her, but he wouldn't believe me. He was aggrieved that I hadn't told him about the bike ride. I tried to explain that the only reason I hadn't done that was because I didn't think it of any importance, particularly as nothing had happened to be worth talking about. There was a distinct cooling in our relationship from then, and I didn't visit him at home any more.

On Sunday afternoons, it was a favourite pastime for my pals and me to catch the afternoon matinee in the Cabra Grand cinema. The following Sunday, Rose and her girl friend were sitting in the row in front of us. I don't know if this was by design or just coincidence. We were chatting before the film started and she told me that she had finished seeing Paddy as well. "So you're no longer his girlfriend?" I asked, as the lights were dimming.

"No," she said, and turned towards the screen. Before I could move back and settle into my seat however, she took both of my hands and pulled them forward, placing them on her breasts. I sat on the edge of my seat all through the picture, with her moving my hands so as to massage her. This had never happened to me before, and by the end of the show I was barely able to stand up, because every muscle in my body had gone stiff. We arranged to meet later that evening after tea and go for a walk. She said she'd be at the end of my road at seven.

Winter was drawing in and it was dark by then. I've always been one for keeping appointments on time and this one was no different. But imagine my surprise when I found Rose waiting for me. We strolled up Fassaugh Avenue, and on up Ratoath Road over the railway level crossing to Reilly's Bridge. The bridge wall curved sharply onto the canal bank and formed a screen of sorts from both the road and the canal bank itself. She stood against the wall and pulled me towards her. We kissed and embraced tightly. She took my hand and placed it on her breast, just as she had done earlier that afternoon. My muscles had relaxed since then and I was supple again. Except for one place and she could feel that against her leg. The excitement was really beginning to tell, and she didn't flinch or object when I slid my hand under her blouse and touched her flesh. I couldn't believe what was happening. Never before had I experienced anything like this. My blood was boiling, and my head felt as if it would explode. Despite the fact that I have five sisters and that we were overcrowded in the house, I had a few fleeting glimpses of the female form, but I never had a chance to touch it. Apart from the fleeting glance of bare breasts that day near the "Broken Arch." I also managed to steal a look at some pictures of nude females in the "Lilliput" magazine. I don't know where this book came from, or which of my brothers had left it lying around but it fascinated and excited me, as it would any young man whose hormones were running riot. Now here I was with a real live female and she was more eager than I was to explore.

We were both only fifteen years of age and yet she seems so much more mature. I remember thinking why my ex-pal Paddy had been so upset when he thought about our bicycle ride a few weeks back. "Let's go and lie down," she whispered.

"Okay," I panted, trying my very best to sound cool and nonchalant. We walked a little further along the canal bank and found a grassy spot. She lay down, taking my hand again and pulling me down on top of her. As I lay on top of her, my excitement overcame me and...

Suddenly I was back to my senses and feeling thoroughly ashamed. There hadn't been any attempt by me to remove my clothing or hers. I honestly never thought of doing that. I was so inexperienced, that I was completely out of my depth. I couldn't wait to part from her, and almost trotted all the way to the corner of the road where she lived. That night as I lay in bed, I clearly remember thinking that I did not want to get deeply involved with any girl. I never had any sex education. However, I knew more from instinct than anything else, that this is how babies get made; and I didn't want that or marriage, at this stage of my life. So, I resolved to finish the relationship at the earliest opportunity. There was also the awful thought of having to tell the priest about this in confession.

In the meantime, she must've either told my ex-pal Paddy or let it be known to him that we were now a serious item; because he challenged me at work to meet him at the company social club and put on the boxing gloves. I agreed, and that Friday evening I was there, waiting for Dessie Hayes, one of the older men to bring the gloves along. My ex-pal had told him that we would be sorting a problem out that night. Dessie didn't turn up. But that didn't deter Paddy, he wanted revenge and he was determined to have it. So he suggested that we fight bare-knuckle style. This was nothing new to me, considering the area I lived in, and so I agreed. We set to it. He caught me with a fair punch in the eye and I gave him a few in return. Before long however, one of the senior staff got fed up with what he was witnessing and stopped the fight, insisting that he would report both of us at work on Monday if we didn't behave. By the time I reached home, my eye had swollen quite a bit. My mother noticed it and asked if someone had beaten me up. "Yeh should see the other guy," was my comment and I said no more. I noticed a wry smile as she quickly turned her head so I couldn't see.

I met Rose shortly afterwards with the intention of telling her that I could no longer see her. Whatever weak attempt I might have made to do this, my intentions were resolved when she approached me wide-eyed and grinning, and asking if it was true that I'd had a fight over her. "No," was my reply in answer to her question. "I don't fight over any girl, and by the way, I won't be seeing you again." Her mouth dropped open and there was a look of surprise on her face as if I had just slapped her. She demanded to know why. I told her I didn't want to get in any trouble and that the priest had upbraided me in confession over our last experience.

"Did you tell him my name?" she asked incredulously.

"Are you kidding?" I replied, "do you think I'm stupid or what? Anyway, we'll only get in trouble if we continue, so I won't be seeing you again... right."

We parted and I breathed a sigh of relief as I walked home, thinking that that was the end of it. She was a lovely girl, good looking, with a well-developed figure for her age. But she was way ahead of me in maturity, at least as far as matters sexual were concerned. I was frightened that I would not be able to control myself and we would both end up in real trouble. So it had to end and I thought that it had. She had other ideas however, and I began to receive anonymous letters through the post, telling me what a rotten swine I was, and calling me names that were far from complimentary. They were written in a very mature hand. The content was such that I was convinced she had to have had someone much older to write them for her. I got so many of them that my mother became concerned, especially when she saw the hand that they were written in. She asked me what it was all about and I told her not to worry; that it was someone acting the fool. She wasn't convinced and told me to put a stop to them. I tried working out where they were coming from by checking the post-mark, without success. They were causing me such anxiety that my stomach began to give me problems. Eventually, I went to a close friend of Rose's and told her that I was putting the matter in the hands of the police. That worked, the letters stopped and my stomach settled down. I liked girls and I was generally very relaxed in their company. Sure, I liked to kiss one at times, but there was never any thought of sex in my mind. I was a total innocent.

During all of this trouble, it was noticed at work that I wasn't looking too well. I was working with Dessie Hayes one day, when he asked me what the problem was. I told him that my stomach was giving me trouble. "Is your stomach or somewhere lower down?" he asked.

"What do you mean?" I enquired.

"Well are you playing with yourself?" was his reply. He seemed convinced that I was masturbating and that was why I looked so wretched. What a strange thing to ask, I thought, funny man.

CHAPTER ELEVEN

THE RESERVE DEFENCE FORCE

Time was moving on, and before long I had reached my sixteenth birthday. There was no big celebration or anything like that. In fact, I didn't have a birthday party until I was twenty-one years of age. Some of my friends had joined the Reserve Defence Force or An Forsa Cosanta Aituil, to give it its Irish name. It was also called the FCA, or "Free Clothing Association," to quote some of the smart alecks around. They asked me if I would join and I told them I'd ask my father if it was all right with him. Before I could do that however, Gerard, an older brother, invited me to join the Fianna Boy Scouts. A whole gang of us set off one evening to the meeting hall that was located on Blackhorse Avenue near to the Phoenix Park, only to find that the police had raided it. It was only then that I realised it was the junior section of the IRA. I didn't have a problem with this anyway, but one of the instructors who met us on our way to the meeting place advised us to keep away until he got in contact at a later date.

A week or so later, I asked my father if it was all right with him for me to join the FCA. He wasn't too keen at first, and he was at pains to tell me that there were no heroes in war. "It's a nasty business and you should keep as far away from the army as you can," he said. But I persisted and he agreed, only if I joined the Medical Corps, in view of my first-aid experience with the Ambulance Brigade. So the following Thursday, I accompanied my pals to Collin's Barracks to sign on. They had warned me that the qualifying age was seventeen years, but if I had a Social Welfare Number, I could lie my way in. I duly took my Social Welfare "Blue Card" with me and tried to look as old as I could.

A Lieutenant Byrne interviewed me and insisted that I was only fourteen years of age. To be fair to him, I did look much younger than my actual age. So much so, that I could still get away with paying half-fare on the bus. I pulled out my "Blue Card," and returning his look, insisted that I was seventeen. "That's your brother's card," he said, "we get that all the time here."

"No Sir, it's mine," I said, "I work for the Electricity Supply Board."

"Okay," he said, "but I'm putting your name down in my notebook alongside all the other under age guys who've joined." I smiled and said nothing further. "Right," he said, "stand against that wall." He pointed at a wall on which were calibrations for measuring height. There was a timber ridge just below the chart and I put my heels on it to give me a bit of extra height. The lads had told me about this before I entered his office. He finally accepted me and issued me with my LA-89 identification book. I resigned from the St. John Ambulance Brigade the very next week.

He took a real liking to me and asked what exactly my job was in the ESB. I explained that among other things, I operated the new photocopy machine. Copying machines were very much in their infancy then. This one was manufactured by Agfa Gaevart, Ltd., and was wet process. I had to mix up the chemicals for it and keep it clean and in good order. It was used to copy confidential documents at times, and it surprised him to know that I would be trusted to that extent. I explained that I had signed a document that bound me to secrecy, and it would cost me my job if I were to discuss any of the Board's business with outsiders, especially since the Board's customers were members of the general public. Their information was strictly private.

He was so impressed with hearing what I had to say that, about six months later, he invited me to an interview with his company. He was a director of Ballsbridge Motors, Ltd., a main Volkswagen dealer and there was an opening in the parts department that he felt would suit my talents better. The problem was… he didn't give me enough time to apply for a half-day's leave of absence from the Board, and he suggested that I go sick. I did this and had a successful interview. If it hadn't worked out in my favour, I would've been in a lot of trouble in my future career. Next day back at work, I was told to report to Mr. C, who proceeded to grill me like a criminal. His abuse upset me so much that when he asked me what my father would think of my behaviour, I told him that it wouldn't do his health any good if my father got to know how he was treating me. He was apoplectic, and I thought he was about to hit me. As a punishment, he transferred me out of the addressing section and into a Hall Porter position. This is where I would have to spend the rest of my working life, he said. My boss in Adrema kicked up a real fuss about this, but he was over-ruled. In fact, he came out to the porter's desk one day and brought me back into his department. The little Nazi kicked up murder, and I was promptly returned to the hall, where I was condemned to rot mentally. I was told specifically, that I was not to read books or study materials of any description while I was at my desk. He was determined that I was not going to progress if he had anything to do with it. Soon afterwards, I resigned and joined the motor company. Many years later, having left the motor company to join my family in England, I returned to the ESB looking for him to give him a piece of my mind, only to find that he had died a short time before.

It seems strange that I was to meet a namesake of his in recent years who was just as obnoxious. It must be in the genes. By this time of my life, I had decided to let him answer to a higher power. His behaviour induced me to retire finally. Now, I thank God almost daily for the freedom that I now enjoy in working around my garden.

While I was working at the porter's desk, I got to see the new intake of female staff, all of whom were from the country areas. One of them seemed to like me very much. It was leap year, a time when a girl is entitled to ask a guy to marry her. Before long, I received a note with a love poem written therein. I can only remember the last line… it said, "If for me there is no hope, then send me back ten yards of rope." She was taking full advantage of the year that was in it, or so it seemed. I had a good idea who it was, but couldn't be sure as it was signed with a nom-de-plume. Considering that I was on a very low wage and that all of the girls had passed their "*Leaving* Certificate," not only would they be paid more than me, the highest I could expect to rise to would be a "Grade C Clerk," (if I ever got away from the Hall Porter job) that was way below what they would achieve. I felt inadequate and besides, I wasn't sure if this might have been a joke. So I wove a hangman's noose out of some parcel cord, and placing it in an envelope I asked one of the girls to pass it to the writer of the letter. It had indeed come from the girl I had in mind. She was lovely, with light blonde hair and bright blue eyes.

We did get around to talking, and she asked me if I would show her around Dublin, since she was new to the city. I agreed and she asked if we could meet the following evening. I told her that I had planned to see a film in the Grafton Cinema. It was called *At the Balalaika*, and starred Nelson Eddie, a favourite of mine. She asked if she could come. I agreed and asked her to be outside the cinema in Grafton Street at quarter to eight, as the film started at eight. This was going to drain my finances, but I was willing to stay home for the rest of the week. I stood outside the cinema until five minutes to eight, but there was no sign of her so I went in. Next day she came over to me and asked where I was the previous evening. She said she had been there and that she didn't see me. I explained that I had in fact been there, and that I could tell her what the film was about if she wished. She insisted that she had turned up, and I felt that she was just messing with me and I told her so. "I waited until five to eight," I told her, "you weren't there at that time, and I don't believe you were there at all. I think it best if you find someone else to show you around," I said and we parted.

She came from Tralee in County Kerry. Her father had a very large farm. I felt so inadequate and thought that I just couldn't entertain her in the standard that she would be used to anyway. My feelings were confirmed when she pulled up beside me in her new car, a few days later and offered me a lift. I accepted and we drove around the block. Her father had bought it for her as a present. I congratulated her and wished her well, while thinking to myself that I had made the right decision, keeping in mind my experience with my previous girl.

When I arrived home with an Infantry Identification Book, known as the LA-89 in the army, my father had a fit. I explained that the Medics were located in Rathmines, on the south side of the city and that it would cost bus fare to get there, he relented. He made it very clear to me however, that I was to serve my full five years or I would answer to him. He also informed me that he had been held prisoner in the Guard Room in what was then "The Royal Barracks," during the Tan War. He was beaten up by the guard and was rescued from serious injury by the Orderly Officer.

That first night in barracks is still fresh in my memory. I cast a wistful eye on the Guard Room as I walked past, remembering my father's story. The feel of the Lee Enfield Mark 3 Rifle was special. There was the unique smell of gun-oil that is still in my nostrils today. Although I had never handled a rifle before, I instinctively knew how to release the safety catch and open the bolt. A couple of other new recruits near me were fascinated as they watched me close the bolt and squeeze the trigger. It made a distinct click as the firing pin shot forward, attracting the attention of a corporal who was standing nearby. "Leave that weapon alone," he roared, with eyes blazing. I swallowed hard and put the rifle down quick. We had our first lesson on the weapon that night and we were told to memorise the various parts, as we would be tested on our knowledge. We were then told to report in on Sunday morning at 11 a.m., when we would be issued with our uniform. The rest of the evening seemed to fly by, and by 10:15 p.m. I was on my way home again.

The uniform, I was to learn, was commonly known as "bulls-wool." It was made up of a thick woollen material that was designed to withstand the roughest wear. Since nobody wore underpants, it was vital to tuck the family jewels into the tails of our shirt, otherwise it became most uncomfortable when the material rubbed against the skin. It was also very difficult

to iron a crease into the trousers, for example, and we had to rely on the older hands to tell us the "tricks of the trade." To get a sharp crease that lasts, we were advised to iron with a damp cloth first, then turn the trousers inside-out and rub a wetted bar of soap down the inside of the crease. Then we were to turn the trousers back the right way, and with a damp cloth use a very hot iron on the crease, followed by brown paper. The paper dried the dampness and at the same time stuck the two sides of the crease together. This gave a razor-sharp crease that lasted for quite a long time.

There was just one problem with the issue that all of us got… the jackets were miles too big. When I told the quartermaster about this he said, "Never mind son, you'll grow into it." The answer to that problem was to get the jacket tailored to fit and that's what most of us did. I sewed on with pride the Red Spearhead Flash of the Eastern Command. This had to be three finger widths down from the shoulder on the left sleeve. If it was more or less when checked, it had to be taken off and redone. The half-moon-shaped Unit Flash denoting membership of the

42nd Infantry Battalion was sown across the shoulder of the right sleeve. The 42nd, we were told, was the successor to the 2nd Battalion, Old IRA. One of the other units in the barracks was the 26th Battalion and this unit contained the sons and other relations of fathers who had served in the IRA. It is mentioned in my father's account of his service. My older brother Gerard served in this unit. I joined the 42nd Battalion because my pals were members of it. The 26th was recognised by the colour of their boots. They used Kiwi Oxblood Polish, which gave their boots a purple hue. The 26th Battalion was one of our bitter rivals in the platoon competitions. One other unit in the barracks was the 7th Battalion... or "the scruffy seventh," as they were known. These presented no threat in competition, as they didn't seem to have the same interest in keeping their uniform to the same standard as us.

Before long, we began to look really smart. We were told to only use Wren's Oxblood Polish on our boots and Wren's Black on our webbing. The web issue was ex-British First World War and it had a pungent smell of must, that only webbing can get when it's a long time in storage. Soon though, we had it gleaming and the smell of polish quickly replaced the old pungent odour. All of the brass buckles and fittings had to be shined with "Brasso."

We got down to the serious business of learning arms and foot-drill, along with absorbing the knowledge of the parts of the rifle and the "Mills Grenade." That was the extent of our armament at the time. My pal Jimmy had no interest in joining the force. He preferred to join Sinn Féin. He was to be found outside the church on Sunday, selling "An Phoblact," the Republican newspaper. I seriously considered joining Sinn Féin myself, but decided against it when the priest condemned the organisation from the pulpit, and threatened ex-communication for anyone who did join their ranks. This coupled with the fact that Jimmy told me, in answer to a question, that they had no provision for looking after individuals or their families in the event of an arrest or worse. I remembered why my father had to join the British Army and decided against getting involved with what was, after all, an illegal organisation. The fifties campaign was in full swing in the North and the IRA had carried out a number of disastrous operations across the border. They had no support from the people on either side of the divide, and their campaign eventually fizzled out. The Army, I would learn later, was highly suspicious of the Reserve, because many of the IRA recruits joined the FCA first, to learn how to fire the weapons and steal small amounts of ammunition when they got the chance. This suspicion was heightened when a serving Lieutenant was killed in a raid on a police barracks in the North. There were all sorts of trouble with our police and army when his IRA comrades tried to have a formal military funeral for him, after his body was returned to his family. He came from Limerick and his name was Sean South. This was the same Sean South who inspired the song, *Sean South from Garryowen.*

My being in the Reserve didn't affect the relationship between Jimmy and myself. He had met Pauline, a new girl-friend who lived on Broombridge Road and I started to hang around with her friend Judy. We just went for walks together and generally hung around. I can't ever remember us going to the cinema, for example, and I preferred the loose arrangement we had anyway. Whatever arrangement we had fell apart after she saw me in uniform. "Lose the uniform or lose me," she said.

"Well, good luck," I said as I walked away. My shyness had all but gone and I was growing in confidence almost daily. No one would tell me what I should do or where I could go in future if I didn't want to. After six months of being among "Army" people, I was cured of my shyness altogether.

Jimmy and me started to attend the dances being held in St. Peter's hall in Phibsboro. I hadn't a clue about dance steps and so got my sister Rosaleen to teach me. Pretty soon I was enjoying the quickstep, foxtrot, tango and the samba, which was my favourite. The dances were strictly supervised by the local priest; who would walk onto the dance floor, tell a couple that they were too close, and part them so that there was a modest gap between them. One night, a fight started close to where I was standing. A couple of guys had been drinking beforehand,

and managed to get passed the security at the door. One of the combatants pulled a bottle of Guinness from his pocket and belted the other one over the head with it. The bottle smashed into smithereens as the guys locked arms and fell to the floor. By this time, a ring of people had formed around them. I was right on the inside edge. The girl I had been dancing with started pushing me forward and telling me to get in and help. I grabbed her arm and swung her into the ring saying, "Now you go and help if you want. I'm wearing a new suit." She was disgusted and that ended what might've been a beautiful friendship.

Fights were not a common occurrence in St. Peter's Hall, I'm pleased to say. It was usually a good night's dancing to a live band and it was very enjoyable. I met Sheila K, and really liked her. She, on the other hand was more interested in playing the field. I arranged to meet her outside of the State Cinema on one occasion and she stood me up. It was a lovely summer's evening, and I decided not to see the film anyway, and walked the short distance from Phibsboro' to Cabra West. I walked along Connaught Street and onto Fassaugh Road. As I approached the bridge at Matt Whelan's Pub, who should come down the hill on her bike but Sheila? She almost fell off with the shock of seeing me. She tried to find a suitable excuse and made a complete mess of the lie she told. "It's alright," I said to her, "let's meet tomorrow and talk about it." The relief showed on her face and she promised faithfully that she would be at the appointed place. Next evening at the time I was meant to be meeting Sheila, I was sitting at home polishing my army boots.

A couple of days later she sent a friend up to my house to ask me to meet her at the corner. I went along and she demanded to know why I hadn't shown up. She was livid with rage. "Not very nice, is it?" I asked.

"No," she said red-faced.

"Well, now you know how I felt, so shag off with yourself, right!" That ended our brief relationship.

I started my new job with Ballsbridge Motors, Ltd. The first six weeks of training were spent in the Spare Parts Department, attached to the Volkswagen factory on the Naas Road. I was told that I would have to learn enough part numbers to be able to deal with a customer at the desk without having to refer to the parts manual. The part numbers were nine digits long and by the time I took up my position in the stores in Ballsbridge, I could serve a customer and write the part number from memory. During my six weeks in Naas Road, I had the distinction of selling the first full set of tools for the saloon car, besides memorising the part numbers. My trainer was highly impressed and informed my boss, Dessie Byrne, of the fact.

I reported to the Stores Manager in Ballsbridge and began work in earnest. He didn't like me because of my association with the Director of the company and didn't hesitate to tell me so. He had a drink problem also, which didn't help his attitude, particularly on Mondays after a weekend of heavy drinking. Matters got worse and worse over time, until eventually he exploded one afternoon and accused me of taking money from the till. Generally, I'm an easygoing fellow and try to get along with everyone, but being accused of thievery really hit me hard. I walked over to the phone and dialled the director's office. "I need to see you right now," I said when he answered. He tried to fob me off, but I said "Sir, I need to see you, it's urgent." He agreed to see me and the stores manager went purple with rage. I stood in front of the director's desk and told him that though I might be a poor kid from a council house scheme, I was an honourable person and certainly not a thief. He promised to deal with the matter, and asked me to return to the stores.

The manager was by this time fit to be tied. "Well," he demanded, "what did you say to the boss?"

"You'll know about that soon enough," I said and walked down the aisle towards the back door to the stores, where I could serve the mechanics with the parts they needed for the jobs they were on.

A couple of weeks went by with no further word from upstairs and no further comment from the manager. Then one of the other staff asked me one day if I'd heard that the guy who worked on the petrol pumps had been arrested. I said no and asked what for. "He's the thief," my colleague said. "He has admitted to forcing the stores door at night, and not only taking odd sums of money from the cash, but stealing parts and selling them." What this guy had done was to take the part and leave the box on the shelf so that it wouldn't be noticed. A full stock-take revealed that hundreds of pounds worth of parts were missing. No one came to me to explain or apologise. I was incensed and lost the respect I had for my "friend," the director. To this day I have abhorrence for thieves, because of the way in which they cast doubt on others who are innocent.

The manager was serving a customer one afternoon, when another one came to the counter. I approached and asked if I could help. He said no, that he wanted to talk to the manager. I began to retreat as I needed to visit the toilet anyway.

"Where are you going?" the manager demanded.

"To the toilet," I answered.

"Get back here and serve this customer," he yelled.

"The customer wants to talk to you," I answered. "You already heard the man ask for you," I said, "and I'm going to the toilet, whether you like it or not." And I walked away. He was fuming when I got back and he began to abuse me verbally. I picked up a flywheel and warned him to behave himself or I would bury the flywheel in his head. He quietened down after that and was very wary of me from then on. The "get" got to know that you don't mess with a Sheridan.

Gormanstown Camp July 1955.

I had joined the Reserve Defence Force on the 14th of October 1954, just two days after my sixteenth birthday. From then until the summer, we trained very hard in weaponry, arms, and foot drill. We held competitions in the various military skills in camp, between the best platoons from every unit in the Eastern Command. To be selected for one of these platoons was an honour, as only the best were considered. One of my school pals had joined the same unit as myself and his mother was an accomplished tailor. She made our uniforms fit as if they had been painted onto our bodies. The crease in the front of our trousers got sharper the more we used the soap and the iron. Our webbing looked terrific, polished black with the brass buckles and studs gleaming. Our boots were like mirrors by the time we had used the special technique of burning the polish on. We even polished the piece of leather in the arch between the heel and the soul of the boot. I was so successful at this that one of my neighbours pointed to my boots as I swung my leg over my bicycle at the curb, as I was about to head off to the barracks, and said, "Look, your boots are all wet!" I smiled widely and told him he was seeing the shine. He was enthralled. Friends and neighbours alike had begun to take notice and I enjoyed every minute of it.

I was picked as a member of the unit "Competition Platoon," after I won the best-dressed soldier of the month award. I wasn't the first to win it as the competition was fierce, but it was sweet when it came. The award consisted of a white web belt and lanyard and it set the green uniform off beautifully. It carried a certain status among my fellow soldiers, and it certainly helped my confidence tremendously. My back became ramrod straight and my head was held high. One of our neighbours, who was in the regular army, was so impressed with my turnout; he presented me with an army tin plate together with a knife, fork and spoon.

The first two weeks in July was our allotted camp time and I applied for leave from my job well in advance of this. I was still working in the ESB at this time, and was entitled to apply for one week with pay and one week without. As we were paid on camp according to rank, etc., and qualified for a ten-pound gratuity, also I was gaining more that I was losing financially. I looked forward eagerly to having what, in fact, would be my first holiday away from home. I gathered, along with all of my new friends and colleagues, in Collin's Barracks and climbed on board a truck with my suitcase. We were taken to Amiens Street, now Connolly Station, where we boarded a train for Gormanston Station in County Meath, approximately twenty miles from Dublin. The excitement was palpable and we chattered with loud voices as we headed off on our great adventure. The station was close to the camp and we put our bags on a truck and marched the rest of the way. Once there we were shown to the long wooden huts or billets, as they were known, where we would live for the next two weeks. The method of heating was with a Pot-Bellied Stove. There were a couple of these approximately one quarter and three quarters way down the hut. Turf was used as a fuel and when the fire was lit, the stove glowed red in the dark. We left our bags and reported to the stores, where we drew our bedding. Back at the billet, we were shown how an army bed is made up; and how each morning, it had to be stripped down, and the sheets folded a particular way, so that the blue line showed to the outside. The sheets then had to be encased in the folded blankets, together with the pillow, so that it formed a neat package. We didn't have sprung beds to sleep in. We were each issued with three wooden planks that sat on wooden trestles, which were only six or so inches off the floor. This was to be the first time in my life that I had a bed all to myself and I loved it… planks included.

Our time on camp during the first week was taken up fully with preparations for the competitions. We had fired on the range some weeks earlier, in Kilbride Camp, County Wicklow and we had qualified to wear two stars on our sleeves. The camp nestled in a valley, not very far from Dublin. It has various ranges on which we fired our weapons. Like all of the camps and ranges around the country, it had been built in the days when the British occupied Ireland. And like most of the ex-British establishments, it had been neglected. The buildings were in a disgraceful condition and we usually ate our food out in the open. The setting however, like all of the ranges, was beautiful.

During breaks for meals, we could look out across the valley towards Blessington Lake as it glistened in the sun. The lake is five miles long. It's manmade and is the reservoir for Dublin. There was also a lovely river running through Kilbride itself. It was a wonderful place to be on a sunny day. But for some peculiar reason, it seemed to be raining most of the time when we were there. Perhaps this was due to it being located in the Dublin Mountains.

There were set tests that had to be passed in order for us to earn our one, then two, and then three stars. These also increased our wages while we were serving on camp. Gormanstown camp was at sea level and the weather had vastly improved. I began to really enjoy the army life and thought seriously about signing on full-time. Here I was among good companions, in a stable job, getting paid for doing what I loved, and with my own bed. I had passed the test for my first star and was presented with it by the commanding officer. I couldn't wait to sew it on the sleeve of my tunic. And when I did, I almost had a creek in my neck from looking sideways at it. I decided to speak to my father about signing on full time when I got home. In the meantime, it was down to the serious business of training. The sun shone from early morning until it set in the evening. It was too hot some days for drilling and such like, and the company commander marched us down to the beach for a swim.

Ah! This is the life, I thought to myself. We made up for lost time by drilling in the evenings. Butlins Holiday Camp was nearby and there was a great buzz among the lads about the shows and the girls available to those who had the money to buy a ticket to get in. The platoon sergeant announced that anyone who wanted to borrow money until payday should see him. There was no scam involved. The CO (Commanding Officer) had organised this, knowing the financial straits that we would be in. Before the sergeant had finished speaking, there was a queue of us having our names and amounts entered into his notebook. Most of us were to be found in Butlins that very evening, enjoying a show first, and afterwards a dance.

Before we were allowed out of camp however, we had to have two NCO's inspect our kit. Our beds had to be made up properly and all of our kit was laid on top so that the corporals could check it. Only after they approved it would we be issued with a pass to leave camp. We had to be back in camp by 23:59 hours or there would be consequences. At the weekend, a group of us visited Drogheda and then Balbriggan where we attended a dance. We learned to look out for each other in both locations, because the local lads didn't like the idea of us Dubliners dancing with their girls. It wasn't unusual to hear someone shout "42nd, Over here," when they were in trouble. That cry for help would bring all of the rest of us to his rescue. The local lads soon got the idea that discretion was the better part of valour, and I'm delighted to say that there was very little trouble once they knew that there were a lot of us around.

Reveille was at 7 a.m. and breakfast on camp was at 7:30. We washed, made our beds, and dressed as for a parade. We then marched to the dining hall, which was an airplane hangar. This was an Air Corps Camp, in fact, and we were there as guests, though we had no contact with Air Corps personnel. They regarded themselves as something special and most of them went on leave when guys like us were about. It was nice to see The Spitfire, my all time favourite aircraft up close. The Corps had six of them at the time that had been bought from Britain after the Second World War ended.

The competitions started at nine o'clock sharp on Monday of the second week. There was great excitement throughout as the first week wore on. Every morning after breakfast, our platoon officer inspected us. Standing there in the warm sunshine had a strange effect on me. Bearing in mind that I was only sixteen years of age and that the hormones were running riot, I would get an erection. My penis would press hard against my trousers, and it was obvious to even the casual observer what was happening. The harder I tried to prevent this, the worse it got. Our platoon officer was homosexually inclined, and he was highly amused at my embarrassment. I wonder if any of the other lads suffered in similar fashion. He looked along my chin against the light of the day and asked if I shaved. When I replied, "No," he told me to get the bum-fluff off my chin. I bought my first razor that afternoon and did as he ordered.

We went through the alphabet of arms and foot drill, threw practice grenades twenty-five yards onto a target, went on a route march that was timed, while referees checked us along the route for any slackness in our lines. We had to maintain our dressing, and keep our rifles upright and in line, among other things. The midges had a feast while we marched. The heat of the day, together with the fact that we were wearing heavy wool uniforms, made us sweat. We were not allowed to brush the midges away, for fear of being seen by the referees and lose points. So by the time we got back to camp, our faces were covered in bites. But we endured to the end. After all, we were soldiers! The culmination of it all was a seven-mile road race that began in Drogheda. The Lord Mayor fired the starting pistol and the race ended outside Headquarters in the camp. By this time, all of the scores for the various competitions would be totalled and the winners announced. Our forte was arms and foot drill, and there was a flag that had been presented by the Lord Mayor of Dublin as the prize. We set our sights on winning this, but fell short by the narrowest of margins. The Pearse Battalion was made up of college boys and they were the successful team this time out. We vowed to be better next time, and were consoled with the two plaques we won for other disciplines.

Our commanding officer informed us that the Commander of Collin's Barracks had asked him if we would consider joining the regular army as a unit, after seeing us drilling on the square. He wanted us as a specialist unit for Guards of Honour and for Tattoos, etc. He thanked him, but refused his offer on our behalf. Many of us would have loved to have taken him up on it but Lieutenant Byrne discouraged any suggestion of it by telling us that only the "scum of the earth" joined the army. True to say that many of those in the army were from troubled backgrounds. Many had come straight from Reform Schools such as Artane and Daingean. Some would have been orphans who had been institutionalised and knew no other life. Some of them were thieves and rogues, but most of them were decent guys trying their best to survive in a bitter world. Anyway... the CO rejected any suggestion of our joining.

There was a great buzz when we lined up that Friday afternoon to collect our pay and the gratuity. I had never had so much money in my hand before and couldn't wait to get home to hand it to my mother. There was a second line also... the sergeant had to be re-paid the money he gave out in loans and this we did gratefully. A bond had been formed. We were soldiers and the spirit of friendship was very strong. We had competed together and won. We were now a "Team," and as proud Dubliners we sung all the way back to our lovely city. Before leaving camp, we were told that we would not need to report into barracks until

September. We would be told of the exact date later on. I looked forward with eagerness to that time when I could earn my next star and become a recognised fully-trained private soldier. Over the next few months Lieutenant Byrne turned up at my home and invited me to go for a drive. Sometimes he would have other lads from the unit with him and sometimes he didn't. He talked on a couple of occasions about a guy at work that liked boys. I suspected that he was talking about himself. On one occasion, he actually put his hand on my thigh while he complimented me on the suit I was wearing. If he was making a pass at me, then the look I gave him soon put paid to any possibilities he might have had in mind.

I broke out in a cold sweat nevertheless, as I recalled an experience I'd had in the Cabra Grand Cinema when I was twelve years of age. As a special treat for helping her with the shopping, my mother had given me the money to go and see *A Christmas Carol*. I had just settled into my seat when an adult male sat beside me. It was the early evening show and there were plenty of vacant seats around me, so it wasn't as if he couldn't have found a seat elsewhere. I noticed that he was breathing hard as he pushed a bag of sweets in front of me. The warning bells began to ring immediately. "Would you like a sweet?" he breathed.

"No thanks," I replied.

"Would you like to earn a few bob?" he asked, placing his hand on my naked thigh (I was wearing short pants).

"What do you mean?" I asked.

"My girlfriend let me down and she had promised me that we would do it… yeh know what I mean? So if you come outside with me, we could go around the back of the cinema and do it. I'd pay yeh. What do yeh say?"

My mind was racing with thoughts and the sweat was rolling down my back. "Don't panic," I said to myself… "Think." Like a shot, I came up with an idea. "I have to go to the toilet," I said to him. "If you wait here for me, I'll be back in a couple of minutes, Okay?"

"Don't be long," he said, this time almost breathless. I knew that if I went to an usher and reported him he would deny it and

I'd probably be thrown out of the cinema anyway. So I opened the toilet door, let it close, and immediately opened it again, as if someone had gone in and someone had come out. I went and sat in a different seat, this time closer to other people and watched my potential abuser. After a few minutes had passed, he got up and went over to the toilet. He was back out within a minute and left the building altogether. Perhaps he thought I would be waiting for him outside, who knows? All that mattered to me was that I had, with God's help, managed to avoid the attentions of a pervert.

Me Ma was delighted with the money from camp when I gave it to her. At that time, a married man's wages for a week was £7.10.0 (approximately €10.00). I handed my mother at least £12.0.0. You can imagine her delight. There was no singing of "Big Head" or slagging from those in the family who had indulged themselves on previous occasions in the past. I really enjoyed the dance in St. Peter's Hall that night, especially as I was wearing a new light pink shirt with my dark navy suit that I bought with my newfound wealth. It was the talk of the night among the girls. Boys didn't wear pink! Next day, Saturday, I asked my father what he thought about my joining the regular army. He was vehemently against, saying that he'd seen enough of that sort of life and emphasizing the perils of war. I wasn't to know at that time that he was intending to move to England.

There was no family discussion about the intended move, although I could understand, to some extent at least, his reasons for doing what he did. First off... he was working three eight-hour shifts and he was finding it very difficult to get a decent sleep when he came off nights. There were so many kids on our road that the decibel level was tremendous. There was constant knocking on our hall door from kids looking for one or the other of us to come out and play. Then there was Mister Solan, whose back garden joined ours. He was in a Pipe Band and he would walk up and down his bedroom playing his pipes. Further up the way was Missus Maloney, playing her fiddle. There was such a cacophony of sound that he used to go nuts at times, trying to sleep. It also came to light that my mother had been borrowing money for some time from an illegal local moneylender.

Only now did I understand why we struggled so much to make ends meet. We should have been very well off with the number of wage packets that were coming into the house, but now it all made sense. It has been stated earlier that the tenement dwellers looked after each other and helped out with finances whenever they could. My mother was as soft hearted as a person could be and her friends took advantage of that. The interest charged by moneylenders was penal and she had gotten in so deep, that a woman named Duffy who lived nearby, called to our door accompanied by two heavies demanding money that my mother had failed to pay. My father happened to be at home at the time and he was shocked to discover the predicament that my mother had gotten herself into. He told Duffy and her heavies to get away from the door before he lost his patience. In other circumstances he would've taken on the two heavies straight away, but I think the shock to his system dulled his reactions. There wasn't any row between my parents, at least not that I know of. But what came to light regarding debts, etc., I believe, was the deciding factor in his moving to England. Perhaps he gave my mother an ultimatum, I don't know, but soon afterwards he resigned his job and took himself off to Birmingham. I cannot, to this day, understand why my father or my older brothers didn't tell Duffy and her henchmen to keep away in future, or suffer the consequences.

One of the ways in which the moneylenders sucked in people was through a "docket" system. The larger stores such as Bolger's and Boyer's in North Earl Street issued dockets to clients with which they could buy goods. It was an early form of the store credit card. Moneylenders would buy up large amounts of these and offer them to poor families as a simple way of shopping for clothes for First Communion, Confirmation, and Christmas, etc. They then charged exorbitant interest rates and the poor people couldn't pay anything off the capital because of this. My mother got involved and borrowed heavily to help her "friends." One of these so-called friends called to our door one evening, and I told her to keep away in future, or else. I was fourteen years of age at the time and my mother had loaned her friend my suit so that she could pawn it. I had asked my mother not to touch my suit, as I needed it to attend a function in the St. John Ambulance Brigade. I was livid when I discovered what my mother had done, and couldn't wait to tell her friend what I thought of her. My mother told me off for speaking to her friend the way that I had, and I told her that from now on, my clothes were not to be touched, especially as I was handing up my wage packet.

We had a nice three-bedroom house, and we kept it and the gardens in good shape. Some of the family had left home, so for a short while there was space and a degree of comfort in our home. May, the sister who had worked in the mill in Lancashire, got married in February 1949. She and her husband rented rooms in a house that my father's relations had in Ventry Park, Cabra West. That didn't work out and they came to live in our house. The space quickly diminished and it was back to overcrowding once again. My eldest sister married in June of the same year. I still remember scutting on the back of the taxi as it left the church at the top of the road on its way 'round the block and back to our house. Frank, her husband, threw a handful of pennies into the waiting kids outside of the chapel, a practice called a "Grush." Most of the wedding parties at the time did this for luck. It used to cause mayhem as kids pushed and shoved each other to get at the fallen money. It was unusual to have two weddings so close together, but we younger kids loved it, especially when we could drain the dregs in the Guinness bottles. There was no booking hotels or anything of that nature. The reception was held at our house and the crowd got so big by the time evening came that the men carried the piano outside onto the footpath and all the neighbours had a "Hoolie" on the road.

Gerard emigrated to Birmingham in England and he got married there in 1953. He was regarded as the "black sheep of the family," (I've never managed to find out why) and so nobody travelled over for his wedding. He had brought his wife Pat, home on holiday before they got married and they stayed for more than a year. He made some money by chopping up planks of timber from old packing cases that my father got from work, and making the sticks into bundles for firewood. The bundles were held together with bands of rubber that had been cut out of old bicycle inner tubes.

He never collected the timber himself and my father didn't seem to demand that he do so. Instead, I would have to walk to Granby Lane near the city centre and hire out a handcart for sixpence from Kehily's. Then I would walk to Glasnevin where Player's factory was, collect the timber, take it to Cabra West, and then return the handcart before the hire company closed that evening. Later on, my younger brother Bill (Willie) had to do it as I was working. Life was tough in our house but we were the stronger for it, even if we resented some of the treatment at times. There was a space under the stairs where we hung our coats and that's where Gerry slept. The door had to be kept open to allow some air to circulate. One night my brother Tom went outside to the toilet. It was located off a porch, outside of the kitchen door at the back of the house. As he opened the door, he heard an awful moaning sound. Thinking it was the Banshee, he burst into the kitchen where Dick was having a cup of tea. He, having heard the sound as well, took after Tom who was running for the door out of the sitting room and heading for the stairs. As he reached the stairs, Dick caught up with him, grabbed him, and pulled him back so that he could get past. Tom thought it was the Banshee as he hadn't seen Dick in his excitement, and he passed out with the shock. We still laugh about this today. On their way passed the cubbyhole where Gerry slept, one of them slammed the door shut to make more room. Gerry had almost suffocated by the time his knocking was heard and things had settled down sufficiently for someone to realise his plight and open the door.

Dick was married in 1954, the year I joined the Reserve. The flattop haircut, or crew cut as it became known, was all the rage then. I had what can only be described as a "shock" of black wavy hair and one of the men at work bet me that I wouldn't get a crew cut. I've never been one to shirk a challenge and so I took his bet. When my brother's wife saw it on the morning of the wedding, she banned me to the back row of the wedding photos.

—ᴍ—

The battalion hadn't been as successful as we had hoped in the competitions on camp in 1955. We trained even harder in 1956 and arrived on camp determined to win the competition outright. That wasn't to be, however. The shooting prowess of the teams from Castlecomer, County Kilkenny, and Tullamore, County Offaly was our undoing. We did defeat all comers at arms and foot-drill, including the Pearse Battalion, our bitter rivals, and we were awarded the coveted Lord Mayor's Flag. The battalion went on to win it so many times in future years that it was given over for keeps. It was used in later years as the flag of the 20th Infantry Battalion.

September 1956 came quickly and having received notification by post, I reported into barracks. After renewing friendships and swapping stories about our summer break, I was called into the office of the commanding officer. He congratulated me on my performance on camp and on my turnout. "You're a credit to the unit," he said, "and I've nominated you for a Potential NCO course that will start next month and run for the next three months."

"Thank you sir," I blurted out, finding it hard to contain my excitement. I was about to jump over the three-star course, and all being well on passing this course, I would become a Non-Commissioned Officer. My father would be proud of me. I saluted and almost ran from his office, eager to tell my pals the good news. By the time the night was over I discovered that Hughie, my school pal, was also on the course. More importantly perhaps, I also discovered who my real friends were. There was a definite coolness emanating from some of those who would not be NCO's. The course itself was terrific. For the first time I learned to take notes and compose a lesson plan. Lieutenant Byrne ran the course with the assistance of a sergeant and three corporals and they really put us through our paces. We were given eight men sections to drill on the barrack square. The section was placed at one end of the square while we were at the other end. We then had to project our voice so that we could be heard at the other end.

—⋙—

Tom was married in 1956 and so some space had been created in the house. He was a devout Catholic and went to the trouble of having a blood test before his marriage to determine his suitability for fathering healthy children. The test was a requirement of the church in those days. On one occasion, Paddy was eating meat for his dinner on a "fast day." "Don't you know it's a fast day today?" Tom asked him, disgusted at the idea of his flouting the church's rules.

"It's not going fast enough for me," Paddy answered, laughing out loud. My mother almost choked, trying to stifle a laugh. I looked at the floor keeping a straight face for fear of getting a belt from him. I wasn't sorry to see him leave, as he was the most difficult one in the family to share a bed with. I had to sleep at the bottom of his bed on one occasion, and he lashed out with his foot at the slightest movement. He didn't like me anyway, and wasn't behind the door about showing it. It was he that I had overheard telling my father that he wasn't going out to work to pay for my schooling. He obviously didn't appreciate the fact that my father had helped to get him a job in John Player & Sons, Ltd. Prior to that he was labouring on a building site where he had to supply his own shovel.

He had also served in the Irish Army during the period in our history known as the "Emergency." The rest of the world was going through the "Second World War," we in Ireland had an emergency. He always seemed an unhappy person. Perhaps it was just my imagination, but I never noticed him enjoying himself except when he was full of Guinness. He accused me one day of stealing his cigarettes. My father happened to walk into the room while I was telling him that I hadn't touched his property. My father asked what was going on and I told him about the accusation. "He knows I don't smoke," I told my father, "but he insists that I took his fags," I said. My father looked a little surprised to hear me speak up in the way that I had. Previously I wouldn't say anything or I might even start to cry. But that was all over now and the real me was beginning to emerge.

"You know that he doesn't smoke," my father said, telling him to leave me alone. He might have been a devout catholic but he was a long way from being Christian, because he never forgot that and we never had a friendly relationship. I did sing at his funeral many years later and hoped that he appreciated that.

My mother looked after my sister May's children while she went to work. Her husband worked in the Irish Raleigh, Ltd., with my brother Dick. In fact it was Dick who introduced them. No sooner had some space been created in the house than it was filled up again by my sister's family. They had to have their own room, my mother and father had their room and that left one bedroom for the rest of us. I don't know how we managed or where we all slept. What I do know is that there were nineteen people living in the house at one time.

On top of all this, we had a constant stream of visiting relations from England. My aunt Annie was my father's sister, and she lived in Oldham in Lancashire. My sister May stayed with her and her family when she lived and worked in Lancashire. Naturally, my parents were expected to return the favour and did so willingly. That was the thing with Tenement dwellers… nobody regarded it as an imposition to facilitate visiting relatives. Or if they did, nobody said so. Anyway, a first cousin arrived at our door one evening. She left her bag open on the table. My brother Willie let his curiosity get the better of him and rooted around in the handbag. He found what he thought was chocolate, and gobbled it down before anyone saw him. Later that evening my cousin announced that a packet of "Brooklax" (an anti-constipation product,) had disappeared from her bag. Everybody sung dumb until a couple of hours later, Willie had to rush to the toilet leaving a trail of "scutter" behind him. The thief was caught and the trail of evidence was on the floor for all to see.

—ɯ—

Jim, who was four years older than me had enough of the crowded conditions and decided to join the Royal Air Force. He had been caught playing "Cowboys and Indians" during working hours in the Raleigh and got the sack. He got a job in Brooks Thomas Wood Mill, at the bottom of Gardiner Street and came home covered in sawdust. That really got to him and when he got his letter of acceptance into the RAF, he took off (to use a pun) and reported to the training camp in the North, before being posted to his unit in England. He would go on to serve in Malaya and Germany.

CHAPTER TWELVE

BIRMINGHAM

Also in 1956, my mother, along with the rest of the family except for my younger sister Olive and me, left for England. I didn't want to leave Dublin in the first place and resisted it for as long as I could. Why they left Olive behind puzzles me even today. My older sister May and her husband had been allocated a Corporation house of their own on Killala Road some time previous to this. Now that our family home on Mulroy Road was empty except for my sister and I, the rent collector informed us that one of our neighbours who had a two-bedroom house had applied for our one, as it had three bedrooms. So my sister May, together with the assistance of the rent collector and the approval of our parents, applied to be transferred to the family home. May and her husband didn't want the responsibility of caring for my sister and I, so we were told that we would have to join the rest of the family in Birmingham. I managed to hold off until the following year.

———※———

I had the regretful task of informing my commanding officer in 1957 that I would have to leave for England. To be fair to the Lieutenant, he didn't attempt any further physical contact and perhaps I misjudged the situation anyway. He now had a girlfriend and they got married within a short time. I was invited to their wedding and met none other than Mr. Charles Haughey who later became Taoiseach. He had been an officer in the same unit as Lieutenant Byrne during the "Emergency." I was surprised at how small he was, though he struck me as a tough individual and one who shouldn't be messed with.

He made the announcement to the unit at the end of our parade one Tuesday evening. Some of the people who came over to shake my hand and wish me well surprised me. The guys from East Wall were tough and hard to manage, but they were all there expressing regret at my leaving. That heartened me and helped me to face something that I had been determined to avoid. I never was presented with my stripes for finishing the NCO course, much to my chagrin. Instability was to become a feature of my life for some time to come.

It also meant that I would have to resign from my job at Ballsbridge Motors, Ltd. I wasn't too disappointed with doing this as the stores manager had been giving me a hard time. To my amazement, he tried every way to get me to stay. I suppose it was his way of showing his remorse at having accused me wrongly of stealing. If somebody had offered me accommodation, I might have seriously considered staying put. The problem with that was money. My wages wouldn't have been enough to rent a place and feed myself. So I was forced to face the inevitable.

My mother arrived home from Birmingham to stay a few days with my sister in what used to be our home, (the house in Mulroy Road was our home and will always be in my opinion,) and I was given a ticket for the boat to England. I had to go. There was no other choice and I wasn't happy about it. That Friday evening, I made my way to Dun Laoghaire via Westland Row (now Pearse Brothers) Railway station. The furthest I had travelled prior to this was to Gormanstown Military Camp and that was via the barracks anyway. So, here I was, on my own, heading for Birmingham. The train was crowded with people from all over the country. They were leaving at the rate of one thousand per week, at the time. All I had to do was follow the crowd. By the time I got on board, every seat had been taken. The "Mail Boat" was nothing like the present day well-appointed liners that operate on the route now. It set sail with the tide at 9 p.m. and it took three hours to reach Holyhead in North Wales. The accommodation was poor, to say the least and to my mind the boat was dangerously over-crowded. Because every seat was taken, I was obliged to sit on a wooden bench on the exposed upper deck and I was lucky to get that. It was freezing cold, so sleep was out of the question. I pulled my overcoat up around my ears and tried to get some measure of comfort, but to no avail. The vision I have of Holyhead as we approached the dock still lives with me even now. All I could see silhouetted against the night sky was tall television aerials on every roof and the screech of seagulls.

I eventually found the train for Birmingham, after asking several people for directions. It was even more crowded than the boat and I was forced to sit in the corridor, close to where two carriages joined. Steam and smuts seemed to permeate the air. It got into my throat and left me gasping for breath at times. My mood grew uglier with every mile. I wondered how anyone could possibly get excited at the idea of travelling on one of these infernal machines.

At approximately six o'clock the following morning, the train pulled into New Street Station in Birmingham. I was stiff with cold and sore from the hard surface of the carriage floor. My father was waiting for me as I walked down the platform to the exit. After the briefest greeting, he led me out of the station and up the Street to a bus stop opposite the City Hall. Everything was grey, the buildings, the sky, and my mood. I stood there looking around me waiting for the bus and I couldn't help but wonder what on earth possessed him to move to a place like this. There was an angry looking stormy sky, which seemed to match the mood I was in and this cast a gloom over the buildings, emphasizing their dirty grey colour "What have I come to?" I remember asking myself under my breath. The journey to our digs didn't do anything to brighten my thoughts. If anything, it made me feel worse. The city had suffered badly during the war and the re-building programme had not yet started. There were demolished buildings all over the place and it looked like what it was… a bombed site.

The house we were staying in had been erected during the Industrial Revolution. Like all of those in the street, it was a red brick structure and it was soot-stained to the extent that it was almost impossible to see the colour of the brick. A Mrs. Pitt owned the house. She was the widow of an ex-Royal Air Force veteran. She knew that my father had served with the 8th Army in North Africa, and it was obvious that she had more than just a soft spot for him, much to annoyance of my mother.

I cannot understand even today, why my parents left a lovely three-bedroom house of their own to live in lodgings. We had gardens back and front, a bathroom and toilet as an integral part of the house. The location was bright, airy, and convenient for the city with a good bus service. This was all given up to live in digs in an unfriendly city still recovering from the effects of the Second World War. It was dirty and the streets were cobbled. They didn't have bathrooms and the toilet was located in the back yard. Worse than all of this, the family was split. I was the only one of my siblings living with my parents. The rest were scattered around with friends and relatives. We became lodgers in other people's houses, unable to express our true feelings for fear of being thrown out on the street.

After I had been introduced, I was told that my room was at the very top of the house and it was suggested that I might like to take my suitcase up to it. I soon understood why nobody volunteered to show it to me. The staircase was almost vertical, like a ladder. One needed to be fit just to climb up to where I was to sleep. It turned out to be the attic. There was no door and daylight came through a small glass roof light. It had a wardrobe and a small dressing table and that pleased me. I never had my own furnished room before, so I was happy to ignore the drawbacks such as the naked light bulb that hung from the rafters, and the fact that there was no roof felt, just slates on timber joists. As a result of this, the room was as cold as a fridge. I put my stuff away and went downstairs for some breakfast. The landlady had kindly boiled an egg and made some toast. She handed me a cup of tea that was so weak, it was almost as white as the milk that was put into it. It tasted funny too, and I discovered that the milk was the long lasting type; awful to the taste buds of anyone who had been brought up on rich creamy milk and butter. The English might drink a lot of tea, but they have no idea how to brew a decent cup. The next few days were spent visiting others of the family who were scattered around friends and relations.

My brother Gerry lived in his father-in-law's house. The address amused me; it was eleven, back of one hundred and twenty three (11/123) Hingeston Street. It was another of the industrial revolution designs. Access was down a lane and along a narrow passageway. The 11/123 was two houses joined together at the back. It was in fact, one house divided to accommodate two families. The rooms were very small and the staircase rose at a very steep angle in similar fashion to my digs. There was a panel in the wall in the uppermost room, which could be broken through in the event of fire. This would allow entry into the bedroom of the house at the front, providing an escape route. The designer of the house obviously realised that the structure was dangerous, should it catch fire, and took some steps to avoid entrapping people in that event. There was a tiny garden, a washhouse, and a toilet in a small building on the left of a narrow concrete path that led to the hall-door. The fireplace consisted of an iron range with an oven to the side that was heated by the fire. Charlie, my brother's father-in-law, had a very gruff sounding loud voice, but he turned out to be a lovely man. He was a painter and decorator and had arranged for my younger brother Bill to be apprenticed to him. The room was sparsely furnished, but there was a television set. It was the first time I had seen one of these apart from on the cinema screen. Its effect was hypnotic and the conversation between people in the house came in short bursts, usually when the advertisements were on. I discovered that Bill slept on two chairs pulled together in the small sitting room and I thanked God for the mercy He had shown me by providing a real bed in my own room, even if it was a garret.

The next day was Sunday and I accompanied my parents to St. Anne's church in Alcester Street. After Mass, we passed several pubs with a crowd of Irishmen waiting for them to open. My father was disgusted and the priests constantly ranted about this practice from the pulpit each Sunday. But these men were far from home and lonely. They socialised with their fellow country-men in this way before having their mid-day meal. Often they had no meal to sit down to and stayed in the pub until closing time. This was one of the great drawbacks of living away from your loved ones. Many of them descended into alcoholism, and lost family and friends as a result. Others took up with local women and had a second family. Needless to remark, the family back in Ireland was neglected. It was essential, in my view, that a family stayed together and not be scattered in the way ours was.

I scanned the classified ads in the newspapers for a job, and before long, I was invited to an interview with F. Keay & Company, Ltd., in Church Street. The letter heading was embossed on what was obviously an expensive paper. The company, as it turned out, was a paper merchant's, located in the heart of the city.

Not being familiar with the street system in Birmingham, I got directions from Pat, Gerry's wife. On the appointed day, I took the bus into the city and got off in Broad Street. I then walked from there to the old Church at the top of Church Street. The sun was shining that Monday morning and I remember how well I felt as I crossed the churchyard, scattering the pigeons as I went. The city was a lot busier than Dublin, with hundreds of people milling about. Delivery vans were stopped outside of the various office buildings with doors open, as goods were taken to the addressees. There was a distinct air of tranquillity as I walked through the churchyard, despite the bustle all around. It was like an island of peace in a sea of pandemonium. I was dressed in a dark navy two-piece suit with a white shirt and wine coloured necktie. My shoes were polished black and glistening in the morning sun. I felt confident and at ease as I approached the front entrance of the company office. The building was old, like all of those surrounding it. But it had character and as I entered the vaulted portico, I was confronted by a wooden coun-ter behind which various people sat at old solid timber desks. "Can I help," asked the young man who came to the counter as I entered.

"I have an appointment with Mr. Neale," I explained, as I showed him the letter.

The company, I discovered, was a subsidiary of Wiggin's Teape, Ltd., one of the biggest paper merchants in the country. Mr. Neale, one of the Directors, interviewed me for the job of junior clerk. His office had that lovely smell of wood that reminded me of the Tin Chapel back home in Cabra West. He was dressed in a dark blue pinstripe suit and I noticed that there was a bowler hat on his hat rack. He was very impressed with the fact that I had passed nine subjects at school and made quite a fuss of me when I showed him my school certificate. I was offered the job and he told me that I would receive a confirmation letter in the post. He was true to his word, and I reported to the office on Monday morning, following receipt of the promised letter. I could hardly contain my excitement when I saw that the wages offered where three times more than I had been paid in Dublin and as an extra perk, the company provided luncheon vouchers. This meant that I could get a decent meal in the middle of the working day. The vouchers were accepted by most of the cafés and restaurants nearby, so there was also a reasonable selection of meals to choose from.

Mr. Neale introduced me to Mr. Eric Balfry, his co-director colleague, in whose section I would be working. He was tall and athletic looking, in contrast to Mr. Neale who was short and stout. I learned later that he was an ex-Naval Commander during World War II. A thorough gentleman, it was a privilege and a pleasure to work for him. He assigned me to an experienced member of staff who wasn't much older than myself. He took me around the other offices within the company and introduced me to the other members of staff. We got along very well together and before long I became familiar with various types of paper and board, together with the finishes applied to them, and was put in charge of the Sample Room.

I became something of a celebrity, or perhaps curiosity would be the better word. Never before had the staff come across an Irish person who worked in an office. They assumed that all Irishmen worked on the building sites. Mr. Neale had informed them that I would be joining the company and made a point of telling them that I had a school certificate. I was complimented by the female staff on my turnout and found myself being invited to join Valerie, Margaret, and Jo for tea break. They were all typists, and like Mike, my trainer, about my own age.

The weeks seemed to fly by, and before long I was invited to attend a staff party. I was told that there would be a dance and that I was welcome to bring a partner if I so wished. The party was enjoyable, though a very mild affair. On Monday, I discovered that I was the talk of the office. The girls couldn't contain their curiosity about who my partner was and the fact that I had only orange to drink.

My partner, I informed them, was my older sister Rosaleen, and I didn't drink alcohol. They were absolutely fascinated by all of this. "Your ears must have been burning all night," they said. When I asked why they said that the comment, "He didn't waste much time," was being bandied about, as I had only been in Birmingham a short while never mind the job. Jo, in particular, found it so interesting, that she asked me a couple of times why I didn't drink alcohol. I later discovered that her father was an alcoholic and her family regularly ran the streets in fear of him.

Christmas came and went. It was a miserable time. As I mentioned earlier, the family was split and I cannot for the life of me remember where, or if I had a Christmas dinner. I reflected on that frosty Christmas morning so long ago, when I made my way to six o'clock Mass to sing with the choir. My poor mother must have been heartbroken. She loved the fuss of preparing the pudding and decorating the house in Dublin. Here she was now, living in digs and unable to do the things she would normally do at this time of the year. So my father decided that we would save for a deposit on a house of our own. I agreed, and I began to give over most of my earnings to him for that purpose.

Mrs. Pitt, the lady we were living with, asked if I might be interested in working part-time in the local pub where she was a barmaid. I said yes, and she arranged for me to meet the manager the very next evening. He liked what he saw and hired me immediately. I spent that evening being taught how to pull a pint and get to know the customers. My father and my brother Gerry came in regularly. After a few weeks or so, I was filling a "shipping order" as it was called; it was a full tray of mixed drinks. As I was topping up the last pint, the customer asked how much it was. I answered immediately and placed the tray of drinks on the counter. The customer checked the price and agreed it was correct. My father, I noticed was standing at the end of the bar talking to the manager. He had come in while I was filling the order and I hadn't noticed. Both he and the manager had broad smiles on their faces. "You'll have to get up very early in the morning to catch him," my father said, looking proudly at me.

From then on, the manager pestered me to consider applying for a pub of my own. "There's just one thing," he said, "You'll have to be prepared to taste the beer to make sure it's alright." I thanked him, but refused politely. One evening, not long after I had taken up the job, a customer came in and asked me for a "Black and Tan." I asked him if he was trying to be funny. My brother Gerry happened to be at the bar also, and quickly informed me that it was a genuine drink. It consisted of half a pint of bitter, with a bottle of Guinness poured in on top. We all had a good laugh as I apologised to the customer. He happened to be Irish and saw the funny side of it.

Before long, Easter was approaching and I decided to return home to Dublin for the weekend. I asked my boss, Mr. Balfrey if I needed to work on Good Friday, explaining to him that I intended to visit Dublin and I wanted to travel on that day if I was free to do so. "Certainly you can have the day off," he said, "but would you remember to change my blotter when you get back?" I promised I would and he wished me well and hoped that I would return.

"There's no doubt about that," I said, reminding him that all of my family were now in Birmingham. His secretary, Mrs. Andrews, happened to be in the office when I made my request and before long, the word of my proposed journey was all round the office.

One of the senior office staff called me and asked if it was true that I was going back to Ireland. "Just for the weekend, Roy," I explained.

"Well, I have to send some samples of paper to our Dublin office," he said. "Would you happen to know where Sir John Rogerson's Quay is, and do you know Armstrong's, the paper merchants and would you be willing to drop the samples in their office for me?" The questions were coming in rapid succession.

"I know the Quay for sure, but I don't know the company. I'll find them though, and I'll be delighted to drop the samples in for you. Are they likely to be open?" I enquired and was surprised to learn that they would, although they closed on Good Friday.

"They'll get a hell of a surprise," he laughed. "They need the samples in a hurry and with the post the way it is, there was no chance of them getting them before Tuesday at the earliest. Don't go letting them talk you into staying and working for them," he joked.

"My sister has thrown me out once already, so there no chance of that, even if I wanted to" I smiled as I took the package. I called in to Armstrong's, expecting to be greeted like a celebrity, particularly as they were getting delivery the very next day. But the office was busy and the guy I spoke to at the counter just took the package and strode off leaving me standing there. I don't even think he said thanks. For sure, no one offered me a job. If anything, I felt as though they resented me. So somewhat deflated, I left, and as it was too early in the day to seek out my girlfriend Kay, I went back to my sister's house in Cabra West.

I had kept the money I was paid from the bar, and saved it for the occasion. I felt that I was playing my part by handing up all of my wages from my full-time job. Before I left Dublin, I had met Kay Storey and I really liked her. We had been writing to each other since I'd left for England. So I bought her a signet ring out of my hard-earned money with her initials engraved on it. I discovered when I got home however, that she didn't feel the same about me and was, in fact, seeing somebody else. So I told her to get lost and to shove the ring. I came to realise anyway, that it was a futile exercise, expecting her or any girl to wait for me, when I didn't know if I would ever be home again. I ached to be back in Dublin and in Cabra West in particular, but there was no prospect of that happening, at least not in the foreseeable future I thought.

I returned to Birmingham on Tuesday morning and went directly from the boat train to work. The journey had been a little more pleasant this time. I managed to get a seat in the lounge on the boat, and as I now knew just where to catch the train, I got there ahead of the main crowd and found myself a seat by the window in a warm carriage. So I was reasonably refreshed when I arrived at the office. Remembering what my boss had asked me to do on my return, I went into his office and changed the blotting paper in his desk pad. Noticing that the container of three by five cards he used for writing messages on was empty, I replenished them also. Around ten o'clock, Mrs. Andrews came into the sample room and informed me that Mr. Balfrey wanted to see me in his office. She was all smiles, so I knew it wasn't going to be a telling off. "Did you have a good time in Dublin?" he asked.

"Yes Sir, it was great," I answered.

"Before you left here on Thursday, I asked you to change my blotter, and I find that you've not just remembered to do that, but you've also filled up my container of cards. Now I want to know how you managed to remember what I asked you to do after a weekend away, and not only that, who told you to fill the card container?"

"Sir, I can't explain, except to say that if you give me an instruction, I'll see to it that it's carried out, and if I see something that needs doing I'll use my initiative and do it."

"Wonderful, fantastic, just great," he smiled. "You're a gem, and I'll see to it that you are rewarded." He was true to his word. My wages were increased by the following Friday and suddenly everyone in the office regarded me as someone to respect.

I was even more popular with the girls now and during the tea break, Jo was particularly attentive, so as I was now free I asked her out. We arranged to meet after work so that I could see her home. She lived within walking distance of my digs. She was nowhere to be seen when I left the office, so I carried on to the bus stop and caught my usual bus home. Next day at the break, she asked if we could meet that evening. Generally, I would be quite ruthless in a situation where a girl had stood me up, and would have nothing further to do with her. But our arrangement had been very loose anyway, and it wasn't as if I had been left standing somewhere. I simply carried on home, once I didn't see her at the pre-arranged place. So I agreed and we met after work. She explained that she had thought that I wasn't being serious, and though she hid in doorway and saw me looking for her, she was too shy to come forward.

Our relationship began to blossom from then on and we began to see each other regularly. She told me about her father and his behaviour and suggested that I might prefer to ask one of the other girls out. It seems that Valerie was very keen on me, but I told her that I was going out with her and not her father, so stop worrying. Valerie, as it happens, was a petite blonde and I met her father on an office outing some time later, and we got along very well. Everyone near us on the bus assumed that Valerie and I would become an item, especially as her father seemed to like me so much. But I had already made my choice, and although Valerie was a very nice person, I was already seeing Jo. And as I'm a faithful guy, I didn't pursue the matter. It might have been better if I had asked Valerie for a date, with the way things eventually turned out. Jo became very possessive and the longer we were together, the worse this got.

Both of her parents were not just against her having a boyfriend, they were virulently anti-Irish. When I went to call for her, my timing had to be perfect, so that when I knocked on the hall door she would know who it was, and answer it herself. Very often, I could hear her father shouting about the "TB ridden Irish Gits," as she quickly closed the door. So they insisted that she be home by ten thirty at the latest, on the nights we went out. This made things very awkward if we wanted to visit the cinema for the evening show. The film usually finished at around ten thirty. So she had to get special permission to stay out until eleven o'clock. This meant that we could get on a bus and be at her house with a few minutes to spare for a quick kiss goodnight. She was embarrassed by all of this, and apologised regularly. I continued to act the "Sir Galahad" however, and the more her parents acted in the way they did, the more I continued with our relationship.

I informed my parents that I was seeing a girl, and that I would like to invite her to tea at our digs. They agreed and arranged it with the landlady. Everyone was on tenterhooks, and we spent a nervous hour or so in a fairly tense atmosphere. I couldn't understand this, as my mother especially was a very friendly good-hearted woman. Later on, she would advise me about marrying "our own kind." She had obviously detected something that wasn't to her liking. I guess it was what's called woman's intuition, although she said nothing to me at the time.

Summer came and my father decided that he would take my mother back home on a holiday. I was delighted for her, but bitterly disappointed to learn that he used all of the savings that had been set aside for the deposit on our own house. I know that my mother would've gladly forgone her holiday in favour of her own house. But that wasn't to be. They met up with my eldest sister Alice and her husband Frank, who were on holiday in Dublin at the same time. They lived in Oldham in Lancashire. When my parents arrived back in Birmingham, they decided to move to Oldham where empty houses were in abundance, so I was told.

I was very happy in my job. In the two years that I had been there, my wages had increased six times. And now the directors had asked me if I would like to attend the College of Arts and Crafts to learn all about "Paper Making, Merchanting, & Usage," and earn a qualification. I was over the moon at the prospect and now my father was talking about moving up North. When I informed my boss about this, he tried his best to arrange a transfer for me to the Manchester Office. He organised an interview with the manager of the Manchester office and gave me a return ticket and enough money to cover my expenses.

I had never experienced such kindness before, and was quite overcome by his generosity. The prospective new boss asked me the question as I sat in front of him in his office… "Where do you see yourself in five years time?"

"Doing your job," was my reply. I knew right there and then, that wasn't what he wanted to hear, and there was no prospect of him employing me.

He had obviously heard how Mr. Balfrey felt about me, and I was being perceived as a threat. In today's world, I would be expected to give such an answer, particularly as the manager would expect to have moved upwards himself. But it was the wrong answer to give at that time. People didn't have ambition then. Or if they did, there just weren't the openings at work. They expected to be in their job as manager until retirement. So, much to my regret, and to Mr. Balfrey's disappointment, I wasn't offered a job in Manchester. Had I been worldlier, I would've found myself a bed-sit and stayed in Birmingham. But I was too naïve, and the thought just didn't enter my head. It broke my heart to have to leave Keay & Company, Ltd. All of the staff wished me well and presented me with a lovely fountain pen, because of my clear handwriting.

My girlfriend's parents would have been delighted at the idea of the move. They would've looked forward to the day when either one, or both of us, would get fed up and give up on each other. My parents would not have been unhappy at this prospect either. But we vowed to remain true to each other, and we would take it in turns to visit each other every weekend. My new address was 10 Coronation Street. The soap with the same name had just started on the television and we used to enjoy it, because of its authenticity. Olive, my younger sister joined us soon afterwards. Alice, my eldest sister and Frank, her husband, lived just around the corner from us in Roscoe Street. And our aunt Annie, my father's sister lived a few blocks further down the road from them.

Oldham.

I had just about gotten used to my surroundings in Birmingham and thought that things couldn't get much worse. But they did. If Birmingham was a step back in time, Oldham was still in the Stone Age. The toilet was like an army latrine. It operated on the basis of a "tippler" system. The toilet bowl was made of concrete and it had a wooden plank across the top, with a hole in it large enough to accommodate one's posterior. There was no "S" bend. Whatever you did, dropped into a shaped receptacle that was quite large, and only tipped over when it was full of water after flushing. But being large, it only tipped over after several flushes. So it meant that six or seven people would have to have used the toilet before the tippler operated. It then dropped the contents directly into the sewers. The first time that the tippler operated while I was sitting on the toilet, almost gave me a heart attack. Nobody had warned me about it and I thought that the whole system had collapsed. I quickly became conscious of the fact that rats had free and easy access to the toilet because of the openness of the system. So one sat down with this in mind; expecting the family jewels to be bitten, at some stage. The summer was very hot the first year after we moved in, and the whole area smelled to high heavens.

I continued to visit my girlfriend in Birmingham every weekend. Her parents had forbidden her to travel to Manchester to see me, so I had to do the travelling. During this time, my brother Gerry and his wife let me stay in their house. It meant sleeping on the floor in the living room and sharing a mattress with my younger brother Bill. But I was glad of their hospitality. The house was overrun with mice, and it wasn't unusual for us to sit in the dark quietly, then switch on a torch and throw our shoes, or anything else that came to hand at the mice that had been caught in the beam. This carried on until we got so tired that we fell asleep. I remember waking one morning and there was a mouse sitting on my forehead.

The train journeys home were a real trial. They were pulled by steam engines that seemed to cover everything in smuts from the burning coal. The Sunday train stopped at every minor station along the way, and took three hours to cover a journey of eighty miles. I came to know the names of all of them and place names like Congleton and Etruria still haunt my memory. Bill was apprenticed to Charlie Hutchings, Gerry's father-in-law as was mentioned earlier. Charlie was the foreman with a large company and he was a very decent sort. He made the mistake of signing time sheets for two guys who went home early one Saturday. The boss found out and Charlie was sacked. Bill left the job shortly afterwards and came to live in Oldham. My other brother, Jim, decided to leave the Royal Air Force after nine years of service, and he came to live with us also while he was on his pre-discharge leave. My younger sister, Olive, also joined us. At last, some of the family were together again. We began to have fun once more, despite our surroundings.

My father was working in a local factory that made plastic raincoats. He spoke to his boss and soon Jim, Bill, and me were working there, too. It was owned and managed by Jews and run on piecework lines. I very quickly mastered the machine that I worked on and was earning upwards of one hundred pounds per week. Very soon afterwards, I bought an engagement ring and proposed to my girlfriend. I continued to visit her in Birmingham and to stay at Gerry's place. Then one Sunday night, as I sat in the carriage of that slow moving train, I began to feel very unwell. I was burning with a fever and was almost delirious by the time I reached home. I said a quick goodnight to my parents and went straight to bed. I'll be fine now, I thought as I fell into a deep sleep. During the course of the night however, I awoke and felt as if I had a ton weight on my chest. I couldn't breathe, nor could I call out for assistance. I managed to bang on the headboard until I woke my parents. My father came into the room and drew back the blankets to see what was wrong. As he did, so a cloud of steam rose towards the ceiling. "I knew he wasn't well when he came home. He's never gone straight to bed without having a chat first," I could hear my mother say. She then went and got a wet towel to put on my forehead, in order to cool me down, while my father went to the nearest phone box to ring the doctor. He arrived very soon afterwards and diagnosed pneumonia. He injected me with penicillin and promised to return later that morning. The drug soon took effect and I settled down to sleep again. The doctor returned around ten o'clock and gave me another shot. He ordered me not to get out of bed for any reason, stating that I had a very bad dose and as long as I did what he said, he would not have me removed to hospital. My mother was present, and he made her promise to see to it that I followed his instructions. After a few days, I was well enough to sit up and I asked my mother to bring me a writing pad and pen so that I could let my girlfriend know what had happened, and that I wouldn't be seeing her for a couple of weeks at least. My mother expressed her concern at the number of weekends I was spending on a floor in Birmingham, and tried to persuade me to stop going altogether.

The following weekend, my girlfriend arrived in Oldham, having finally taken the courage to tell her parents what she intended doing. I could see that my mother wasn't best pleased. She felt that I needed complete rest and that meant not seeing anyone. She had always been concerned by the fact that I was busy with some project or other, all the time. I remember her asking me at home in Dublin if I would just relax and rest for one evening, at least. Both she and my father were even less pleased when I announced to them that I had proposed and that I had given Jo an engagement ring.

My father had collected my wages on Friday, and he was very upset when he saw the amount of money on my pay envelope. He felt that I should've been handing up a lot more towards my keep. That really annoyed me, and I told him that I was giving up more than him. Also, I was now saving to get married. I was nineteen years of age and I'd had enough of being ordered about and having my life disrupted by this man, and his thoughtless moves. So I had decided that I needed to get out as soon as it was feasible to do so. A two-bedroom house came up for sale in Roscoe Street at the princely sum of two hundred pounds. It wasn't in bad condition, considering its age and I decided to buy it. I wasn't prepared to live under somebody else's roof when I got married, so I was intent on having my own place, no matter how humble. It needed some work and my intention was to carry this out before I moved in. Suddenly, I found I was the talk of the family. Not one of them had bought a house in the past, and some of them at least were speculating about the price and wondering where the money had come from.

Jim met his future wife while working at the plastics factory. He had gotten used to better conditions in the RAF, and decided to sign on again. His decision was helped by the fact that my mother took in a lodger. We awoke one morning to discover that there was a stranger in the spare bed that was in our room. He had met my parents in the pub the previous evening. My mother took pity on him because he had been thrown out of his digs that afternoon, and she invited him to stay with us. The tenement attitude to the homeless was still with her, by all accounts. The fact that he was Irish didn't cut any ice with us, but we didn't want to upset her, so we didn't make a fuss about it. Jim had been undecided up until then, but this made up his mind finally.

When he told our parents that he was rejoining the RAF, my mother took in a second lodger. This lad was a product of the Orphanage School system in Ireland. He was a brilliant pianist, but a raving lunatic. My younger brother Bill and his pal Peter took him under their wing, and arranged gigs for him, drinking free beer all evening as their share of the fee, at the two local hotels where he played. Then my sister Olive found that a coat she had left hanging on the back of her bedroom door was cut to shreds. Con, our lodger was the culprit, and we encouraged him to move on. When he moved out my, mother was clearing out a chest of drawers that he'd been using. My sister was helping, and as my mother opened one of the drawers, she found some tissues wrapped around something that was beginning to smell. She peeled back the layers and clutching her breast said, "Oh, dear Jesus he's gone and mutilated himself." She was holding what for all the world looked like a penis. On further investigation however, and much to her relief she discovered it was a piece of tripe that had rolled itself into what looked like a piece of the male anatomy. My sister almost fell down the stairs laughing. What he was doing with tripe in his drawer in the first place, no one has ever been able to figure out.

Bill was also an excellent darts player. One evening, he was practising in the hotel bar when his dart landed in the "Bull."

He threw the second one and it stuck into the back of the first. "Do that with the third and it's free beer for the evening," the Landlord said. He threw the third dart and low and behold, it stuck into the back of the second. The landlord, true to his word, honoured his bet and wouldn't let anyone touch the board for the rest of the evening. Needless to remark, Bill was first choice for the hotel darts teams from then on.

—✖—

I made up my mind to move as soon as it was possible to do so. But first, I had to get my girlfriend's parents' permission to marry. She was eighteen and I was just a year older. They finally relented, amid great jubilation between my fiancée and me. My parents reluctantly agreed also and we set about planning our wedding. She was a member of the Church of England and had been taking instruction in the Roman Catholic faith. So, in celebration, she decided to be baptised into the Roman Catholic Church. That removed any problems we were likely to encounter when making arrangements to get married. The day came, and on the 19th September 1957, we were married in St. Anne's Roman Catholic Church in Alcester Street, Birmingham. The reception was held in the church hall, the hiring of which had kindly been arranged by the priest who had been instructing her. Our friends from Keay & Company were there, together with members of both our families. Her father disappeared before the service, along with my brother Gerry. They were both in need of a drink and found a pub nearby to slake their thirst. They spent the rest of the day together, like long lost brothers. All went well and we spent two weeks honeymooning in Dublin.

On the way across the Irish Sea aboard ship, she informed me that she wasn't a virgin. But she quickly added that it was due to the fact that she and her family had run the streets so much, because of her father's behaviour. Her doctor, she assured me, could confirm this. I wasn't a total idiot, and while I accepted her explanation, I took it with a large grain of salt. While we were on O'Connell Bridge one afternoon, she left me to visit the ladies toilet just off the bridge on the quayside. When she was in there, four of the girls I knew from the Friday night dances in St. Peter's Hall came walking past. "Hey, there's Éamonn," one of them shouted and all four were around me like bees to a honey pot. We had exchanged a few words and they asked me if I would be at the dance, when my wife came out of the toilet.

"Oh, meet my wife," I said and before I could say anything else, they disappeared as if by magic.

"Who were they?" she demanded to know, looking as if I had done something wrong. I explained, but she was in no mood to accept my explanation and got into a hell of a huff that lasted for the rest of the day. I knew that she was a little possessive, from previous experience, but this was nonsense, I thought. I was learning things that might have changed matters regarding our relationship, if I had been aware of them before marriage. I might have waited longer, except that my hormones were running riot and we had become intimate of late. I felt that I was obliged to marry her as a result. Such was the influence of the religious teaching that I'd been brought up with. We returned to the little house in Roscoe Street, and set about furnishing it, etc. I returned to Rose Weatherproof, Ltd. the plastic coat factory.

One day at lunch in the factory canteen, I was sitting across the table from my father and the factory manager. Just right of them sat a young woman. She asked in a voice loud enough for all to hear, "How do you like living in a brick house instead of a mud hut?"

I could see my father watching what I would say or do. "How old are you?" I asked. Before she could answer, I said "About my age, I reckon… right?"

"Yes," she answered.

"Does your brick house have a garden?"

"No," came the reply.

"Does it have a bathroom?"

"No."

"Does it have electric light or gas?"

"Gas," she said.

"When you want to take a bath, do you go to the local council bathhouse?"

"Yes," she said.

"Well, I was born into a house with gardens back and front. It also had a bathroom and an indoor proper toilet. Not one of these harbingers of disease called tipplers. We also had an electric cooker to compliment our lights. My father is sitting two seats away from you, ask him why he gave all that up to come and live in this backward kip!" Both my father and the manager burst out laughing and applauding at the same time. The manager turned to her, and confirmed that he had visited Dublin on a few occasions and he could never figure out why any of us would leave such a lovely city. If looks could kill, I would've died right there and then.

Gerry came to Oldham on a visit one weekend while my wife was visiting her family in Birmingham. I showed him around the house and he noticed that there were gas pipes in the cellar. "Do you use gas?" he asked.

"No, we have electric," I answered.

"I'll strip all that away for you and get rid of it," he said.

"Fair enough," I said.

"Right, leave me to it and I'll see you later."

"I'll be in me Ma's if you're looking for me," I said, as I left to go. "I'll be back soon," I shouted as I closed the hall door. I returned within the hour, but there was no sign of Gerry. He had stripped the place clean of the lead pipes and gone to a local scrap dealer. I never saw any of the money he got for the lead, and he had his drinking money for the weekend.

My sister Rosaleen got married the following March. We all travelled to Birmingham for the Saturday wedding. It was the most hilarious wedding that I've ever been at. She had to make her way to the chapel on a Birmingham Corporation bus. She was dressed in her white wedding dress, and accompanied by her bridesmaid. My brother Bill was best man, and he likewise had to get to the church on the bus, while the groom and his parents travelled in a taxi. Her husband, whom none of us had met previously, and who looked like an out-of-work jockey, was one of the McCormack's from Gardiner Street in Dublin. We had humble origins, but these were common as muck and behaved accordingly. Their attitude and their language were appalling. They liked to portray themselves as tough guys, perhaps because of the famous boxer called "Spike McCormack," who came from the same street.

My mother and father kept asking how their daughter managed to get mixed up with this bunch of "scallywags." My aunt Annie wore a wide brimmed hat especially for that day. A few of the groom's people were heard asking loudly in a broad Dublin City centre accent, "Who's the *Hoor* in the hat?" The reception was held in his parent's house. When we got there, they pulled a sheet off one of the beds and threw it across the kitchen table to use as a tablecloth. That was bad enough, but when my mother pointed out that there were skid marks on it, my aunt Annie fainted. We all fell around the place laughing. The laughter grew more intense and a lot louder when we discovered that the wedding breakfast consisted of stew. There was only enough food for half a dozen people anyway, and there was no drink whatsoever. His parents and mine were offered food and the rest of us were told to f... off and get our own. Most of us headed for the chip shop. I thanked my lucky stars that my wife wasn't there. She had gone to visit her mother. The 29th March 1958 is a day that will live in my memory forever. A couple of years later I called to see my sister and her husband one Saturday and caught him knocking her about. I stuck him against the wall and taught him a lesson he's never forgotten. You don't mess with the Sheridans.

—m—

Back in Oldham, my eldest sister and her husband had taken my lead and bought an old house that was bigger than the one they rented in Roscoe Street. Frank, my sister's husband set about cleaning it up. After making it habitable, he set about cleaning up the rubbish that had been left by the previous occupants. There was a fireplace in the cellar and he lit a fire and began to pile the rubbish on to it. Among the items that had been left, there was an old armchair and he pulled this up in front of the fire and settled back to enjoy a cigarette. Suddenly, there was an explosion, and the contents of the fire were blown out into his lap. As luck would have it, the explosion extinguished the fire, but it blew loads of soot into the cellar, covering Frank from head to foot. My mother was upstairs visiting my sister, Alice. They got a hell of a shock at the sound of the explosion and looked towards to cellar door in trepidation, wondering what had happened to Frank. As they approached the door nervously, it opened and Frank stood there looking like Al Jolson, the famous jazz singer, who dressed up as a "minstrel." His hair was standing on end and all they could see was the whites of his eyes and the white around his mouth where he had licked his lips. Both of them collapsed laughing. Frank wasn't very amused to begin with, but saw the funny side of it when he saw himself in the mirror. And what might otherwise have been a tragedy turned into a great joke. My mother had trouble amid bouts of laughter, trying to tell the rest of the family that evening about what had happened. Better yet, when they were relaxing with cup of tea after Frank had cleaned himself up, my sister switched the television on. As they watched the programme Alice, pointing at the screen said, "Look that guy has a face like your Dick." He had just taken a mouthful of tea, and it spurted everywhere as he burst into laughter. My mother spilled her tea on her lap as she roared with laughter. Frank had a brother named Dick, and my sister meant to preface her remark with, "your brother." Just goes to show how careful we all need to be in what we say and how we say it.

On returning to the cellar next day and checking through the rubbish, he discovered that there was still a large quantity of .303 rifle ammunition mixed through it. He collected all of the remaining bullets and took them to the local police station, and was promptly arrested. The IRA had only recently called off its campaign in the North of Ireland. One would have to wonder about the police. Why would an IRA suspect present himself at a police station with a handful of bullets? Frank was trying to be a good citizen. Sometimes a guy can do nothing right.

—⁓—

Jim was married on the 26th December, 1961. It was his twenty-seventh birthday. He was on leave from the RAF, and the wedding was held in St Mark's Roman Catholic Church Aston-under-Lyne, near Manchester. The reception was held in the upper room of a pub in Ashton. This time, we had a proper meal and the drink flowed freely. All went well until the end of the night, when we were leaving. His wife had too much to drink and insisted on having more. When Jim told her that the bar was closed, and that she had had enough anyway, she flew into a terrible rage. "Ooops!" I thought, "This should prove to be an interesting relationship." My mother was absolutely disgusted by this and felt that Jim had made a big mistake in marrying her in the first place. He, however, being the gentleman that he was, sorted things out with his wife very quickly. It was the talk of the family for a long time afterwards.

He served for eighteen years and spent time in Malaya and Germany. The RAF ran a scheme that allowed family members to visit their relatives serving abroad for £10.00. Jim invited me and I stayed with him on a camp in Berlin. It had been an officer training camp for the German Army and it had wonderful facilities, including an Olympic-sized swimming pool. I was fascinated to see the double-glazing in the married quarters. They were light years ahead of the rest of us. Pity they allowed a maniac to take over and ruin the country. In a way, I was sorry that the Nazis hadn't invaded Ireland. We would've driven them nuts with our casual attitude to everything, especially timetables. When Jim returned to the UK, I visited him at the camp in High Wycome where he was serving. His wife and family hadn't returned from Germany as yet. I was allowed to stay in his billet overnight, and almost got arrested by the Military Police.

He gave me his bunk while he used the one next to it, with the permission of the lad whose it was. He had gone on a weekend's leave. I was shaken awake at five o'clock in the morning by the policeman and told to report for duty. My brother had forgotten to tell me that this would happen. I told the MP that it wasn't me and to call my brother. But he was having none of this and threatened to arrest me if I didn't get up. Just then, Jim awoke and explained what was afoot. The MP accepted his explanation, albeit reluctantly. I was sorely tempted to join up myself when I saw that they had eight choices for breakfast.

Back to Birmingham.

I had successfully applied for a sales job with a US company, which manufactured printing machines. They had a vacancy in the Birmingham office and my wife persuaded me to apply for it. So we sold the house in Oldham and went to live in digs in Birmingham. This was against all my previous intentions, but I was swayed by my wife's claim that she would find work easier in her own city, and the fact that Oldham was way behind Birmingham in its social development. The company didn't supply a car, so I arranged to buy one. Well, it was more like a motorbike with a roof. It was known as an Isetta Bubble Car. There were two types of bubble car on the road at that time. The one I had was a two-seater. It was rounded in shape and the passenger sat beside the driver. It was commonly referred to as a "Spitfire" cockpit. "Heinkel," the German bomber manufacturer of World War II fame made the other type. The passenger sat behind the driver in this car. Both models had three wheels and it was very difficult to control the car in icy conditions.

I had taken driving lessons while living in Oldham and I am delighted to say, I passed the driving test the first time and was awarded a full driving licence. I picked up the bubble car from the man who sold it to me and was heading home to show it off to my wife, when I found myself in trouble. It was a left-hand drive vehicle and I found it tricky to manage at first. I turned into a street where there were cars parked on both sides.

I noticed a Rolls Royce entering the street at the far end. I pulled in, giving way to him. But he did likewise and I then moved forward. As I did so, he also moved forward resulting in us making contact. I immediately stopped and got out to see what the damage was, only to discover that while my wing had been fairly badly dented, the only damage to the Rolls was a streak of blue paint from my car.

The chauffeur began to berate me. While I was trying to explain that I thought he had given way to me, a gentleman in the back of the Rolls got out and asked what was wrong. It was obvious that he'd had a liquid lunch, since he was unsteady on his feet, and slurred his words as he spoke. But he was very nice. It turned out that he was a director of Avery Scales, Ltd., a very large manufacturing company not too far away from the scene of the accident. He told the chauffeur to be quiet while he asked me how long I had my car. I explained that I had just picked it up. I could see that I immediately struck a sympathetic cord, and he suggested that we just forget the whole business. We shook hands as I thanked him and he climbed back into the rear seat and told the driver to move on. The chauffeur wasn't very happy, but he could do nothing about it and got back into the Rolls and left. "Thank God for decent folk," I said in silent prayer as I headed home, this time being extra cautious.

While it was nice to have a "car," I quickly discovered that I was being regarded as the family chauffeur. Certain members of the family took it as a given that I would drive them home after a night out; this was one of the problems I experienced, because I was a non-drinker. My parents thoughtlessly told people that I would drive them home. At one stage, I had six people crammed into this little car that was designed to take two adults comfortably. The final straw came when I was visiting my mother in Oldham; I was wakened from a deep sleep and asked to drive a couple of my mother's friends home after they'd had a boozy night in the local pub. I was livid, and while I did what I was asked, I told my mother off when I got back to her house. It hurt me to do this, but it was necessary to get the message across that I was not a free taxi ride for anybody.

So in a way, I wasn't sorry to have moved to Birmingham after all. I was driving a friend of mine from work back to the office one day when there was a clicking sound. Before I could figure out what it was, smoke began to fill the cabin. I opened the sunroof and it poured out of it, just as if I was flying a spitfire that had just been shot down. I told my friend not to panic as I tried to manoeuvre to the side of the road. But he ignored me, opened the door, and jumped out. Had the door been at the side of the car I wouldn't have bothered but it was at the front. The steering wheel and column was on a universal joint that went forward with the door, when it opened. So the steering wheel went out of my hands and the car zigzagged all over the road. I finally managed to get it to the side of the road, thanking God that there was no traffic about. I lifted the seat, which is where the clicking sound was coming from, to discover that a lead to the battery had caught fire, and the rest of the wiring was in danger of doing the same. I pulled at the cable to remove it. It was red hot and burned into my hands. I held on and managed to remove it, at the same time cursing my workmate for opening the door when he did. As luck would have it, the cable was one that a parking light could be attached to for use at night. This was a requirement under law if a car was parked on the street when it was dark. The lead had two prongs that fitted into a socket, which was attached to the end of the lead, which in turn was connected to the car battery. The metal collars into which the prongs were inserted were making contact with the base of the seat and sparking. This is what made the clicking sound. Thankfully, the fire didn't affect the workings of the engine and I was able to drive on. My colleague was very reluctant to get back into the car again. I decided it was time for it to go. I drove forty-thousand miles in the bubble car before I sold it. As a matter of interest, bubble cars are now collector's items and they are worth a lot of money today.

—∿—

My boss advised me to contact a car hire company in Bir-mingham city and discuss a contract-hire arrangement with

them. Contract hire or leasing, as it is now known, was an inno-
vation, and the company was anxious to get the business. I took
his advice, and to my delight, I qualified to rent a new car. The
"Mini" had just been launched, and this was the car that I was
supplied with. Apart from the lovely smell of a new car, it was a
treat to drive. I picked it up on Friday and on the following Sunday, I decided to take it for a run down the M1 Motorway, which
had just been built. I was thrilled with the speed that I got out of
it, and delighted with the feeling of safety I felt as it hugged the
road. On Monday, I happened to be talking to the boss and staff
of a Motorcycle Transport Company located at the back of our
office. He drove a Humber Hawk and had noticed my Mini as
I drove into the car park attached to both premises. "Here," he
said to me as I walked passed wishing them a good morning, "I
see you're driving one of those new Minis, how do you like it?"

"It's brilliant," I answered, beaming all over my face.

"I was driving down the M1 yesterday with the pedal to the
floor," he said. "I must've been hitting seventy when a little red
roller skate passed me by as if I was standing still."

"What time was that at?" I asked him.

"Around three o'clock," he replied.

"Shake hands with the owner of the roller skate," I said,
holding my hand out and smiling from ear to ear.

"Well bugger me," he said, "I think I'll have to get rid of
the Humber." The three men on his staff had a good laugh at
his astonishment. The Mini was the pride of my life. I drove it
all over the country and was really sorry to let it go eventually.

I was called to a meeting at Head Office in London. I
assumed that it was a Sales Meeting and the usual pep talk. But
I was nicely surprised when I was told that my salary was being
increased, and that I was to pick up a new car immediately afterwards. The car was a Renault Dauphine. It was blue and it was
just lovely to drive, except on a windy day. The engine was at the
rear, like the Volkswagen, and the front was so light that I had to
keep a bag of cement in the boot to stabilise it. But it was nice
to have that "new" smell again. It meant that I had to terminate

the hire agreement on the Mini, but sufficient time had passed to enable me to do this without a problem.

When I got back to the office in Birmingham and told the secretary what had happened, she threw her arms around me and kissed me on the lips. This took me by surprise, especially as she was ten years older than me, but I put it down to exuberance and thought no more about it. Shortly after that, I was told that I would be needed to work on the company stand at the print exhibition in Earl's Court in London. Arrangements were made for me to stay in a hotel close by and I spent the week enjoying the atmosphere and the excitement of my first exhibition. During the course of the week, I demonstrated the machine that I was working on to a few Cypriot visitors. They explained that their workshop had been totally destroyed during the troubles on the island. They were very impressed with my demonstration, and having visited other stands, they returned next day and wanted to buy nine machines. You can imagine how I felt as I asked them to take a seat and have a coffee, while I spoke to the General Manager about the best way to handle payment and shipping. He spoke to them and asked them to return the next day. When they had gone, he told me to forget the deal. I wanted to know why and when I asked him to explain he turned his back as he told me to, "Just forget it." I spoke to my immediate boss and he told me that the visitors were Turkish Cypriots and that the General Manager's mother was Greek, and he would not do business with the Turks. His prejudice cost me a whole heap of money in commission; not to mention considerable embarrassment when the customers arrived back on the stand next day. But, he was the boss and I had to "grin and bear it."

The branch secretary arrived on the stand on Saturday, and I was asked if I might drive her home when the exhibition closed. I was delighted to have some company on the long journey, and I readily agreed. I took the road that runs through Aylesbury, Bicester, and Banbury. We stopped in Aylesbury for dinner, and laughed about the fact that there was none of the famous Aylesbury Duck on the menu. The meal was very good however, and we were very relaxed in each other's company. "Do you mind if I share something with you?" she asked.

"No," I replied, "Sure aren't we friends?" I said, not knowing what to expect and thinking of that kiss.

"It's very sensitive," she said, "and I don't want to cause offence." I didn't know what the heck was coming next and fully expected that I was about to learn something about myself that was annoying or upsetting her, and possibly others in the office.

"I'm intrigued," I said leaning forward so that she could speak in a lower voice.

"I've two pieces of news for you. First, you remember Arthur Helbing, the representative from the finance company who called on us last Wednesday?"

"Yes I do," I said, "He was a very nice guy and I may have some business for him soon."

"Don't bother," she said, "He's been arrested for murdering his girlfriend." That took me totally by surprise. He'd been such a gentleman when he came offering finance for machines that we sold to clients. "It appears that she wanted to end their relationship and he phoned her, pretending that his car had broken down and asking her to help. When she picked him up, she drove back to her flat where he appealed to her to stay with him. When she refused, he strangled her."

"Oh, my God," I said, "He seemed such a timid guy." I sat stunned for a few moments and after gathering my thoughts, I asked her what the next piece of news was.

"You're a lovely guy, and I hold you in very high regard. I think that you ought to know how Ray and Jill feel." My wife and I were lodging with the Branch Manager and his wife at the time, and there was a distinct atmosphere lately, which made me feel very uncomfortable. I told her this. "You're very perceptive," she said, "Jill phoned me the other day to tell me that she had gone into your bedroom to tidy up when she noticed a pungent smell. She discovered that it was coming from a chest of drawers, and when she opened one of the drawers she found that it was stuffed with used sanitary towels."

"Oh, my dear God," I said, with mouth wide open as my jaw dropped. "I had noticed a smell alright, but thought that it was coming from the bathroom, which was right next to our bedroom." I felt ashamed and disgusted and didn't know where to look.

"Jill said that she had heard all sorts about the *dirty Irish*, but was very quick to add that this wasn't true. She greatly admires the fact that you shower every morning, and that you're as tidy as though you were living in a barracks. She's appalled that one of ours should not have learned basic hygiene, particularly where sanitary matters are concerned."

I was dumbstruck. "I'd better get to hell out of there quick before the relationship between Jill, Ray, and myself is completely ruined."

"I'm sorry to have told you, but I felt that it was important for you to know."

"You were right to tell me and I appreciate knowing, I'll straighten her out as soon as I get home. That explains the reason why I found the house locked up when we got home last Wednesday. I had to get through a downstairs window. I thought that they had forgotten that we were out. Oh, my God!" I was in shock and couldn't eat, at least not for a while. This was worse news than the murder she had just told me about.

The secretary was very supportive and tried to reassure me as we drove home. "It's not your fault," she kept saying. "How could you have known what she was like? We all have our secrets." Nothing she said could ease the pain that I was feeling. When I eventually arrived home after dropping her off, it was too late to do anything about this matter. I resolved to sort it out next day… Sunday. When I talked to my wife about it next morning, she didn't seem to take on board the seriousness of the matter. Nothing I said seemed to be getting through to her. Then she announced that she was pregnant, and she wouldn't be using sanitary towels for the immediate future. So I wasn't to worry, as if that was the answer.

After Mass, I drove over to see my brother Gerry and his wife Pat, and asked if there was any way that they could put us up, at least temporarily. They had moved to a newer bigger house and had a spare room that we could have for as long as we wanted. I immediately drove to the home of my boss and announced that we were moving out, straight away. The boss and his wife seemed relieved and we parted on good terms.

As I drove away with our few possessions, I made a resolution to get a house of our own as soon as I possibly could. In the meantime, we gratefully settled in to our new digs at the top of my brother's house. His wife was very welcoming and tried to make us feel at home. Although the house had been redecorated and repaired by the Council, it hadn't been fumigated and was infested by bedbugs. I was forced to get some empty bean tins and place the legs of the bed into these to try to prevent the bugs from crawling up the legs of the bed. Another quick move was decided on, there and then. Soon afterwards, we found digs near to where my wife's family lived. We thanked my brother and his wife and packed our suitcases once again.

We shared a house with an old couple who were struggling to make ends meet. It was nearer to my workplace also, but uncomfortably near to my mother-in-law. Despite the fact that she didn't like me, she decided to use my flat as a place of refuge from her husband. I would arrive home each evening to find her asleep in my armchair. I soon got fed up with this and told my wife to get rid of her. She did, but only to the extent that her mother left just before I got home every night. I knew this because the chair cushion was still warm. My wife denied that her mother was there at all when I asked her about it.

My wife insisted on us visiting her mother's house every Saturday, despite the fact that there was no welcome there for me. I was reluctant to do this but complied to keep the peace. There were a number of reasons for my reticence, not the least of which was that her father would arrive home drunk. Also, there was never a fire in the grate, and used cups and saucers littered the dining room table. Her mother would sit at the table wearing two overcoats. The first time I agreed to accept a cup of tea, she shuffled out of the room and came back carrying a kettle. She poured some of the hot water into one cup swished it around a few times before pouring it into the next one. This was her method of washing the dishes. I could've lived with that, after all I was used to hardship. But the tea she made was as weak as could be and it tasted vile, especially to one who had been used to drinking strong army tea. She was so lazy that she didn't bathe, and she began to smell so badly that local shop-keepers barred her from their shops.

One Saturday when my wife was nearing her time, her father came home in his usual drunken state. Some words were exchanged between them, and he took a swipe at her. Quick as a light, I was out of the chair and grabbed him by the throat. I dragged him outside, into the yard. "Now you drunken scum, let's see what sort of a man you really are. Go on, throw a punch at me."

"You wouldn't hit an old man," he groaned.

"I've had enough of you, and have put up with your snide remarks about the Irish. But you crossed the line when you raised your hand to my pregnant wife. Now, let's see what you can do."

He was stunned and rooted to the spot. "I'm sorry," he said. "I didn't mean any harm."

"Let's get something straight right now," I said, "You behave yourself in future, or I'll bury you in this yard. Do you under-stand me?"

"Yes," he said all sheepish, "I'm sorry."

I went into the house and told her to get her coat; and leave right away or stay for good. From that moment on, his attitude to me changed totally. All of a sudden, I was his son-in-law and a hero who didn't take nonsense from anybody. He would tell his friends… "You don't mess with the Sheridans."

At a later stage in our relationship, I began to understand his reason for behaving as he did. Shortly before our wedding, I was allowed into my future in-law's house. Every Saturday morning before he went to the pub, I noticed that he cleaned the house from top to bottom while my mother-in-law sat on her fat backside. They didn't share the same bed and hadn't for years, according to my wife. They never spoke except to snarl and argue. They had three children, all girls. He had been told that she had done her duty and that was the end of any further sexual activity. There was also the strange notion going around that a man wasn't a real man unless he had a son first. No wonder he was drinking heavily, and causing problems at home. My wife's two sisters began to look on me as their hero and they became very attached. So much so, that at one stage, the second eldest who was a staff nurse in Birmingham General Hospital told me that she was considering having a baby. If she came to a final decision on this, she said that she wouldn't mind if I was the father. "How cold and calculating is that," I thought to myself, although I must admit to being flattered. This coldness was to manifest itself in my relationship with my wife, not many years later.

Then, happy day, our daughter was born. She was a lovely healthy ten pounds and I was thrilled with the whole idea that I was her father. From the first day, after she came home from the hospital I nursed her, sung to her and when she was old enough to sit up, I took her everywhere with me. She was named Catherine, after my mother. This didn't please my wife or her mother but I insisted and that was that. As she grew older, my wife became terribly jealous of my obvious love and displays of affection for our daughter. Then she passed a particular remark to me one day about my relationship with my daughter. It suggested that the displays of affection were unhealthy. I was disgusted and I began to suspect that the relationship that she had with her father wasn't as healthy as it ought to have been. I remembered her explanation about the loss of her virginity and wondered. Her remarks annoyed me, and I became self-conscious about holding my daughter. So much so, that it took me many years before I learned to hug my children. But this was after I had entered a whole new relationship.

Just about this time, it must have been around the year 1960; an article appeared in the *Letters to the Editor* in the Birmingham Sunday Mercury. A guy by the name of Monroe wrote it and it was virulently anti-Irish. Perhaps he was related to the ex-governor of Mountjoy Prison in Dublin, who was given a hard time by the IRA when my father was incarcerated there. It annoyed me so much, that I sat down immediately and penned a reply. I pointed out that my countrymen were not just in the process of re-building their cities and doing many of the menial jobs that the natives wouldn't do. But they had earned the right, in any event, through their service in the British Armed Forces. A total of 250,000 of my countrymen served during the First World War. Two of them were uncles of mine. One was killed and the other lost a leg at the Somme. My father, I went on to argue had served in the 8th Army in North Africa, Sicily, and Italy, and had been wounded while helping an English colleague who had been hit. As for me, I argued further, I never wanted to come to England in the first place and would be returning home at the earliest opportunity. In the meantime, should the security of the state be threatened and my services required, I would not hesitate to join the armed forces. My attitude is… if one is making a living in England then the least they can do is to help in times of need.

The repercussions from my letter that was listed under the title in the newspaper, *In Defence of the Irish*, amazed me. I was invited to travel to Valentia Island, off the coast of Kerry, to speak to the people there. My daughter's godparents were from Valentia. The husband was visiting his parents at the time that one of them was ill. His wife posted a copy of the newspaper to him and he showed the letter to his neighbours in the local pub. The Irish workers in Guest, Keen & Nettlefolds, a large engineering factory in Birmingham, where my sister Rosaleen worked, wanted me to speak to them in the canteen during lunch. I became something of a celebrity among the Irish. But some of the local Birmingham people saw me in a different light, and many of those employing Irish workers were becoming concerned at the reaction of their staff. The neighbours stood in a group outside of the house where I lived as I left for work, and nodded to each other as a couple of them said in a voice loud enough for me to hear, "He's the guy who wrote to

171

the Mercury." If this behaviour was meant to intimidate me, it didn't work but it certainly had its effect on my landlord, who asked me to leave his house. One of the guys at work refused to believe that I had the command of English to write such a letter. When I said that I had indeed written it, he then insisted that I'd had my schooling in England. Feelings were running high all around. The newspaper editor was so inundated with mail that he published an editorial, stating the matter was now closed and no more mail on the subject would be accepted. Hindsight is a great thing, so they say. If I hadn't been so naïve, I might have capitalised on the situation and entered politics. I would've had no problem with garnering the support of the Irish at large.

CHAPTER THIRTEEN

A NEW HOUSE IN NEWPORT

I had made it clear to Jo from the start of our relationship that I would be returning home as soon as an opportunity arose, and if she wanted to be my wife, she would have to get used to the idea of living in Ireland. The letter and the behaviour of the neighbours strengthened my resolve to seek employment back home, and I informed her of my intention. She didn't seem to have a problem with this. If she did, she never said so. In the meantime, I began to scan the newspapers for new digs and noticed an advertisement for new housing in Newport Shropshire. The developer was having trouble selling the houses he'd built; he was offering to pay the deposit and help with the mortgage for suitable couples. The very next weekend, we drove the thirty-eight miles to Newport and had a meeting with the representative on-site. He was confident that we would qualify and we filled out the necessary paperwork.

A week or two later, we were contacted by the mortgage company, inviting us to come and pick up the keys for the house we had chosen. It would be a bit of a chore to drive that distance twice a day to get to work, but I was happy to do it. Within days of receiving the keys, we moved out of our digs. I had been attending a Judo Club for some time to keep fit and Reggie Bleakman, the black belt instructor with whom I had become friends, brought his van around to help with the move. Good people like Reggie, Mr. Balfry, and others proved to me that there were more decent English people about, than the other type. The difference, I found, laid in the degree of education, which the person had, or whether they had served in the armed forces. If they had, the odds were that they had Irish men and women serving alongside them, and they appreciated the contribution made by their Irish comrades. It amused me how naïve some of the English could be where the Irish are concerned. I remember being asked by a fellow office worker one day, if I missed the Saturday Night Fights in Dublin. He seemed awfully disappointed when I explained to him that this didn't happen, at least not in the area where I was raised.

Newport was a growing village and the local people were concerned that there was little for the youth to do. I had a sign on the rear window of my car, advertising the Kyu Shin Kan School of Judo. I was approached by some of the local adults and asked if I would consider setting up a club in the village. A meeting was arranged with the interested villagers; soon afterwards, a committee was formed, and a club was founded. One of the members of the committee had a connection with a local army camp, and arranged for us to borrow their mats until such time as we could afford our own. We met in the parish hall and I arranged for Reggie to attend on Saturdays, to instruct the members. About three months later, we entered a number of members for "Grading."

The first belt is white in colour, followed by yellow. The organisation doing the grading was different from the one I was a member of, so I had to grade along with the rest. As I held a yellow belt with the British Judo Council, it didn't count with the British Judo Association, the local organising body. I applied to contest for two grades and was successful. The rest of our club entrants won their white belts, and we returned to Newport a very happy bunch. The army unit whose mats we borrowed were leaving to serve overseas and they donated the mats to us at no cost. We found Brian Evison, a local farmer who was a black belt, and he was willing to act as our permanent "Sensai" or teacher. He was a great character and the club progressed very well under his tutelage. The year was 1963; as we made our way to a demonstration evening in Shrewsbury, we stopped at a petrol station. The station attendant informed us that President John F. Kennedy had just been assassinated. We carried on to our destination with heavy hearts. That same evening Brian, our instructor, was demonstrating how to disarm an assailant wielding a knife. The opponent tried to be smart, and deviating from the rehearsed routine, he began switching the knife from hand to hand in the crouching position. Brian simply punched him on the nose, knocking him out. When he came to, he complained that that wasn't Judo. "Maybe not," said Brian, "but it was effective and that's all that matters." We had a great laugh about it later over a pint in the pub.

The next grading brought us further success. I was now a green belt, while the other members won yellow. The Shrewsbury Chronicle, the local newspaper, reported our progress much to the delight of everyone involved. Because of this, the club secretary approached the managing director of Audco Valves, Ltd., the company he worked for as an engineer and asked for financial help. His boss agreed to help, provided we fought under the title of Audco. Stan also informed me that one of the members of the company sports committee objected to my being the club captain, because I was Irish. He was promptly told that there would be no deal if I were removed.

At the following committee meeting, all members agreed with the proposal to accept the new name, and we became Audco Judo Club. The managing director was true to his word, and he arranged for the company to build a club premises on the company land. It was fully equipped with showers, etc., and soon became the focus of much attention in the village. The club returned his kindness by becoming County Champions within the next eighteen months. All was going well, and we trained five nights a week. We also had a weekend session every month with the Olympic Coach. All the clubs in the County gathered for this, and for two days training, all we paid was half a crown (two shillings and sixpence). A couple of my neighbours joined the club and Brian asked me to help with their instruction. I was demonstrating a throw and had one of them in front of me, as I pointed out the correct way to unbalance an opponent, and throw him. I had him under my point of balance, and was telling the rest of the class that all he now needed to do was continue

bending, and the throw would be complete. Suddenly and without my telling him, he slammed me into the mat. Not being prepared, I landed awkwardly and as a result hurt my arm. Thankful
that I had reacted fairly quickly, the damage wasn't as great as
it might have been. A couple of evenings later, one of my other
neighbours approached me and asked how my broken arm was.
I assured him that my arm was far from broken and asked where
he got such an idea. "Oh, Colin across the road told me that he
beat you on the mat at the club the other night, and that he had
broken your arm."

I showed him my arm, explaining what had happened and
telling him that it was my fault I got injured and that I should've
been ready for what he did. The following evening, I bowed in
front of Colin. The bow in Judo indicates a challenge, and an
opponent is not allowed to refuse. He nervously stepped onto the
mat and as I took hold of his jacket, he asked me to go easy with
him. "I'll be as easy as you were with me," I said as I threw him.
He no sooner stood up than I slammed him down again... and
again. When he was completely exhausted and could no longer
carry on, I told him to be very careful with his tongue in future. I
also warned him that I would be informing the neighbours about
his performance that night. That was the last I saw of him in the
club. He'd learned not to mess with a Sheridan.

Things were going so well that I decided to settle down
in Newport. The locals had taken to the Irishman who was a
member of the church choir, and who was also responsible for
setting up their very own Judo Club. Then, as luck would have
it I received a reply to a letter that I had written earlier to a firm
in Dublin, inviting me to an interview. I found myself in something of a dilemma, having decided only a short time before
that I would settle in Newport, now I had to make up my mind
whether I should resurrect my plan to return to Dublin. I felt
that there was nothing to lose by at least attending the interview.

By this time, I could run a printing machine and make
plates, etc. The application that I had written was in response
to an advertisement in the Evening Press, an Irish newspaper.
The company was looking for a machine operator. As already

stated above, I decided to attend and at least find out what the conditions were and what wages was on offer. When I presented myself at their office, I was given an IQ test and a mechanical aptitude test before the actual interview.

The general manager was friendly and we got on very well. He perused the results of the tests and stated that he was very happy with them. He was so pleased, that he offered me the job of Department Supervisor. He explained that the printing department was a new addition and that he needed someone who could get it up and running. He felt that I was the right person for the job. The wages started at £900 per annum, with the promise of a bonus at Christmas. This may seem very small money, but in 1964, it was a decent wages. It was £150 more than I was earning in my present job, and it meant that I could come home at last. I was given a month to wind up my affairs in England.

I returned to Newport, overjoyed at the prospect of what lay ahead and I could hardly contain myself as I told my wife what had happened. I would be sorry to leave Newport and the club and my friends; I realised that I had decided that I was going to settle permanently there. My wife was not aware of this however, as I hadn't said anything to her. I probably would've stayed if it hadn't been for the fact that her mother and sisters came visiting a short time previously and I overheard her mother saying that she would love to come and live with us. "Not on your life," I thought, "That is never going to happen." My wife seemed to be in favour of my taking the job. That's what I thought at least, because she never raised any objections. So I went to see the local auctioneer and put the sale of the house in his hands.

Back to Dublin.

The month flew past and before I knew it, I was waving goodbye to my wife, my daughter, and our son, Eamonn Junior, who had been born in Newport and was now four years of age. I hated to leave them, but it was necessary to do so while I set about finding a house in Dublin, etc. The Judo club secretary was almost in tears when I told him that I was returning home. He felt that it might have had something to do with the comments passed by the person who didn't want me as team captain. I assured him that it had nothing whatever to do with his racism, and that it had all to do with my wanting to live in my own hometown. I had arranged to stay with my sister May, who now occupied the old family home, and arranged to pay her what she thought was fair.

Before long, I was immersed in getting the printing department set up. There was much to do and it kept me busy late into the evening at times. The company was very efficiently run. Most of the staff was of Leaving Certificate Standard and the layout of the plant, (it wasn't permitted to call it a factory,) was excellent. There was a first rate Restaurant (not Canteen) that was heavily subsidised. It meant that the staff could buy a hearty meal at a very reasonable price. It also took the onus off my sister, as she didn't have to cook any meals for me except on Sunday.

I spent Saturday afternoon visiting housing developments, and soon found a beautiful four-bedroom house in the suburbs. It had a double garage and under floor heating and at £3,500.00, I felt that it was a bargain. I went to visit my Bank Manager and ask if he would be prepared to advance me sufficient funds for a deposit. He wasn't too keen at first, but I convinced him after telling him that I had a house in England that was up for sale. He recommended a solicitor and after giving him the same assurances with regard to repaying the loan, it was arranged. I didn't wait until the following Saturday, but arranged to leave work early enough to catch the sales people on site that Monday and secured the house.

I phoned my wife to tell her the good news but she didn't sound very enthusiastic. "Perhaps she was tired," I told myself. "After all, she has the two kids to look after." "Any word from the estate agent?" I enquired.

"No, nothing yet," she said. That was the usual comment as the weeks went by. The new house was almost ready and I was getting concerned that the builder would be looking for the rest of the deposit. So I decided to arrange to take a Friday off and travel over on Thursday night. I would go speak to the estate agent, and try to get things moving.

Imagine my surprise when he informed me that my wife had told him the house was no longer for sale. "I had a couple who were prepared to pay more than the asking price, because they had family living on the estate." he said, showing a good deal of annoyance.

"Can we get in touch with them now?" I asked.

"It won't do any good," he said. "When your wife told me the news, I went knocking on doors and found a couple who had been thinking of moving and they decided to go ahead. The deal was done very quickly, so that's that I'm afraid."

"Could you put mine on the market again?" I pleaded, trying to conceal my frustration. I'm not given to using violence against women, but I felt as though I could wring my wife's neck as I walked the mile or so back to my house. She flatly denied any knowledge of what the agent said. She was so convincing in fact, that I believed her. "After all," I thought, "haven't estate agents as bad a reputation as second-hand car dealers?"

I arrived back at work in Dublin early on the Monday morning, tired and worried. "What the hell am I going to do now?" I thought. There was nothing else for it but to bluff my way with the bank manager and hope that the house in England sold quickly. But somehow, I felt the opportunity wouldn't come again so soon. It was time to bite the bullet.

The new house was ready, so I paid the remainder of the deposit and arranged to draw down the mortgage. There was nothing for it but to move the family over. I realised that this would add to the difficulty of selling the house in Newport, but I needed my family with me. In any event, the longer my wife stayed in England, the more difficult it would be to sell, if it was true that she had already put the estate agent off once. So I went to the bank manager again and borrowed the money to pay for the furniture removal. I was getting further and further in debt, and this began to cause me some concern.

I travelled over once again. Leaving on Friday evening, I arrived in Newport on Saturday in time to meet the removals people and help to pack our belongings for the journey home to Dublin. I had little or no sleep, but the excitement of the move and having my family with me again boosted my adrenalin to the extent that I didn't notice any tiredness. I realised that the furniture would not reach our Dublin address until later in the week, and as my wife wanted to say goodbye to her family it was agreed that she would stay with them until I took delivery. By the following Wednesday, the truck had arrived outside the new house and I set about preparing the house for my family. I phoned my wife after arranging the flight from Birmingham, and told her that I would be at the airport to meet them on Saturday. All went well, and my heart leapt as I saw my family come through arrivals.

Almost as soon as I arrived back in Ireland to take up my new job, I phoned my old company commander in the Army Reserve. After visiting him in the barracks, he insisted that I sign on again. He was also a director of Ballsbridge Motors, Ltd., as mentioned earlier and when he heard that I needed a car, he kindly arranged to supply a ten-year-old Volkswagen at a very reasonable price. So I met my family, and with joy in my heart drove, them to see their new home.

The house was in immaculate order and as I proudly opened the hall door, I thought my wife would be as excited as myself. I was to be disappointed, however. She didn't show any emotion. Matters were soon to deteriorate to a stage where I felt that I was on my own, as far as worries where concerned. The house in England sold eventually, but for much less than the asking price. By the time the agent and the solicitor got paid and the mortgage was cleared, there was very little left. I can't remember what the actual amount, was but I do know that it didn't go anywhere near clearing the debt in the bank. When I visited the bank manager to pay what money I had, and to explain the situation, I got no sympathy. He suggested that I sell the house and pay my debts. I countered with the suggestion that his idea wouldn't help matters as there were still houses for sale on the estate and there was little or no chance of making a profit. I informed him that I was an honourable man, and that he would get paid if he would just wait a little longer. When he insisted on my selling, I told him that I would declare myself a bankrupt, and that he would have no chance of getting his money. His face lit up like a beacon, and I thought for a minute he was about to hit me. He demanded that I report to him on a weekly basis to discuss the situation. I asked my wife if she would consider getting a job to help out. She was rightly concerned as to who would look after the children. I explained that my mother and father wanted to return home, and that they could take care of the kids. She agreed and promised to start looking for work straight away.

While all of this was going on, I was trying to run my department at work as efficiently as I could. I was working long hours and getting nothing extra in my pay packet because I was a staff member. Being a member of "staff," in my opinion, is a way of being screwed by the employer. My apprentice had more money in his pay packet some weeks because he wasn't staff and got paid for overtime. I had no complaints, however. My belief, rightly or wrongly, is that if one agrees to take a job, knowing what the terms and conditions are, then you just get on with it.

Bombs and Bums and Buggers with Guns.

I was also progressing at a rapid rate in the army reserve. My corporal stripes had been restored within weeks of my signing on again, and I was nominated for a sergeant's course almost immediately after that. Time was flying by, and at the end of summer of 1964, I had my sergeant's stripes up. Earlier in the year, I had been a member of the most successful 81mm mortar team ever. Our score had been higher than anything previously achieved in either the regular army or the reserve. During the course of the shoot, there was a misfire in the number two gun. A bomb was jammed in the tube. The gun controller called out misfire, and both gun crews quickly ran for cover in accordance with procedure, in case the bomb blew up. After waiting the required time with nothing happening, the gun crew are then obliged to disarm the gun. The crew approached the gun, and gently undid the collar-locking device. This frees the barrel and allows it to be turned so that the number two on the gun can raise it. By so doing, the number three puts both hands in front of the barrel opening, so that he can catch the bomb as it slides out. This is a highly dangerous manoeuvre, and an officer must supervise it. In this case, it was the duty of the regular training officer to oversee things. He stood there behind the gun crew as Private Willie Phelan raised the barrel but nothing happened. The bomb was stuck fast. So Willie gently shook the barrel from side to side. Still nothing happened. So he shook it violently saying, "Move, yeh f….r." On seeing what he was doing, the officer retreated backwards at a faster rate than I've seen some guys run. The final shake did the trick, the bomb was dislodged and the number three caught it before it hit the ground. Everyone breathed a sigh of relief. Here we were on "Cemetery Hill," and if the number three hadn't caught the bomb, there would have been bodies blown all over the place. The handling of the misfire was noted and the crew complimented for their efficiency. The officer got one hell of a slagging afterwards, and didn't live it down for years afterwards.

The following year, 1965, around the same time of the year, I was back in the Glen of Imaal, this time as a sergeant. We arrived in Coolmooney Camp on the Saturday afternoon and offloaded the ammunition, putting it in the camp magazine. After tea, we were back in the magazine priming the bombs in preparation for the shoot next day. This involved taking the detonators from a box, setting the fuse on instantaneous, and screwing the fuse into the top of the bomb. This might sound dangerous and it is, but not as much as one might think. The bomb is detonated when it strikes the ground. It is shot from a tube that is set into a base plate. After reaching the zenith of its travel, it falls back to earth and explodes when it hits the ground. Everything within a hundred-yard radius, depending on the type of ground that it lands on, is in danger. The idea behind it is to drop a pattern of these on an enemy position, causing death and terror. So unless someone drops the bomb while it is being primed, there is no danger. We made sure that the bombs stayed in their cases while the priming was taking place, as a precaution. The only other way they would explode is if someone hit the fuse with a hammer or something similar, and none of those present had a death wish. So there was not a lot to worry about when a corporal lit a cigarette while he worked. I told him to get the heck out of the magazine anyway, as the younger private soldiers were about to panic. Besides, he hadn't asked permission to smoke. He left the force not long afterwards and joined the Gardaí. The last time I met him he had been promoted to sergeant in the motorcycle section. He'll be in no danger there, as long as he doesn't light up while riding the bike.

Our job was finished within the hour and I reported to my commanding officer that all was in readiness. He was pleased that it had been done so quickly. He informed me that one of the senior officers was returning to Dublin shortly. As my wife was due to have our third child very soon, he thought that I might like to spend the night at home. The colonel would be returning to camp next morning, and he would give me a lift back. I thanked him for his kindness and accepted the lift with gratitude. I met the colonel shortly after that, and we headed out of the camp in his car. Just as we turned left out of the gate to head for Dublin, we passed a group of four hikers. He stopped the car. "You'd better tell those lads that we'll be dropping high explosives into the Glen tomorrow and they need to get up over Table Mountain tonight for their own safety."

"Right sir," I said and got out of the car, calling to the hikers. They stopped and turned round to face me. As I explained the situation, I realised that one of them was an electrician who was carrying out maintenance work at the plant where I worked. "Hi," I said smiling.

"Hello," they replied...

"Ah, howareyeh?" said the electrician, "I didn't know that you were a member of the Free Clothing Association. What are yeh at." I explained about the shoot and ignored his smart-ass remark. "No problem and thanks for the warning" said the one who appeared the leader of the group.

Back on camp next morning, I thanked the colonel for his kindness, and set about getting the teams ready for the shoot. Everything we needed was loaded onto trucks and we headed off to Cemetery Hill, which would be our firebase. The hill is so named because of an accident that occurred there during the Emergency. An officer was demonstrating how to arm a landmine to a platoon of soldiers who were seated amphitheatre style on the side of the hill. He did something wrong and the mine exploded, killing him and most of those seated nearby. The remains of many of them are buried on the top of the hill. The graveyard acts as a reminder to all of how careful we need to be when handling weapons or explosives.

The sun shone in a cloudless sky that morning, displaying the beauty of our surroundings. Mother Nature was at her best as she raised the curtain of early morning mist from the land to expose the exquisite beauty of the scene set out before us. The sun warmed our bones as it took the chill out of the air, promising a day that would be remembered with fondness by all who were privileged to witness the sight before them.

It seemed that the sacrilege of doing this on Sunday would be compounded by the assault that was about to be perpetrated on this beautiful scene. I was reminded of similar days in Kilbride Camp in the Dublin Mountains when, during a break, I sat on a rock in the rushing waters of the river that runs through it. I was prompted to pen the following verse as I looked at discarded rubbish that was polluting the crystal clear water.

I wonder if man will ever see
That a river, running wild and free
Is far more beautiful than he
Or, does he know, and through jealousy
Pollutes it.

Back at work on Monday morning, the electrician approached me. "Your shooting wasn't very good," he jibed.

"What do you mean?" I asked, ignoring the mocking attitude he had adopted.

"Me and the boys were sitting on the side of the hill opposite, watching you through binoculars and your bombs were landing all over the place."

"If you knew anything about mortar fire, you'd know that the whole idea is to drop them in a pattern on an area, so as to catch the enemy as he tries to run in any direction. Anyway, I thought you and the boys were supposed to be heading over the mountain into Glenmalure?"

"Oh yeah we did that last night and spent most of the night stripping and assembling the Thompson Sub-Machine Gun in the An Oige Hostel. We told the rest of the boys there about the shoot and it was decided to watch how you did."

"What boys are you talking about?" I asked.

"The IRA boys, who else?"

"Would yeh get lost," I said, in as derisory a tone as I could muster. "The IRA are dead and gone, so you're just shooting your mouth off... right!"

"You can mock all you like," he said, taking a step nearer, "but we have a surprise in store next year for you and your guys, just wait and see."

"Oh, give over will you?" I said, half laughing. "You lot weren't up to the task in the 50s and you won't have any success in the future. So what's the big surprise, or are you just talking through your hind-quarters."

"We're going to blow Nelson Pillar down, and that same night, we're going to wipe out the high-ranking army officers and politicians. So how will you like taking orders from us in the future?"

"Would yeh ever go and get yourself seen to?" I said mocking him, "You're raving and you'd best see a shrink before you lose the run of yourself altogether. Now get lost, I've got work to do."

"We'll see," he said as he walked away his face red with anger.

I thought long and hard on what he'd said to me as the day wore on. The business about Nelson certainly tied in with what a school friend had said to me ten years previously. He was a member of Sinn Féin, and I hadn't put any store by what he'd said at the time. But now it was being repeated and I supposed that there had to be some truth in what I'd just heard. I want to make it clear to the reader that I didn't like the idea of a British Admiral looking down on us from a pillar in the middle of the main street of our capital city. To be honest, I wasn't too concerned about whether they blew up the pillar or not. But the rest of it concerned me very much. We had experienced the horrors of a civil war once already, and the legacy was still alive to a large extent in the 1960s. There had been no contact with my father's uncle, or his side of the family, since that time when he was part of the escort, which took my father to the train that would take him to prison during the Civil War. I didn't want to see that happen to anyone else's family. So I decided after pondering on it for three days, to phone my company commander and discuss it with him. I was at pains to point out that I felt what I'd heard was bravado and may not amount to anything. He agreed and asked if I would be in barracks the following night for the usual parade. I confirmed that I would, and he said we'd talk further then. Feeling a bit more relaxed I got on with my work.

The next day, Thursday, seemed to fly by. There was lots of work on and we were busy all day. The only break in the schedule was a visit from the General Manager, who told me that a new girl would be starting work on Monday and that she lived on the same estate as myself; he asked me if I would be willing to give her a lift in the mornings and drop her home in the evenings. I agreed and he thanked me. I didn't say anything to my wife when I got home. It slipped my mind and I didn't think it was important anyway.

When I arrived in barracks that evening I was met by the Company Sergeant, who asked me to report to the CO's office. The place where we paraded (gathered,) for training was the top floor of a very large three-storey block. It was a total shambles when we took it over, with paint peeling off the walls and generally filthy. The post-colonial thing was very much in evidence.

A chapter in the Crane Bag talks about the neglect that happens when a country throws off the yoke of oppression. The contempt held by the newly freed people for the buildings, etc., of the oppressor leads to complete neglect and vandalism to a large extent. This is because the new occupiers don't view the buildings as being theirs. In our case however, the unit got together at the request of the CO and stripped the walls and woodwork and painted them. One of the other sergeants in the unit was an accomplished artist and he painted the cap badge on the end wall of the billet. It was four feet in diameter and done in black and gold on a cream background and it looked magnificent. We were very proud of what had been achieved, particularly as it was done in our own time. The CO of the barracks tried to take it off us when he saw it and give it to the regular unit for their use. But our CO was made of sterner stuff and told him where to go.

I knocked on the door of the office and waited until I heard the CO invite me in. He stood behind the table that acted as his desk in that dingy place. It had an army blanket thrown over the top of it to mask the damaged surface. A single light bulb with no shade hung on its original flex from the very high ceiling, casting shadows in the corners of the room. The only thing that lent any cheer to the surroundings was a lighted fire in the large grate. Standing next to the CO was a tall man, wearing a greatcoat over his uniform against the chill of the night. I noticed that he had what we other ranks referred to as "custard" on the peak of his cap. "Ah… hello sergeant," said my CO. "This is Colonel Fitzgerald, the Brigade Commander. He's interested in what you told me on the phone yesterday."

Before he could say any more, the Colonel stepped forward as I lowered my hand from the salute I had just given both of them. He held his hand out and took mine. His hand was bony, but his grip was firm. There are some people who are the wrong shape for a uniform. No matter how they try not to look like a sack of potatoes, they just don't succeed. Not this man. He was tall and slim and the uniform hung on him as though it had been painted on his frame. He held his head high and looked every bit a soldier.

"Would you mind repeating what it is you told the Commandant?" he asked, while looking me straight in the eyes.

This man could read what is imprinted in the back of your brain, I remember thinking to myself. I told him the story and how it came about that I should be talking to an alleged member of the IRA. He was particularly intrigued when I told him that a school friend had told me practically the same story ten years earlier, all except the bit concerning a possible coup d'état.

"You're probably right about this fellow being a braggart, but I'll report it to the Garda Special Branch anyway and we'll see what they have to say." He thanked me and I saluted and went about my duties.

—ᴍ—

During the next week or so, I set about contacting my parents and arranging for them to return home. I got their room ready and awaited their arrival. My mother's face lit up when she saw me waiting on the pier at Dun Laoghaire. "Howareyeh Ma?" I asked, "Did you have a nice trip? Hi Da, are you well? Was the journey alright?"

"Yes," they both replied, not showing any sign of the tiredness that I knew from experience was a feature of travelling by boat and train. We headed for home and after they had settled in, I invited my father to accompany me to the local pub for a pint and a chat.

"It's great to have you home, and I'd just like to ask a favour of you, if you wouldn't mind," I said, as we sat down with our drinks.

"What's that?" he said with a puzzled look on his face.

"I want you to promise me that if a problem should arise, no matter what it is, that you will ask me down here for a pint and tell me. There may never be a need to do this, but I'm just making sure that you know there is nothing that can't be sorted out over a pint. It's possible that there might be a disagreement with two women in the kitchen, who knows, but whatever it is, we can resolve it by discussing it. Will you do that for me?" He agreed and I felt that all would be well, as I trusted him to keep his promise. Next day was Saturday, and I took them to visit the rest of the family who were living in Cabra West, Finglas, and Dorset Street in the city centre. Everything seemed to be working out fine, and I returned to work on Monday, happy in the knowledge that at last my wife had the babysitters that would allow her to find a job. I could at last see some light at the end of the tunnel. My job was going very well and I was happy that I had been able to help my parents in a small way.

—⧢—

The company commander called me into his office when I arrived in barracks the next day. We paraded on Sundays from eleven until one o'clock, and on Thursday evenings from eight until ten. "I've just had word that a potential officer course will be starting soon, and I want you to go on it."

"Thanks sir, but I'm happy as a sergeant," I said.

"I'm not effen asking you, I'm effen telling you," he said, while blowing a stream of smoke from the long draw that he had just taken on his cigarette. "There's an interview in Army Headquarters on Thursday next at eight... be there."

"Right sir... and thanks again."

"Here, have a fag," he said holding out the packet of Player's.

"Thanks, but I don't smoke," I said politely.

"Have an effen fag," he insisted. So I took one, wondering if this was a test of my obedience. If it was, he needn't have worried. All he had to do was give me an instruction and I would carry it out. He would have known that anyway. We puffed and made small talk until we'd finished our cigarettes and I returned to my duties once again.

—⧢—

My parents were proud to see me in uniform. My mother said that she was delighted to see that at least one of her sons had put on the "green jacket" that her husband had left off. This was a reference to his IRA service. I got the camera out and had my wife take a photo of me with me parents standing in the front garden. They were delighted to hear that I was nominated for an officer course and wished me well for the upcoming interview. Life was great, I thought, and it would be a whole lot better if my wife could get a job and help out with the finances. But she kept claiming that she was being discriminated against, because she was English. I found that hard to accept. Most Irish people were inclined to go out of their way to be polite to visitors. But she insisted that this wasn't the case. Then one evening when I arrived home, I noticed that me mother had been crying. I asked her what was wrong, assuming that she'd had a disagreement with my father. She said that she had a cold. I didn't want to pry, so I accepted her explanation, though I knew in my heart that a cold wasn't the problem. I thought that there had been an argument with my father and I didn't want to interfere.

The interview at Army HQ was in front of a panel of senior officers, and it went so well that the Battalion CO rushed back to the barracks to inform my Company CO that I had taken first place. There was great jubilation. Anyone would've thought that I'd won a major battle. But learning later that my performance would reflect on both of my senior officers, I understood their reason for celebrating. It gave me great satisfaction also, I have to admit. The course would start in a couple of weeks and I looked forward to it with great anticipation. I was to learn from my boss later that one of the senior officers in the battalion was a close friend his. They apparently compared notes on my performance, both in the force and at work. My future seemed assured.

Back at work the following day, one of the male staff came into my department and asked if I had seen the new girl in quality control. I said that I hadn't, and he said just wait and see... she's a beauty. There was a tea break at ten o'clock each morning, and I promised I'd check the QC department on my way to the dining hall. Ten o'clock came and I headed for the dining hall, via Quality Control. I saw a new girl and wasn't particularly impressed. She was nice enough, but not someone that I'd

be excited about. After the break, the same guy came over to my department and asked me if I'd seen the new talent. "I did and I'm not impressed," I said in answer to his question.

"You're one fussy bugger," he said, and disappeared as quickly as he'd come.

Later however, as I made my way back from lunch, I realised why he was so excited. Two new girls had started, and the one he was talking about was standing near one of the folding machines, surrounded by six guys who were behaving like dogs in heat. I decided that she needed rescuing and poked my head between two of the guys and asked, "When?"

"When what?" she asked smiling.

"When you're finished with this lot, call over to the printing section and I'll tell you the rest." I had just reached my desk when she appeared beside me.

"So do you have something to say to me?" she asked. I must admit that I was aroused just to be standing beside her. Her name was Linda and she was seventeen, I learned. "Is that short for Belinda?" I asked.

"No, just Linda," she said.

"Never heard of it before. It's beautiful." She seemed amused and we talked rubbish for the remainder of the lunch period. "Talk to you again," I said as the bell went to signal the end of lunch break.

"Looking forward to it," she said, as she walked away. For the rest of the afternoon, I kept getting phone calls from the other guys, calling me a dirty so and so. How people's minds work! If there's nothing to talk about, they'll make things up. We were very busy over the next week or so, and things soon quietened down again.

When I got home, I noticed once again that my mother was crying, and she tried to hide her tears from me as I walked into the sitting room. "What's the matter, Ma?" I asked.

"Oh, it's nothing," she said.

"Are you having trouble with me Da?" I asked.

"Yes," she said.

"Is there anything that I can do?" I asked.

"No," she said. So I let it go again, not wanting to interfere. Little did I know what was to come.

The following day, I got a visit from my eldest sister Alice, accompanied by May and Dick, the two older siblings. Dick was fired up and ready for a fight.

"What going on with me Ma and Da?" he demanded. I could see that there was trouble afoot from the faces of all three, especially as Alice lived in England.

"Just hold on a minute," I said to Dick. "Come with me and let's have a chat." I walked out into the hall and up the stairs. When we reached my bedroom, I told him that he could have trouble if he insisted, but first tell me what this visit was all about.

"Right," he said. "Are you telling me that you know nothing of the way that your wife has been treating me Ma and Da."

"What do you mean?" I asked. "She's been giving them a terrible time since they arrived, and your daughter keeps asking them when are they going home. Now, I know that she's too young to make that up herself. She's obviously been put up to it.

Me Da opened a letter addressed to J. Sheridan, thinking that it was for him. When he discovered that it was for Jo, she abused him terribly over opening private mail." There was a whole list of things he told me that left me dumbfounded.

"You can believe me or not, but this is the first I've heard of any problems." I told him about what I'd asked my father to promise.

He knew nothing of that, of course. "We're here to take them away," he said, "They're going back to England with Alice tonight."

"What?" I said, "They can't do that. Let me talk to them."

"It's too late," he said. "They've already made their minds up."

"Right," I said, "I'm going for a pint." I was fit to be tied as I sat in the bar sipping my beer, not knowing what to do for the best. I decided to try to talk to my father, and at least ask him why he didn't keep his promise.

"I didn't want to interfere between man and wife," he said.

"I wouldn't have considered it interfering," I said. "What's going to happen to my mother? She's not able for this."

"I'll look after her, as always," he said. "Won't any of the family put you up here in Dublin? You can't be taking her back to that awful place."

"We asked, and the answer is no, so Alice has a house for us, next to hers in Oldham."

It had only been two months or so since they had arrived. Now in this cold October, they were heading back to England. I was devastated, particularly when I thought that they didn't even get to spend Christmas in Ireland. The seeds of separation between my wife and myself had been sown much earlier, and now they were blossoming. It took all of the control that I could muster to keep from exploding into a rage. Again, my wife denied everything. No, she hadn't prompted our daughter to ask her grandparents when were they going home. No, she hadn't verbally abused my father for mistakenly opening her letter. No, she couldn't get work, because she was being discriminated against. Finally, no… she no longer wanted any sexual relations with me because she had, "done her duty." If she felt that way, she said, she would let me know and as we were practicing Catholics, any contact in future would have to be at the safe time of the month. Love and all that flowed from it was a spontaneous thing, I told her. I wasn't about to be controlled in that way. I couldn't compartmentalise my love life, in spite of the disciplined way I ran my job and behaved in the Armed Forces.

I arrived in work on Monday, mentally bruised and quietly seething with anger. No one would've known from my demeanour, however. I was good at disguising my feelings and in any event, all of what had gone on was private, and I didn't believe in bothering others with my personal problems. As things turned out, I found myself standing next to the new girl, Linda, in the queue for lunch that day. She seemed as pleased to see me, as I was to see her. After some small talk, I asked her if she liked Chinese food. Chinese Restaurants were new to Ireland at that time and they were regarded as a novelty.

"Yes," she said.

"Well, how would you like it if I took you to one?" I asked, fully expecting her to laugh it off as a joke. After all, why would a beautiful girl like her be interested in a guy ten years her senior, when she could have the pick of the crop.

My heart leapt in my breast when she said, "Yes."

There were others around us on the queue, and from the looks that we were getting; I thought I'd better end the conversation good and quick. "I'll ring you later," I whispered. We had reached the top of the queue anyway, collected a tray, chosen our lunch, and moved on. I could hardly wait to finish lunch, as I felt that everyone in the dining room was looking at me. Back at my desk, I wondered as I eyed the telephone, whether she would reject me if I made the call. She'll have taken it as a joke, I kept telling myself. Don't ring, you'll only make a fool of yourself, my inner voice kept saying besides… you're a married man.

I resisted the temptation and congratulated myself on my self-control. Just as well that I did, because the word had got around about our conversation, and she was being watched like a hawk watches his prey. In fact, one of the older male staff came to me during the course of the afternoon and reminded me of my obligations as a married man. I had seen him in the local church a number of times when I'd called in to offer a prayer before starting the day's work. He reminded me about this, and pointed out the consequences of what I was doing. I thanked him for his concern and informed him that I wasn't doing anything except having a laugh with a young woman that I admired. I reminded him about the scandalmongers and what their fate should be, according to the Bible. I also told him as politely as I could to mind his own business.

When I got home that evening, I found my wife sitting by the fire, staring into the grate. The breakfast dishes were on the draining board unwashed, and there was no dinner prepared. It was usual for me to get up very early and prepare breakfast before I left for work. I saw to it that the kids were fed, and that my wife got some tea and toast in bed. The unwashed dishes had now become the norm. But no evening meal was a new departure. When I enquired of my wife why this was so, she said that she had been too busy. Now, I knew that it couldn't have been from cleaning the house, because that was my job on Saturdays, (shades of her father in Birmingham). The children were well-behaved so it couldn't be them. She obviously wasn't interested, and she constantly reminded me that we didn't have money problems in England, and that she would easily find a job if we were to return. I must admit that I gave it serious thought. The bank manager was at me again, too; and the strain of it all was beginning to wear me down.

I had finished the potential officer course and though I'd passed it, I was somewhat disappointed with my performance. I finished eighth in a class of ten. The pressure that I was under was affecting my performance, and I realised that I needed to keep things together. Whatever about my hobby, and that's what the reserve was, in effect, I wasn't going to allow it to affect my job. So I took whatever steps I needed to in order to keep on top of things.

There was free medical cover available to all of the employees at work. The doctor would visit twice a week, on Monday and Friday. I was running a temperature, and decided to pay him a visit. My head felt is if it was about to explode. After checking me over, the doctor asked why I had come into work in the first place. I told him that a simple cold wouldn't keep me away. He said that it was anything but a cold, and told me that my temperature was dangerously high. I was ordered to go home straight away, get into bed, and call my local GP. I reported to my immediate boss and then to the General Manager. They insisted that I leave for home immediately. By the time I got there, I was sweating profusely, and my chest felt as if it had a ton weight on it. My GP called, and confirmed that I had a bad dose of pneumonia. He was quite concerned, particularly when I told him that I had had pneumonia previously. He visited me every day for the next week to make sure that I didn't need to be transferred to hospital. I was completely run down, and to add to my woes, I had an abscess on my elbow, and to make things even worse, I got shingles.

During the second week, the young lady that I gave a lift to every day called to the door enquiring about my health. It was a lovely sunny Saturday and I was sat on the settee in the living room watching the television. My wife showed her in with a look of distain on her face. The young woman apologised for disturbing me and told me that her mother, who was waiting at the bottom of our driveway, insisted that she call. It was the least she could do, in return for my kindness in giving her a lift, she said. We talked only briefly and I informed her that I would be off work for at least another week. Following her visit, my wife went into a jealous huff. When I enquired as to what was bothering her, she informed me through gritted teeth that she knew about me and the other woman. One of the neighbours, whose house faced up the road had seen me pick the girl up and drop her off each day, and she reported this to my wife.

"All I do is give her a lift," I explained, "and that was at the request of my boss. She lives on the estate. Don't you think I'd be more discreet if we were up to anything?"

"You weren't discreet when this was taken," she said, handing me a photo. I almost had a relapse. It was a picture of me sitting beside the secretary from work in Birmingham. It was taken at the last office Christmas lunch. We were sat beside each other, and I was looking at her. Both of us were obviously enjoying whatever remark had been made, but that's all. Where she got the photo from, I will never know. I still don't know to this day. No amount of explaining on my part would mollify her. Perhaps I should've told her about the lift right at the start. But it just didn't strike me as important. Besides, I was also picking up a woman who lived on a nearby estate. When I told her this it only made her worse. She began harping on about returning to Birmingham and how much better off we were over there. I told the two women about her comments, fearing that she might be at the top of the road one morning, making a show of herself. They immediately dropped me and found other means for getting to work. It caused me considerable embarrassment when my boss approached me and mentioned it.

It was three weeks before I was fit enough to return to work anyway. The abscess that was followed by shingles had followed the pneumonia. Just as I thought I was clear, I went for a drive on Friday of the second week at the doctor's suggestion, and struggled back to his surgery with pleurisy. My boss was very understanding, and insisted that I was not to worry about missing work. It was nice to have a friend. Particularly as I was feeling so isolated. My wife was of no help, and I couldn't talk to my family. They didn't want to speak to me since my parents went back to England. If I am totally honest, I didn't want to speak to them either.

CHAPTER FOURTEEN

FALLING IN LOVE

A s luck would have it, I found myself next to Linda in the lunch queue on the Monday that I returned to work. She enquired as to my well-being and looked genuinely concerned. I thanked her and confirmed that I was fully fit again. "By the way," I said, "are you on for that Chinese Meal?"

"Yes," she smiled and my heart leapt.

"I'll ring you later," I said. After lunch and back at my desk, I picked up the handset of the phone and dialled her extension. She answered after the first ring. "How are you fixed on Wednesday night?" I enquired.

"I'm busy Wednesday," she said.

"Here it comes," I thought… "The brush off."

"But I'm free Thursday, if that would suit."

"Great," I said. "Tell you what, if you get a 16A from your house, it will leave you at the Ballast Office in Westmoreland Street and it's just a short walk from there to McBirney's Store on the Quay. Would eight o'clock suit you?"

Her answer was in the affirmative and I was delighted, if not a little guilty.

I arranged to have the night off from barracks and told my wife that I was attending a reunion, and so I wouldn't be wearing my uniform. At about quarter past eight, I saw Linda arrive and stand outside the store. The lights were on in all of the display windows, so she was easy to spot. By the time I got out of my car, which was parked by the curb right outside and walked over to her, some scumbag was already trying to pick her up. "Is this guy bothering you?" I asked and he took off down the quays like a bat out of hell.

"Sorry you were bothered," I said. "I didn't realise what it was like around here."

"That's alright," she said with that lovely smile, as I held the car door open for her. We had a wonderful evening. We talked about anything and everything.

"You know that I'm married?" I asked. That didn't faze her and we carried on chatting. I couldn't remember when I felt so relaxed and comfortable in anyone's company in the way I did with her.

We met a couple of more times, and I knew that I had to finish things for both our sakes. She was seventeen and I was almost twenty-eight, and I was falling in love with her. Well, who wouldn't, she was beautiful, and vivacious, and she smelled so fresh. Unlike my wife who had long since let herself go. I was obliged on one occasion recently, to insist that she have a bath, because of the odour that was emanating from her.

"We can't go on like this," I said. "It's going to bring grief for both of us and the last thing I want is that."

She agreed, after all she did have a boyfriend. So we parted as friends, promising to keep in touch whenever we got the chance. We managed to spend a few hours together when the company closed down for the Christmas Holidays. We finished work at mid-day and we spent the afternoon together. There was no exchange of gifts or anything like that, just a few drinks and a chat as usual.

The year 1966 arrived and I found myself missing her company over the holiday. When I got back to work in January, my boss called me in to his office and asked me if I would be willing to spend six weeks in our London Plant. "They've lost a manager and would like you to fill the gap until they find someone suitable."

I agreed and arrangements were made for me to travel over to London at the end of the month. My wife was all in favour, thinking that it might lead to a permanent move. When I was shown to my desk by the General Manager London office, I found that the staff had left a welcoming present for me. It was neatly wrapped in Christmas Paper and bound with a silk ribbon. I opened it as the staff eyed me over the partitions that separated one area from another. There was a roar of laughter and loud applause as I smiled widely at what it contained. There on the desk in front of me had spilled a gross of Condoms. "Hey you guys," I said "I'm staying longer than a weekend." That brought a loud roar of approval.

We got along very well after that, and they arranged to take me to see the nightlife during the course of my stay. On one occasion, we went to a strip-club. They knew that nothing of that nature was allowed in Ireland, and were anxious to see how I would react. I sat right in the front row of the dingy little theatre with Taffi, a Welsh colleague, while the rest of the lads stood at the back. Taffi told me that he didn't make friends easily. He was a hard drinker, and liked to keep to himself. "Don't worry," I told him. "I won't be bothering you. If you want to be alone, I won't pester you." By the time the six weeks were up, we were the best of buddies. Suddenly there was a scuffle as Barry, one of our company, tackled a guy who was rubbing himself up against him. The bouncer quickly grabbed the pervert and threw him out and things settled down again. It's surprising how quickly you get bored looking at the same thing over and over. But, so as not to disappoint the company, I told them how marvellous the whole experience was. We had a great laugh over a pint about Barry and his admirer.

On the morning of the 8th March, Taffe asked me where I'd been the night before. "In my bed, recovering from the debauchery I was up to with you guys," I said smiling. "Why do you ask?"

He threw a newspaper on my desk. There on the front page was a picture of what was left of Nelson's column under a banner headline. "Holy Moses," I exclaimed, "they've gone and done it. There may be a phone call from Dublin for me during the course of the morning."

"Why would that be?" asked Taffe.

"Oh… I'm in the army reserve and they might want me back in case of further trouble," I said, not wanting to tell him too much.

"Bugger off," he jibed, "you're not that important." There was nobody more surprised than he when within the hour, he picked up the phone and told me that there was a call from Dublin. He listened intently to my conversation with my CO, albeit one sided.

"I'm due a weekend off this weekend," I said into the phone, "and I'll be in barracks on Sunday if that suits, sir," I said.

Before I knew it, Taffi had the word all around the office that I was some sort of special agent, else why would the Irish Army be looking for me to fly home as soon as possible. Suddenly I became a celebrity. "Give 'em hell," the lads shouted as I walked past.

When I arrived into barracks on the Sunday morning, I found the Brigade Commander waiting to speak to me. "Well… you were right after all," he said in his lovely Kerry lilt. "The Gardai want you to stand in a dock and point the finger at the fellow who gave you the information. How do you feel about that?"

"If you order me to do it, I'll obey your order, Sir," I said. "But if you give me that order, then I suggest that you issue me with a weapon right now, because that's how I'll have to live the rest of my life." He looked at me for what seemed minutes. In reality it could only have been seconds.

"You're right," he said. "We gave those f'rs more than enough notice. They told us that there was no truth in what you heard. So they can f…off now." He thanked me once again for what I'd done. It didn't do anything to help how I felt about being a possible "Informer." I discussed this with my own CO after the Brigade CO had left.

201

"Look," he said, "if there's truth in what you told him and by the looks of it there certainly seems to be, we can't have another Civil War. That's what will happen if they carry out the second part of their threat. So don't you be concerned. All you've done is your duty."

My wife wanted to know why I had to attend the barracks when all I had was the weekend to spend with my family. I didn't want to worry her, so I passed it off by telling her that it had to do with my upcoming promotion to the officer ranks. She wasn't happy about this and didn't hesitate to emphasise her displeasure, citing my neglect of the children, especially as we had Martin Desmond, our new addition to the family. He was only a few months old by this time. I reminded her that I had been home since Friday evening, and that I had been with her and the children since then, and I would be with them for the remainder of the day. I wasn't due to catch a plane back to London until Monday morning.

—⟶⟵—

Back in the London office, my colleagues surrounded me, eager to know what had occurred in Dublin over the weekend. They were disappointed when I told them that I couldn't discuss it. That led to all sorts of speculation and the word went around the plant that I was some sort of hero. People were looking at me admiringly. It became a little embarrassing, and I tried to quell any notions they might have had in that regard. I had more invitations than I could handle to go out for the evening. Things got even more intense when I announced that I had just received a letter from my commanding officer that I had had indeed passed the course, and would be commissioned within the next few weeks. I seemed to be in a permanent alcoholic haze as a result of the constant celebrating. One thing that will always be in my memory was that one of our customers gave me a ticket for the re-match for the Heavyweight Championship of the World between Henry Cooper and Cassias Clay (later known as Muhammad Ali). It was held in the Arsenal Football

Club Grounds. Diana Dors, the film actress and Stanley Baker, one of my favourites walked passed me on their way into the grounds. What a night it proved to be. Unfortunately, Henry lost the bout. He put on a gallant performance, but his cheekbones were very sharp and I witnessed the spurt of blood from his cheek that finished the contest. To give Clay credit, I have never seen anything as fast as his fists before or since. He was a true champion, though I reckoned that Henry would've beaten him in their first match, if Clay's second hadn't slit his glove. This gave him enough time to recover from the punch that Cooper had landed on his chin, just at the end of the previous round.

One Saturday, when I was waiting in the resident's lounge, the owner of the hotel came in, accompanied by a young couple who were about to have their wedding reception in the hotel. Having been told by my colleagues that I was an Irish Army Officer, he introduced me to intended groom. He was a lieutenant in the British Army, and assumed that I was on United Nations business. "You must come to our wedding," he said. "It would be lovely to have you there. You could sing us a few good Irish songs," he beamed. He gave me the date and I apologised that I had to be back in Dublin then. He was very disappointed, and asked me if I couldn't rearrange things so I could be with them. What the owner of the hotel had told him, I'll never know but he seemed terribly impressed and anxious that I should be at his wedding. Again I apologised, and told him that I had no choice in the matter.

"Phew!" I thought, "You managed to duck that one." It would've been great fun at the wedding if I had attended and it had come to his knowledge that I was a Reservist and had nothing to do with the UN.

—៳—

Back at work in Dublin, my boss was delighted with the reports that he received from London. "This won't do your career any harm," he said. "There are great things in store for you."

Things were moving along apace. My CO called me to check that I would be in barracks on Thursday. I said that I would. He told me that the Brigade CO would be there and wanted to speak to me again. When I got there, I found that all of the members of the potential officer course were present. The Brigade CO was there to administer the Oath that officers needed to take before they are officially commissioned. After he did that, he asked me to stay behind, as he wanted to speak to me.

When we were alone, he told me that the Gardai had been back on to him and they were claiming that I was a member of the Provisional IRA. They also claimed that I was involved in the operation to blow up Nelson Pillar, and that I had gotten cold feet when the rest of the operation was mooted. He looked at me in that way that he had, and asked how I felt about their allegations. I looked him straight in the eye and asked him how he felt about them. He waited a few moments in that way he had that would unnerve some men. "I don't believe them," he said, with conviction. "If they try to approach you or if you even suspect that there's a garda in your company that you don't know about, you are to phone me, and I will have the Military Police arrest him. Will you be sure to do that?" he asked.

"I certainly will, Sir," I said. I saluted and departed his company. I was so disgusted with the police, I vowed to myself that no matter what information came my way in future, I would keep it to myself, and I would not be cooperating with them. The rest of the guys were anxious to know why I had been held back. I explained very briefly what it was about, thinking that I was in good company and that it would be safe to mention some of what had gone before. To my utter disgust, they moved away from me as though I had an infectious disease. "I'll know who to avoid should we find ourselves in a conflict in the future," I thought. Nothing was ever mentioned again about what I had said. Not by them and not by me.

The next big occasion was the commissioning ceremony. It went very well and I have to admit to a certain feeling of pride, despite the fact that I had dropped eight places on the course as I mentioned above. This was due, not so much to the health problems at the time, as to the idiocy of one of the captains from the Military College.

The task that I was set on a tactical exercise involved my leading a point section of a point platoon. This, for the uninitiated, is the group of guys who are ahead of the main body, checking that it is safe for the rest to proceed along the route. We came under fire from a cottage that lay at the edge of a wood. There was a steep hill running down from the front of the cottage to a river. On the opposite bank, the ground rose steeply to a low hedge atop a ditch that masked the road that we were travelling along. Once the firing started, we went to ground, under cover of the ditch. I got the guys to back away until we were safely out of sight and under proper cover. "Right lads," I said to the machine gunners, "Get set up and keep those buggers' heads down." They moved forward to the place that I had indicated and got the machine gun going. "The rest of you follow me on your bellies, along the ditch until we are past the far line of trees. That would put us out of sight of the enemy in the cottage." I had told the machine gunners that we would make our way down the field under cover of the ditch where the line of trees was. We would then cross the river and carry on up the far field still using the cover of the trees. When we reached the wood, I would explode a smoke grenade just before we attacked from the rear. The machine gun would stop firing at that stage and allow us to get in and finish the enemy off, without being fired on by our own troops. I drew it out in my notebook for the examiner.

"That's not the College solution," he said.

"Would you mind telling what the College solution is, Captain?" I enquired.

"You were right to back off. You brought your machine gun into play and that's fine. But instead of going forward, you should've moved further back to the line of trees at the other side of the field."

"That's okay," I thought. The section could do exactly as I had done, except at the other end of the field in question. What came next shocked me.

"You take your section into the river," and just when I thought he was going to tell me to cross to the far bank he said… "You wade down the river until you're in front of the cottage. Climb out and charge the cottage."

I began to laugh.

"What are you laughing at?" he said. "This isn't funny."

"You're dead right it isn't," I said. "Is the College still teaching First World War tactics?" I asked.

"What do mean?" he said with a look of consternation that I should question the *College Solution*.

"Have you ever tried to run in wet boots uphill on grass, and do it under fire? Every one of us would've been dead before we had a chance to stand upright after climbing out of the water." He was disgusted and submitted a report about me that was not complimentary, to say the least. My CO was highly annoyed with me when the Battalion CO told him that I had failed in my tactics. But when I drew it out for him, he changed his mind, using the usual expletives that he reserved for the regular force. See the diagram on the opposite page and judge for yourself.

I was to meet the "College Captain" at a later date with similar results. I was a second lieutenant at this stage, and I had been told that I was to be Orderly Officer on camp. (This is the officer who is responsible for the camp security for a twenty-four hour tour of duty). I reported to Battalion Headquarters and there he was, sitting behind the administration officer's desk. He handed me a file containing my orders and told me to read it. When I'd finished, he asked if there were any questions I wanted to ask.

"Yes," I replied.

"And what's that?" he asked.

"It says that there's a pistol in the safe located in the officer's mess should it be required."

"That's right," he said.

"Well, let's suppose that I am at the far end of the camp when I'm set upon by a bunch of subversives. Do I ask them to hold off and play fair while I run all the way down to the other end of the camp to get the pistol out of the safe?"

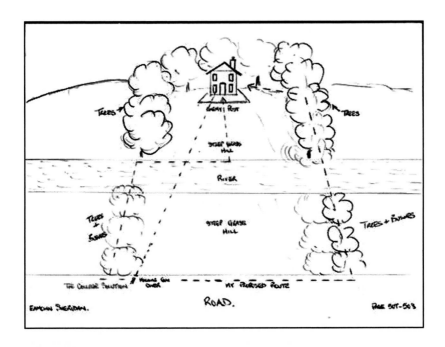

"That's not funny," he said.

Déjà vu," I thought. Here we go again.

"The reason the gun is in the safe is that you are not quali-fied to fire it."

"Well, would it not be a good idea to take it and me to the range right now, and test me on it so that I would be entitled to carry it?"

"But the Reserve's are not allowed to fire the pistol," he said.

"Oh, don't bother your backside," I said, "I can do more damage with my hands anyway."

"What do you mean?" he demanded.

"Attack me sometime and you'll find out for yourself." This sort of nonsense was typical of the attitude of the so-called pro-fessionals. They were paid extra money to train us, but I never once witnessed them earning it, except perhaps when I did my captain's course in later years. The reserve army was only allowed to use weapons or equipment that they had as a last resort. This had nothing to do with whether we were capable or not; on the contrary, we generally performed better in all areas. Maybe this was due to the fact that we were interested in what we were doing, and wanted to perform to the best of our ability, just as we would be expected to do in our civilian jobs. But it is my firm belief that it was nothing more than jealousy. My CO described the regulars as, "Civil Servants in Uniform." They were inefficient and lazy and were found wanting when the one opportunity in recent history arose to test their metal. But more about that later.

—ɷ—

Before I knew it, the long awaited fiftieth anniversary of the 1916 Easter Rising was upon us. I had been kitted out with my new officer pattern uniform, just in time for the military parade that was to take place in honour of the men and women of that great period in our history. We had been rehearsing for weeks and there was a buzz of excitement in the barracks on the morning of the parade that was palpable. My company commander complimented me on my turnout and then told me to report to the battalion commander at Headquarters. I did as I was told and the battalion CO told me that I would be marching with Headquarters Company that day. He indicated the place that I was to occupy on the march.

"Is this not reserved for a more senior rank, Sir?" I asked him with a look of surprise on my face.

"Yes, usually," he said, "but today you'll take that spot. A threat has been received from the IRA that they are going to take the National Colours away from us today. You're there because they'll recognise you, and go after you first. That'll give us time to draw our weapons and take care of things. Live ammunition has been issued to certain Officers and NCOs."

"Do I get a weapon?" I asked.

"What good would it do you if you're dead?" he replied.

"Is this the thanks I get for risking my life?" I asked.

"That's a soldier's life. You'll be a hero," he said smiling.

"Thanks a lot, Sir," I replied, wondering why the IRA would recognise me. The implication in his statement was worrying, to say the least. If the IRA knew what I looked like, who the hell had given them my name or my picture?

The CO went off to visit the toilet before we set off. It was nearing the time for us to move to the point where we would join the main body of troops coming from the barracks in Rathmines. I was chatting to the other officers present when a commandant who had just come out of the mess marched up to me and told me to get into the back rank. I did as ordered and carried on my conversation with the other lads.

The CO arrived back and almost had a fit. "What are you doing there?" he demanded. "I told you where I wanted you to be on this parade."

"The commandant ordered me to move," I told him, nodding in the direction of the senior man.

"Let the lieutenant back there and you take his place," he ordered the commandant.

"But I'm a senior officer," he said.

"I don't give a f... what you are; the lieutenant is to be in that place, so do as I'm telling you." If looks could kill, I would have died right there and then. The other officers knew nothing of what was going on and looked puzzled. I wasn't about to make them any the wiser, especially not the arrogant idiot (who was coincidently, a very senior *Civil Servant*,) that stood behind me fuming. As he was a commandant, the CO relented and let him march in the front rank, but on the right edge, not the left where I had been placed. Maybe the CO thought that he'd get a bullet too, should anything start that day.

The parade was magnificent. There was no attempt by any group to take the colours. The feeling of pride among the people at their army strutting their stuff was electric. I doubt if they would've tolerated any interference with us for whatever reason. As an added precaution, armed army officers in civilian clothes took up strategic positions throughout the crowd. If anything had happened, there would've been mayhem. But we were determined that no organisation, particularly an illegal one, would be allowed to interfere with us in any way. Heaven only knows what the consequences would've been had anything untoward happened. The civilian casualties as a result of panic would've been enormous. Perhaps the subversives took this into account and decided against taking the proposed action... who knows? Perhaps it was never on in the first place and was simply a rumour, like the alleged coup. I guess we'll never know. What I do know is... that there was resurgence in National Pride among the people in general.

Rebel ballads were to be heard in every pub, and groups such as the Dubliners and the Wolfe Tones were at the peak of popularity. It saddened me that my parents weren't at home to enjoy all of what was going on. My father would've loved to have been here for the celebrations. He would've been impressed with the interview of Commandant Tom Barry of the West Cork Brigade. When the interviewer asked Barry if he had any regrets about what he'd done to the Black and Tans, he left him and everybody else listening in no doubt that he would do it over again, if it were necessary.

It was a momentous year in many ways. I was commissioned into the Officer Ranks of the Reserve Defence Force. My commission was one of the last ones to have the signature of Eamonn De Valera, the only surviving Leader of the 1916 Rising. I believe that I was instrumental in averting the threat of another Civil War. I was put in charge of the company rifle shooting team, and we won the Battalion Shoot, against the odds. The company formally known as the "Pearse Battalion," now "D" company 20th were odds on to win. They had been successful in past years and fully expected to repeat their success. The company was composed of graduates and undergraduates from the various third-level colleges. Many of their number joined when they were attending Clongowes Wood College, in County Kildare. It didn't sit too well with them when a company that was mainly composed of working class Dublin Gurriers beat them.

My company commander overheard the battalion commander telling the commander of "D" Company not to be too concerned. "It was just a stroke of luck for them," he said. "Sure they're only a crowd of Cowboys."

We were so incensed at this remark that we saw to it that they didn't win a competition for the next ten years. We won the Battalion, Brigade and Command shoots, and came second in the All Army, during the course of the following years. To add insult to injury, our Light Machine Gun Team repeated our success and went one better... they won the All Army competition. The Sub-Machine Gun team also enjoyed considerable success. We became thoroughly unpopular and the opposition tried every trick in the book to beat us. On the day that the Bren-gun Team won and the Rifle Team came second, the battalion commander invited us all into the officer's mess for a drink to celebrate. "What'll you have?" he asked Private Fullam, one of my team.

"I'll have a brandy, Sir," he said.

"Will you have something with it?" the CO asked.

"Yes Sir, I'll have another one," answered Fullam. That was the last time the CO invited other ranks into "His" mess.

Despite the pressure that I was under from the bank manager, (he was at me again to sell the house,) I couldn't help but have a broad smile on my face at work. I asked Linda if she would join me for dinner to celebrate. She agreed and as we dined she told me that a couple of the other guys at work were trying to get her to go out with them. I informed her that she was free to do as she thought best. I had no problem with the fact that she had a boyfriend and so what if others wanted to take her out. I didn't think that I had any claim on her. She had refused the others she said, since she preferred my company. We began to meet at least once a week for the next while. I found her so pleasing to be with, that I had a wonderful relaxed feeling whenever we parted. It helped me to cope with the pressures I was under. During this time, I picked her up at her house so as to ensure that there wasn't a repeat of the experience outside of McBirney's Store. I got to know her parents. They were lovely people and I regretted the deception that I was perpetrating.

Before long however, the deception was exposed. One of the guys at work who was also married and who wanted to take Linda out happened to meet two of her aunts in a pub one evening. He was trying to pick one of them up, and they got into conversation. He told them that he worked in the printing trade, in answer to a question. They said that their niece had a boyfriend who worked in the trade. When they told him my name, he informed them that I was married and had a family. The next time I showed up at her house, her father asked me if what he had heard was true. I admitted that it was and apologised for any hurt that I might have caused him and her mother. When he told me how he came to know, I told him that the other guy was married also and that he had been pestering Linda to go out with him.

"I'll take care of that *Rat*," I told him.

"No, leave that to me," he said. He made me promise not to see Linda again and I agreed. He then called her, and told her what we'd discussed, and told her not to see me again. I left the house feeling partly relieved that the worry of our relationship and all the deception was now at an end. In contrast to that, I was broken-hearted that I had lost my closest friend.

Before I could tackle the other guy about running his mouth off, he was beaten-up. He spent the next week in hospital. During that time, my wife received a phone call informing her of my clandestine meetings. Her reaction was to arrange for me to see a psychiatrist. She informed me that I either kept the appointment, or she would leave me. I agreed, provided that she saw the psychiatrist, also. There has to be something radically amiss with a woman who deposits used sanitary towels under her pillow, and down by the side of the bed, etc. That's what had happened again only recently. I awoke one Saturday morning to discover that there a pungent smell in our bedroom. She had gone downstairs to make some tea. On investigation, I found the offending linen and almost got sick. "This could not go on," I told her. "I don't care what you say, there's no excuse for behaving in that way." She agreed to my demands, fully confident that the doctor would clear her, and have me committed.

The consultant from St. Patrick's Hospital held a clinic in the Health Centre in Ballyfermot, not too far from Clondalkin where we lived. After we had chatted for about thirty minutes, he asked me why I had come to see him. I told him that my wife had decided that it was necessary.

"You're saner than me," he said. "Is your wife here with you?" he asked.

"Yes," I said.

"Well, send her in to me and wait outside, if you would. We'll chat again when I've spoken to her."

After he had interviewed her, she came out of his office and told me that he wanted to speak to me again. I sat myself down in front of his desk again. "Did you know that your wife is seriously schizophrenic?" he asked.

"I had absolutely no idea," I told him.

"I want you to sign her in as soon as you can, tonight if possible." he said. I was dumbfounded and he could see this from my reaction. "Perhaps you would prefer to hold off for a week and try to talk her into coming in voluntarily. If not, you should bring her back here next week and we'll section her."

On the way home in the car, she asked me what the doctor had said. I tried to put his comments to her as best I could.

"That's what he told me about you," she said. She flatly refused to see him again and I didn't have the heart to section her. It would've been better all round if I had, as things turned out. During the next few months, she created chaos by telling my family what a whoremaster I was. She also contacted Linda's parents and tried to make trouble for her. She phoned the bank manager, and told him how I was behaving. Then she also phoned my boss and tried to have him pay my wages directly to her.

She then got on to the parish priest and made an appointment for me to see him. "Hell hath no fury," is certainly true. My wife was doing all that she could to cause me maximum damage.

"Your wife is a very cold person, if you don't mind my saying," he smiled with an, *I understand your problem* look on his face. When I agreed, he asked me about Linda. I told him that she was totally opposite. She was warm, and loving, and very understanding, I explained. "Well look, if she needs a bit of company, get her to ring me and I'll see to her," he said.

"Am I hearing this reprobate right?" I thought to myself. "He's as bad as the two in work who thought that because she was seeing a married man, she was anyone's. No way am I bringing her anywhere near you or your kind," I thought.

I wasn't the most popular guy around where they were concerned, anyway. Some time back, I had agreed to join the "Planned Giving" campaign that they had instituted in the parish. The parishioners were treated to a meal in one of the airplane hangars at Baldonnel Aircorps Camp. During the course of the meal, a professional fund-raiser delivered a very convincing speech. "The purpose of the campaign," he said, "was to raise enough money to pay off a twelve thousand pounds debt on the church building that was now one hundred years old." The parish priest also promised that a community centre for the youth and the aged of the parish would be built, as a matter of urgency. Despite my straightened circumstances, I agreed to get involved. However, when I received the statement of account at the end of the financial year, the debt on the church had not been cleared. Neither was there any sign of the community centre. They had used the funds to build two four-bed-roomed houses opposite the church, to accommodate one priest in each. When the priest's representative called to my door to ask me to sign on again, he got very agitated when I challenged him about what I considered to be the misuse of funds. I also informed him that they were spending millions on a Cathedral in Galway, when there were people living within walking distance of it that couldn't afford shoes. He almost had a fit, and asked me with a red bulging face if I was a communist.

—∭—

Clerical Abuse.

Around that time also, one of my niece's phoned me in a very distressed state and ask if she could call out to see me. I agreed and we made an appointment for that very evening. Her boyfriend accompanied her, and I fully expected to hear her say that she was pregnant and would I inform her parents. That wasn't the case however, and what she had to say left me shocked and incensed. She was ill in bed for almost two weeks, and she was in a very weakened state, she told me. I can confirm this because I had called to visit her mother, my sister, a couple of weeks previously and she told me that her daughter was very ill, and both of her parents were very worried about her. Knowing that my sister and her husband were both working, I asked if anyone was looking after her daughter during the day. She told me that the priest from the parish youth club, which her daughter was a member of, was calling. She had given him a key to the hall door.

I never thought that there was anything wrong with this. Sure didn't we all trust the priests? Now I had my niece sitting in front of me in one heck of a state, telling me that the priest had forced himself on her, and raped her. That was bad enough, but worse than that, (if anything could be worse,) he gave her a dose of the "Clap."

"Have you told your Ma and Da?" I asked.

"No," she answered, "I'm too ashamed and they won't understand."

"My first bit of advice is that you tell them as soon as possible. Or I can do it for you, if you wish. My next bit of advice is that you not tell anyone else about this, especially not another priest. If you do tell another priest, he will warn this guy off; they will move him elsewhere and somebody else will fall victim. Is he living in the parish house?"

"He stays there when he's visiting the parish. He lives in London and only visits to conduct Retreats."

"What connection has he with the youth club?" I asked.

"He's the club chaplain," she said.

"Is he in town at the moment" I asked.

"No, he's gone back to London, but he'll be back again soon."

"Right... then let's do it this way. When he gets back, make an appointment with him to come to the house. Let me know when you've done that and what time he's due to arrive. You go for a walk and I'll deal with him. He will never bother you again, I promise. Now remember, do not tell anyone about this."

She agreed and went away feeling better in herself. Two weeks later, she was back. When I asked her if the arrangements were in place as previously discussed, she apologised and said no.

"What's happened?" I asked.

"My boyfriend told his mother, who's a friend of the parish priest, and she went to him and told him. So the visit has been cancelled and I don't know if he'll ever be back." My disappointment showed and I would've grabbed the boyfriend by the throat if he had been there. But they had split up. He had dropped her on his mother's advice. My niece was in a worse state now, because of his rejection. She felt dirty and ugly. I arranged for her to visit my GP, who was a friend of mine. He prescribed some tranquillisers but could do little else. Shortly afterwards, she was admitted to Grangegorman Mental Hospital and spent some weeks there. When I visited her, I discovered that she had taken the advice of the psychiatrist and informed her parents. They were devastated, but didn't know what to do about it. I advised them to take a case against the priest. But they were too intimidated by the clergy in general to proceed.

Her mother accompanied my niece to the general hospital to have the venereal disease treated, and witnessed the reaction of the nun who was treating her. She had the look of disdain of one who was dealing with a prostitute. Not ever being one to stand up to the clergy, she found the courage to tell the nun that her daughter's condition was due to one of her kind. For years, I tried in vain to get my sister to persuade my niece to take an action against the corrupt bastard who had left her in such a state. When she finally agreed, the man assigned to deal with clerical abuse in his particular order informed me that the offender had died.

"I hope he made his peace with God," I said as I walked away in disgust. The reader should note that this was in the sixties... long before clerical abuse came to the notice of the public. It shattered my respect for the clergy and undermined my belief in religion to the extent that I no longer attended Mass.

Well, that's not quite true. The battalion held a Mass in September each year, to commemorate the deceased of the various units. It was open to members and ex-members alike; and after the ceremonies, we returned to the barracks and had a drink to celebrate with the retired members. I attend this Mass out of respect for those who have served their country and those who continue to serve. This year, we gathered in the mess as usual. George Colley, a Fianna Fail TD always attended, being an ex-member himself. On this particular occasion he was Minister for Defence, and as usual he was enjoying the company of his colleagues. The mess was jammed solid and the Battalion CO pushed his way through the crowd to talk to the Adjutant, who was standing drinking a pint and smoking his pipe, close to where I stood. "I hear that some of the civvies here are not officers. Is that true?"

The Adjutant took a pull on his pipe, stretched to his full six-foot plus height, and looked over the heads of the crowd in the direction of the civilians who were gathered at the bar. "Mmmm, I think you're right, Sir," he said.

"Well, get them out of here and send them over to the NCO's mess where they belong."

The adj' took another pull on his pipe. "Does that order apply to everyone without exception, Sir?"

"Yes, now get over there and get rid of them."

"While I'm doing that, would you mind telling the Minister to leave, since he was only a corporal when he was in the unit." All of us stood within hearing distance burst into laughter. The CO went away red faced and muttering.

The year 1966 drew to a close, and Linda and I got together as we had done the previous year–end. I know that I was breaking the promise I had made to her father, but I felt that I had to see her. We spent the afternoon in a pub in the Dublin Mountains, drinking and chatting. I told her how sorry I was that she had been in trouble because of our relationship. She assured me that there was no problem, and that I shouldn't worry so much. We kissed for the first time as we parted, and my heart went on fire. I was falling deeply in love and I couldn't help myself.

Amidst all of the turmoil, I was offered a new job. My boss had asked me to attend a "Trade Evening" in a South Dublin Hotel on his behalf. An American multi-national company conducted the evening. They manufactured printing plates and chemicals, among other products. When the representative conducting the evening heard that I was actually using their plates, he asked me if I would be interested in applying for a job with them. He told me that the company was looking for a Technical Sales Representative to cover Ireland. The money on offer was twice what I was being paid in my present job. They also supplied a top of the range car and expenses. Of course I was interested, and after writing down the details of to whom and where I should apply, I sent off an application the very next day. After several interviews, the final one in London, I was offered the job. What a way to start the New Year. I was over the moon.

When I told my boss, he told me that there was no way he could match the salary that I was being offered. Nor could he provide me with a car and expenses. He did say that there was something lined up for me within the company but he couldn't tell me about it. I would have loved to have stayed on, but in the circumstances I had little choice. This new job would enable me to finally sort out my financial problems, among other things. "I shouldn't have asked you to attend that trade evening," he said. "But I wish you well and trust that everything will sort itself out in your private life."

I thanked him and set about preparing to hand over the department to whoever might be appointed in my place.

Not everything was going to plan however, and I decided because of the pressure I was under from the bank manager, that I would have to sell the house and buy something more affordable in another area. So I placed an advertisement in a national newspaper and used a "Box Number" for privacy. Besides, I didn't want to get involved with another estate agent, if I could avoid it. The evening that the ad appeared, I was working on the front lawn when a guy came toward me.

"You've got a house for sale," he said.

"I have," I said, wondering how he could know since I had no phone call from anyone enquiring about it. So where did he get the address, I wondered?

"I'm an estate agent and I have some people who are interested in buying houses on this estate," he said.

"Where did you get your information from?" I asked.

"Don't bother about that," he said, "Do you want to sell your house or not?"

"If you have some people who are interested, then we can do business, but don't try to mess me about."

He didn't have anyone, as it turned out, but he pleaded with me to let him represent me. I relented, thinking that it might be better to have someone of experience to do the job. He eventually brought along a client to view the house. He was a managing director of a large company who wanted to buy a house as a wedding present for his son. Nothing happened for quite a while after his visit. So I called into the office of the agent one afternoon, and he informed me that the man who viewed the house wanted to buy it.

"But," he told me, "He doesn't want to pay what you're asking."

"Then you can tell him to forget it," I said.

A couple of more weeks went by and the agent contacted me and asked me to call into his office once more. "You're a hard man to do business with, but the client says he'll go ahead and buy."

So I agreed to sell and asked him to contact my solicitor to arrange the purchase contract. I had no sooner done that, than another man appeared on the scene and offered me more money if I would sell to him. I told him that I had given my word, and I wasn't prepared to break it. As things turned out, it would have been better if I had. The first guy just delayed things until I reached the point where I told the agent to tell the customer that I was cancelling the deal.

While I was away on business in Cork, the solicitor called my wife into his office and she signed the contract of sale without contacting me to seek permission. After doing that and arriving home, the hall-door bell rang. She opened and found it was the guy on whose behalf the house was being bought. He told her that the house was now his, and she had until nine o'clock that evening to clear out. She phoned me in a panic to tell me about this. I told her that she did not have my permission to sign, and that the solicitor was wrong to get her to do so. I cancelled my hotel booking, got into my car, and drove at breakneck speed to get home in time to meet the purchaser. I told my wife to go and visit a neighbour, and not to come back until I came for her.

When I opened the door to his ring, he almost fainted on the spot. "Come in," I said, "I'd like a word with you." He stepped into the hall and I closed the door, applying the latch at the same time so that he wouldn't be able to open it easily. "You've terrified my wife, and upset my kids with your behaviour today. Now let me hear you repeat what you said to her earlier."

His eyes were wide and his mouth open from the moment he saw me. "The house is mine and there's nothing you can do about it," he said.

"Here's a present from me and my kids," I said as I dug my fist into his solar plexus. He screamed like a stuck pig, as I continued to pound him below the belt, concentrating on his genitals. When I'd finished, I opened the door and threw him out into the garden. "Don't mess with the Sheridans," I told him.

I left the house, locked the door, and went to the neighbour's house where my family were waiting for me. As I told my neighbour what had happened, I asked if we could wait with him for a while, since I expected that the guy would be back. After a short while, two cars stopped outside my door. He was driving one and the other contained four Gardai. They tried the bell and knocked on the door, and when they got no answer, they got back into their cars and waited a while, perhaps to see if I would open the door thinking that they'd gone, I don't know. After a while, they got fed up and left.

Next morning around ten o'clock, I received a phone call from my solicitor telling me that the buyer's solicitor had informed him that his client would be charging me with assault.

"Let him go ahead," I said. "I look forward to having my day in court. You can explain to the judge how a deal can be completed with my wife's signature, when the house is in my name. I also want to hear him explain his behaviour to the court, and I will enjoy seeing him show his bruises." There was a pregnant silence at the other end of the phone as I hung up.

About an hour later, my solicitor was back on the line. "I've persuaded them to drop the charges," he said.

"I didn't ask you to do that. I told you I want my day in court." He spent the next half-hour talking me out of that. It is now and was then, my firm belief that there was collusion between the estate agent, the buyer, and both of the solicitors to facilitate the managing director of a very large company. His son was not an innocent bystander in all of this, either. He proved to be as arrogant as his father. I would've pursued the affair through the courts, except I was worn out after my illness. But he learned not to mess with the Sheridans. Neither did I have the funds nor the experience of court proceedings. I insisted that I be given time to find other accommodations and got their agreement on that. I spoke to my wife about all of what happened, and told her that she shouldn't have signed anything without getting their agreement to allow us time to move. She insisted that she was right in what she'd done.

To add to my woes, I had a call from my father to say that my mother was seriously ill and was in Oldham General Hospital. I told him I'd be over on Friday and went about making the arrangements. My mother looked reasonably well when I got there, and although she hadn't been eating, she had a full lunch while I sat by her side.

"Are you happy being back in Oldham?" I asked her.

"Yes" she said and told me not to worry.

"I'm sorry that things didn't work out in Dublin," I said.

221

"That's alright," she said. But I could see from her face that she was still hurting from the experience. I left her promising that I'd be back in two weeks to see her again.

She gave me a look as I departed that said, "If I'm still here."

I told my father that she had eaten her lunch while we chatted. He was delighted and we both felt that it was a sign that she was on the mend. The following week, I got a phone call at work telling me that my mother had died. It was the 21st February 1967, and it shattered me. All of the positive things that had happened in 1966 came to naught. To make matters worse, my wife continued to complain about her lot. There was no expression of sympathy about my mother from her or from her family. I was incensed, and decided that it was time to finish our relationship as soon as I got home after my mother's funeral.

The new house that we'd looked at was on a new estate in Tallaght County, Dublin. It had three bedrooms and was at the end of a row of eight other houses. A friend of mine in the army reserve knew the builder, and he arranged with him to get us a house in a nice location with the extra space at the end of the terrace. (This friend was later to prove his worth when I needed help urgently on another occasion). I liked the house and it was certainly within my budget. My wife complained that it wasn't to her liking, and I reminded her of the circumstances that brought this about. Besides, it was better than anything that she had been used to in Birmingham. Unfortunately, it wouldn't be completed for about three months, so I had to find somewhere to rent in the meantime. The agent on site was also a friend of my friend, and he put me in touch with a friend of *his* who rented out mobile homes. This was an example of a typical Irish way of "networking." If you want anything done, you ask a friend if he/she knows someone who can help. It works very well and it's a way of getting someone who's reliable. I phoned the mobile-home owner and had a look at what he had to offer. It was fine, and I arranged to move in straight away. We didn't have far to go, either. He had a site right in the village, about a mile from where we lived. This didn't please my wife, and she complained bitterly. "What can I do?" I asked her. "The house will be ready in a few months, the weather is fine, and this can hardly be described as a hardship." The kids thought it was a great adventure.

Soon after moving into the new house, she decided that she needed a holiday. So I booked her and the children on a return flight to Birmingham. Two weeks later, not having heard a word from her since she left, I sat at the airport waiting for them to arrive. They weren't on the flight that I had booked. So, thinking there might've been some problem, I waited there until the last flight, but in vain. That was the last I saw of them. I phoned my sister Rosaleen, who lived in Birmingham, and asked her to call at my in-law's house and ask my wife to contact me. She discovered that my father-in-law had died, and the rest of the family had moved to an unknown address. I eventually traced them and tried in vain to get my kids to talk to me. My wife had done a thorough job of poisoning their minds against me. We haven't had any contact whatsoever to this day. Does it hurt? You bet your life it does!

The bank manager was delighted to have the debt off his books. "Stick with me and I'll make you a very rich man," he said. But I was in no mood for him or his platitudes, and told him to take a hike. At the same time, the estate agent sent me a bill that was outrageously high. I insisted on having an itemised account, and when I checked it out I discovered that he was charging me for block advertisements, when the details of my house only took up one line of the ad. I told my solicitor about this and he advised me to pay him what I thought was fair. I did this and my solicitor phoned to inform me that the estate agent had arrived in his office, threatening him with physical harm. He was obliged to call the Gardai and have him removed. The saga regarding the sale of my house was at an end, as far as I was concerned. I had other problems to deal with now.

I contacted Linda and asked if she would be willing to meet me. She agreed and I told her about recent happenings. I thanked her for her expression of sympathy regarding my mother's death. She had phoned me on the internal phone at work when she heard the news. We just sat in my car and I poured out my heart to her. She was ten years my junior, but her mature attitude belied her tender years. "How serious is your relationship with your boyfriend?" I asked.

"Not serious at all," she replied.

"Maybe I've no right to ask this, but would you think about getting serious with me?"

"No need for me to think about it, I'd be delighted to," she smiled.

I explained that my marriage was over, but that I wanted to get my kids back if I could. She had no problem with this, and suggested that she would take care of them for me if I wished. She also had no problem with my travelling to England to try and track down the whereabouts of my children.

I checked the fees of a Private Detective Agency in Birmingham and found them exorbitant, so I decided that I would have to do the job of tracing myself. Knowing that one of my wife's two sisters worked for Birmingham City Council, this was my first port of call. Her work colleagues informed me that she was attending a full-time course at college. They gave the address of the college and I made my way there. The lady in the registry listened to me sympathetically, as I explained the reason I wanted to contact her. She told me that she wasn't allowed to give out the address of any student, but she would check with a superior if an exception could be made in this case. She had taken the details of my sister-in-law from the file and left the card on the counter as she went to make a phone call. Whether it was deliberate or not, I can't say. I prefer to think that it was. I was able to read the address up-side down and etched it into my memory. She did tell me what room number she was in, and I made my way there. I knocked on the door and entered and asked the lecturer if I could speak with her, after first apologising for interrupting his class. I couldn't see her among the room full of students and she didn't acknowledge me. He asked me to leave, as there was no one of that name in his class. As I reached reception, again I was met by a security guard and escorted off the premises.

I wasn't about to be put off that easily, and I asked my brother Gerry in whose house I was staying, if he would accompany me to the address that I'd acquired. We decided that it would be better to leave it to the following day, as the evening had drawn in and it was dark by now. The new address was on the opposite side of the city from where they used to live. I phoned the local police station, and told them what I was about to do, and advised them that I was not seeking to cause trouble of any sort. The desk sergeant thanked me and wished me luck. As my brother and I made our way down the road towards the address that I had, I saw my two sons standing at a bus stop. The older one recognised me, and shouted to his brother to run. They both took off like hares. But being very fit myself, I caught up with them quite quickly. They looked terrified and the older boy began to shout awful names at me at the top of his voice. I tried to calm things down, and told them that I only wanted to talk. No amount of appealing would persuade him to stop.

"You'd best leave things as they stand," my brother advised. "Walk away and let them be. I've never heard anything like the poison he's shouting at you. His mother has certainly made a good job of turning them against you."

I reluctantly agreed and left them, hiding my tears as I went. I've tried unsuccessfully to make contact over the years, including using the services of the Salvation Army. My heart was broken and I was having great difficulty sleeping. So many years have gone by now, I often think that murderers get a lesser sentence than I got. I pray still that one day, one of them at least will make contact. I became very hard hearted, and swore that I would never marry again despite being head over heels in love with Linda.

CHAPTER FIFTEEN

NORTHERN TROUBLES

The outbreak of the "Troubles" in the North of Ireland began in 1969. The students from Queens University in Belfast organised a march to seek Civil Rights. They headed off from Belfast with the intention of meeting the students from the University of Coleraine, in the city of Derry, and holding a joint rally. When they reached the bridge at Burntollet, they were attacked by a mob led by the so-called "Reverend" Ian Paisley. They used homemade cudgels of every description. Some of them were axe handles with nails driven through, and they were designed to do maximum damage. The police (RUC) stood by and let Paisley's mob do their worst. When the marchers began to defend themselves, the police joined in with Paisley and used their batons on the students. Once the students in Derry got to hear of this, they started a riot so as to take the pressure off their fellow students at Burntollet. The rest, as they say, is History. Very few historians or political commentators I have read or listened to over the years since then have recognised this as the beginning of the turmoil that was to follow over the next thirty years.

It has been said that the "Troubles," as they became known, actually started in April/May of 1968 in the village of Caledon in County Tyrone. A Catholic family were squatting in a house that had become vacant. They had been on the Council waiting list for so long, that it had gone beyond endurance. The Council evicted them, and allocated the house to a young single Protestant mother, who happened to be secretary to the local Tory MP. Her brother, who was a member of the Royal Ulster Constabulary took part in the eviction. Perhaps the spark was lit then, but the flame took hold at Burntollet, in my view.

The IRA was reformed and eventually split into the "Official IRA," a left-wing communist-influenced organisation, and the "Provisional IRA," described by some as a "Green Fascist" group. Whatever the labels, both were intent on getting the British out of Ireland. The Provisionals became the dominant group, and they began to raid homes and shops where they knew that arms were kept. One of my business colleagues was a gun collector, and he became very nervous about keeping the collection, so he sold it to a gun dealer. All except for one revolver, that is. He kept that for me; knowing that I was an officer in the army reserve, he wanted it to go to someone that would appreciate its historical significance. It was, he told me, the personal weapon of Dan Breen the leader of the Old IRA's Tipperary Brigade. I was delighted to have it. It served me well on a few occasions.

On the day that I picked it up, I visited my sister who lived near to where he had his office. Not wanting to take a chance by leaving the gun in the car, I took it in its brown paper bag into the house with me. My sister opened the hall door and it was obvious that she was upset. She invited me in, excused herself, and went into the kitchen, leaving me in the sitting room with her husband. The atmosphere was taut, to say the least, as I sat down. I put the bag on the floor between my feet. Then for the sake of making conversation, I told him I had something to show him. Picking up the bag, I took out the gun. He went white as a ghost, pleading with me to put it away. Just as I put it back in the bag, my sister re-entered the room. I stood up, taking my parcel with me and excused myself, saying that I'd call back another day.

Next morning I got a call at work from my brother Dick. "What did you do to Paddy?" he asked.

"What do you mean?" I asked.

"He's in a hell of a state since he got into work this morning. He said that you pulled a gun on him."

"I never did any such thing. There was obviously a problem with him and May, and I showed him the gun as a way of making conversation. What was going on anyway?"

"He took nearly four hundred pounds out of her purse and drank it. When you arrived, he thought that she had sent for you and when you pulled the gun, he thought he was a gonner. Anyway, I told him that if you pulled a gun on him, he was lucky to be alive. He's been crying and says he needs help. So I told him that if he went to see the doctor and arranged a cure, I'd talk to you and you might forget about the next visit."

"Right," I said, "Let him do that and tell him to be sure he does... or else."

He did and he never stole from my sister again. It's an ill wind... as they say.

Matters began to get out of hand in the North and it looked at one stage, as though the Irish Army would cross the border to prevent the Nationalist Population from being wiped out. I happened to be in Belfast on business and for a friend's Stag Party, when the people on the Falls Road decided to riot, in order to relieve the pressure on the people in Derry. I sold printing plate chemicals and film for the American company mentioned earlier. The firms I called on in Belfast included the Daily Mirror Newspaper Group, McCaw, Stevenson & Orr, and William Finlay, Ltd. These firms were protestant owned and they employed only protestant workers. That meant that the employees were anti-catholic and vehemently anti-republican. Since I came from the Republic and used the Irish version of my name, it would've been assumed that I was both Catholic and Republican. Northern Ireland had been set up as a "Protestant State for a Protestant People," and those in power had sworn to keep it that way. The British Government had approved of and assisted in the formation of this state following the War of Independence that took place in the 1920s. All three of these firms had asked me to call to sort out some technical difficulties that they were having. The Mirror had a problem with film, and I spent an hour in their darkroom sorting out the correct exposures with the camera operator. The guys in the planning department were polite, though I noticed that someone had crossed through the Irish Tricolour on the Flags of the Nations in a print above one of the workbenches. Apart from that, there was nothing to be concerned about. One of the staff asked if I was married.

"Yes," I replied smiling.

"How long?" he asked.

"Almost seven years," I answered.

"How many children have you got" he asked looking around the room at his colleagues.

"Two," I said.

"What does the Pope have to say about that?" he asked.

I knew immediately what he was getting at. The Catholic Church teaching on contraception is emphatic. It simply is not allowed.

"F... the Pope. If he wants a load of kids, then he can have them; because I can't afford any more than I've got."

"Did you hear what he said, lads?" he called to his colleagues. "You did say f... the Pope, didn't you?"

"Sure I did, and f... him again if that makes you feel happier."

This was unheard of and they were astounded to not only hear me said but repeat it. I could see the reaction that it brought all round the room.

"How many of you have visited the Republic?" I asked.

"None," they replied.

"Well it's about time you did, fellas. There's a different generation now that doesn't take orders from the clergy any more. Why don't you come and check it out for yourselves."

They were dumbfounded and sure enough, they promised they would.

That one conversation did more for inter-state relationships than one could imagine. From that day on I was welcomed into their company and got their cooperation.

There was another tale to tell in McCaw's. Their company printed labels, and one of the machine men in particular, was having great difficulty keeping reverse prints from filling in. The print was quite fine and would be a challenge for any printer. The manager, Billy Madders met me in reception. A pleasant older man who had a ready smile and an honest face, he greeted me warmly and with a firm handshake. "Don't be alarmed when you enter the pressroom," he said smiling, "and let me do the talking if you don't mind."

I understood his comment immediately on entering the "Works." There was a Union Jack flag hanging from the back of every machine. This indicated that Republicans weren't welcome. There's a strange anomaly regarding the six Northern Counties of Ireland. Despite the fact that the inhabitants are born on the island of Ireland, those of the Protestant Faith regard themselves as British while the Catholics regard themselves as Irish. When the Queen of England refers to her territories she speaks of the Kingdom of Great Britain and Northern Ireland. So strictly speaking, all those born in Northern Ireland are Irish. But those of the population who are loyal to the Queen refuse to be regarded as such and the vast majority of them are protestant.

"I see the flags are out, Billy," I said, smiling, "Now where's the Guard of Honour?"

He had a good laugh at that. He then introduced me to the machine operator who was having the problem. "Could I see a printed sheet," I asked Billy.

He then asked the operator to show me a sheet.

"Would you ask him to take out the top dampening roller so that I can measure it?" I asked. He did and I checked the circumference with my Vernier Scale. My company manufactured a special type of dampening cover that would sort out his problems, providing the roller was of the correct dimensions to take it. It was, and I ask Billy to get him to drop out the bottom roller and leave it out of contact while I fitted the new sleeve. The sleeve had to be shrunk on with water and when this was done, I asked for it to be reinstated.

He started the press up and dropped the top roller into contact with the plate and tripped in the paper feeder. He pulled a sheet out after ten copies to check it. There was no improvement and he fully expected things to deteriorate rapidly with no bottom roller in contact.

He said as much to Billy, and Billy looked at me.

"Let it run for one hundred," I said.

He looked at me with the eye of a sceptic, fully expecting to say, "I told you it wouldn't work." Things weren't much better when we checked the hundredth sheet. I was beginning to have doubts myself, at this stage. But something prompted me to ask him to continue. At one hundred and twenty the image was as clear as a bell.

"That's it," I smiled, "Now keep it going." This time he ignored Billy and looked at me in awe.

"How did you do that?" he asked. The other pressmen saw him take my hand to shake it, and they quickly gathered around, as I explained how the sleeve worked. If there had been any hint of racism beforehand, it went out the door very quickly when they saw that I had provided an answer to their problems.

Billy thanked me profusely, as we walked back towards the reception area. I had also cured a headache for him. "I have a feeling that you'll be welcome here at any time from now on," he said as we parted.

I made my way up the Ballygomartin Road, to the William Finlay printing works. The plant manager explained that they had recently ordered plates made by my company, and he would like me to demonstrate to his staff the proper way of making them ready for press. It was lunchtime by the time I had finished, and he invited me to have something to eat in the canteen. I gratefully accepted and after collecting our food, we sat at a table where there were two vacant seats. He introduced me to the other two and we continued to talk. Just then, one of the others began a tirade against the Republic.

"Our men answered the colours in two world wars and they would sort out any threat to their security in the future," he said. He also said what a wonderful man Ian Paisley was. The manager looked quite embarrassed.

Looking the other guy straight in the eye, I said. "Your remarks are obviously addressed at me. Now answer me one question…

have you ever worn a uniform in your life?" I knew that he would have to reply in the negative because he had a hunchback.

He answered no, as I expected.

"Let me ask you another one then. Have you studied the history of both wars?"

He again replied in the negative. "I have, and it will surprise you to know that a total of 255,000 Irishmen and women served in the First World War. The vast majority of them were from the Republic. They served with such regiments as the Royal Dublin Fusiliers, the Leinster Fusiliers, the Munster Fusiliers, and the Connaught Rangers, etc. Two of my uncles served, one was killed, and the other lost a leg. In the Second World War, between seventy and one hundred thousand of our men from the Republic served. Many of them were deserters from the Irish Army. Please note that our guys only ever desert going towards the enemy. My father served with the 8th Army in North Africa, Sicily, and Italy. Where did your father serve?"

He was dumbfounded.

"Finally, I am a serving officer with the Irish Army Reserve, so if you are going to address me then make sure you call me *Sir*."

The others broke into loud laughter. "You've found your match at last," they said.

When lunch was over, the manager apologised to me as we walked towards the door leading to reception. "That guy has been a pain in the neck since this recent trouble started. Thanks for putting him in his place. He'll be careful about who he shoots off his mouth to in future."

"It was my pleasure," I said. "Look at the troublemakers of the past. He reminds me of Goebbels, the Nazi propaganda Minister. He looks at lot like him. Those that claimed racial or religious purity as a reason for starting a war were either sick in mind, or body, or both."

That was the last contact I had with any of the three companies, since my company barred me from going to the North of Ireland for safety reasons.

—〰—

Back in my hotel on the Upper Newtownards Road, I showered and had dinner. The owner of the hotel was a retired British Naval Commander and he came over to my table to ask if I would mind moving my Dublin registered car to the back of the hotel for safety reasons. He advised me not to go out again during the day until things had quietened down in the city. When I told him that I would be going to a stag party later that evening, he was astonished. He calmed down, however, when I told him that my friend was local and that he would be picking me up. As it happened, my friend was a serving Petty Officer in the Royal Naval Reserve, and the commander knew him, so he was relieved that I would be in safe hands. My friend arrived soon afterwards and on our way to the hotel near the city centre, we called to pick up two brothers who lived with their family on the Malone Road. I was ushered into the house, and introduced to their father who sat by the fire in a very expensively decorated lounge. When he and the younger of the two sons heard my name, there was a distinct cooling in their attitude. As if by magic, I found myself sitting in an empty room. It seemed like an hour had passed before my friend and his Best Man-to-be came back and said, "Let's go." There was no comment made about their absence, as we made our way to the hotel where the party was to take place. But there was a distinct atmosphere.

When we got to the hotel, we found that the front doors were locked. My friend rang the bell and a porter appeared soon afterwards. He told us that all the bars and hotels within the city limits had been closed under a curfew, imposed by the security forces. Arrangements had been made, however, with a hotel on the outskirts of the city to accommodate us there. The car was parked very close to the Protestant enclave of Sandy Row and as we walked the short distance to get it, we saw the residents erecting a barricade at the end of the street. While they were doing that, there was a rattle of machine-gun fire in the distance.

We were just about to move off when a young man came walking up to us in an excited state. "A guy with a Dublin accent has just asked me how to get to the Falls Road," (The Falls Road is a Catholic enclave), he said nervously, "and when I asked him why he wanted to go there, he said that their pubs were still open. He must be a raving nut case."

"Here's another one," I said, smiling.

When he heard my accent, he took off running down the road as though his pants were on fire, shouting as he went, "You're all nuts." We had a good laugh about that as we got into the car and headed for the hotel in the suburbs.

When we got there, we could barely find a parking space for the number of cars that were in the car park. The porter checked the name on his register and allowed us in. The lounge was absolutely crammed full of people. It seemed as if the whole of the drinking public in Belfast had found their way there. But the atmosphere was relaxed and I found myself sitting on a low stool with my back tight up against two lads from Birmingham. They were very interested to hear that I'd lived there for seven years as we chatted. My friend insisted on buying treble measures of spirits to save us having to go to the bar too often.

After his best man's brother got enough into him, he stood up, pointing at me, and shouted at the top of his voice, "He's a Fenian." (Now I understood why I had been left on my own in the lounge at his house). Nobody was paying any attention to him and he got quite annoyed. "You're a Fenian, aren't you?" he roared.

"Yer right," I laughed, "Now sit down and behave yourself like a good lad." The two guys from Birmingham were highly amused and thought it was all a joke, and part of the stag celebrations. But he wouldn't be placated, so we were asked to leave. It was just as well anyway, as we'd all had more than enough to drink. When we got outside there, was a scuffle between himself and his brother. I learned later that he was insisting on going to the Falls Road to teach the "Taigs" some manners. (Taig is a colloquialism for Catholics or Republicans).

My friend went to help after he'd first flagged a taxi and pushed me inside. He told the driver to get me back to my hotel, just as the troublemaker punched him in the face. A police Land-rover appeared as if by magic and pulled to check what was going on. But the taxi driver took off and didn't stop until he reached my hotel. When I saw my friend next day, he was missing his two front teeth. He told me that the three of them had spent the night in the cells. He was more concerned about getting his teeth replaced before his wedding in three days.

"Did you hear what was on the news yesterday evening?" he asked. When I said no, he informed me that the Taoiseach of the Republic had announced on the evening news that he would not stand by and see our people being gunned down in the streets. It was expected by all and sundry in Belfast that the Irish Army was about to cross the border. "What am I to do?" he said.

"What do mean?" I asked.

"Well you're an Irish Army Officer aren't you?"

"Oh, I see what you mean," I said. "Well, don't worry, if they do cross, you can take me into barracks and hand me over to your commander. I will only surrender to him not the police... right?"

"You won't mind then?" he said, sounding relieved.

"Not one bit," I said, remembering that I had a length of pickaxe handle under the driver's seat of my car. If he had made any attempt to take me in, he would've had that across his head and found himself on the Falls Road among Republicans and my prisoner.

I stayed in the hotel for the rest of the week at the commander's request. On Friday morning, I arrived in the dining room for breakfast. "Where were you last night?" he asked as he took my order.

"In my bed asleep where all good people should be," I said. "Why do you ask?"

"There was absolute mayhem during the night, with shots being fired and a supermarket across the road was burned out."

"You're kidding," I said.

"You must be a very innocent man if you could sleep through all of what was going on. All of the rest of the guests were down here drinking my whiskey."

"You should've given me a call. I'd have helped," I said.

"Bugger me," was all he could say in return as he shook his head and walked away. I stayed in the hotel until Saturday and left early in the morning, hoping to avoid any trouble on my way home. The streets were very quiet as I headed for the border. People were obviously tired after a week of shootings, burning, and looting, and were sleeping it off.

I never felt so relieved as I did when I crossed the line at Carrickcarnan and headed for Dundalk. It's a strange phenomenon, but there is a distinct difference in the atmosphere between North and South. As soon as that border is crossed into the North, one can feel the tension in the air. I should add that most of the people who live there are honest, hard working, and law abiding. But they have allowed a lunatic fringe to operate among them, and they are hell bent on maintaining the status quo.

I headed straight for the barracks when I reached Dublin, thinking that the army would be on stand-to, at the very least. To my dismay and utter disbelief, I found that there was just the usual weekend guard on duty. "Everyone's gone for the weekend," the gate policeman informed me.

I discovered later that when the government met with the army chiefs to discuss the situation, they reported that of the eleven thousand regular troops, fewer than four thousand were in any way fit for combat. Despite the fact that there were thirty thousand reserves, these were never even considered. The reason, I have been told, is that the economy of the country would suffer too much if we were all called up. What a mess it was, and I for one was thoroughly ashamed of the lack of action taken. In more recent times, the regular army have referred to the reserve as "Sandbags." This is meant to imply that the reserve is only fit to be used as such in the event of a conflict.

It is a sad reflection on the ones who had the opportunity to face the enemy but couldn't or wouldn't, because they weren't up to the job. The Reserve at least was willing to have a go and we were a hell of a sight fitter than our counterparts in the regular army. But one can only expect the same reaction from a force that has done no actual soldiering for so long, as happened with the French Army at the beginning of the First World War. They were fat and stale, with no incentive to fight, and paid dearly for their mistakes in the beginning. The Reserve was called on by the powers that be, to guard vital installations and take part in Border Patrols. I got so involved that some weeks, I would report to barracks after work to take over from the regular orderly officer, stay up all night and report to work next morning. The regular army in the main worked from 09:00 to 16:30 with weekends off, and there was no way they were going to let the Northern thing interfere with that. I thought of the *College Solution* from the course that I had done and shook my head as I thought of the consequences of people with that attitude going into action. What a disgrace they are, I thought to myself. What the hell use is an army when it isn't able or willing to defend its citizens in times of trouble.

CHAPTER SIXTEEN

THE THREAT

Back at work on the following Monday, I had a colleague call on me and invite me to visit a new German Bar in the Dolphin Hotel in downtown Dublin. That evening, as I walked into Essex Street in the city after parking my car, I found my way blocked. A car had parked partly on the footpath and the driver's door was open, blocking the path completely. As I approached, the driver got out and asked if my name was Sheridan. It was a winter's night and I was wearing my overcoat. I have a habit of putting my hand inside of my coat resting it on the top button. Some of friends used to refer to me as "Napoleon." I placed my hand inside my coat as usual. "Hold on hold on, I only want to talk," he said, obviously thinking that I was going for a gun.

"What do you want," I asked, catching on very quickly to the reason for his nervousness.

"Are you the Eamonn Sheridan who used to attend St. Finbarr's School?" he asked.

"Yeah, what of it?" I replied.

"Don't you know me?" he asked.

"No, and I suggest that you identify yourself good and quick before I lose my patience."

"I'm Billy Wright," he said.

"Well bugger me Billy, what the hell are you up to?" I asked the question, knowing that he was a member of the IRA. We had been at school together and his father and mine served together in the Dublin Brigade Old IRA. But unlike myself, he had joined the new crowd and didn't care who knew about it.

"Look, I'm sorry but I've been sent to give you a warning. You've been talking to the wrong people and you could be in serious trouble."

"I don't know what the hell you're talking about Billy. But this much I'll tell you... your mistake was in not doing me tonight. Because by the time you get home, I'll have arranged for you and... I named three others to be wiped out within twenty-four hours of anything happening to me." Just then the friend that I was meeting came along. "Hi Jack," I called to him. He was on the opposite footpath and the lighting in the street was very poor. Billy immediately jumped into his car and took off with a screech of tyres.

"What was that all about?" Jack asked as we made our way into the German Bierkeller.

I related the story over a pint and he looked at me in astonishment. "Don't worry," I said, "You're perfectly safe." We met on many occasions after that but never a word was mentioned about the episode.

I'm no hero, I hasten to add, and I shook all over as I made my way home that night. I wondered how best to handle the situation. My mentor, Colonel Fitzgerald had died and I didn't have another contact. The poor man had been suffering from cancer and it finally took its toll. My own commanding officer had moved from the unit to Area Command. He didn't approve of me anyway, since I began to live with Linda. So I phoned my father and told him briefly what had happened. "I'm leaving a note of the addresses of the four individuals," I said, "If anything happens to me you'll know where to look." He was happy with that and asked me to call and see him as soon as I got the chance.

Having given the situation much thought that night, I decided to face Billy Wright next day and do whatever was necessary to sort him out. Call me a head-case if you like, but I won't be intimidated by anyone. So I set off early next morning and arrived at his barbershop on the Cabra Road at five minutes past nine. I wore a military style rain Mac and tucked the .45 into a holster in front of my left hip. It would be easier to draw it from that position, as I am right handed.

I was surprised to find that there was a man already in the shop having his hair cut. So I took a seat and wondered why Billy didn't recognise me. He didn't greet me in the way that I'd have expected. As I watched him however I began to realise that the guy I was looking at wasn't Billy at all. He had an identical twin brother that I'd forgotten about and that's who I was seeing. "Is Billy due in?" I asked him.

"No, he's got the day off today," he replied.

"When you see him tell him that Eamonn Sheridan was looking for him and I'll be back."

"Right," he said as I opened the door to leave. Before I managed to visit him again he was machined-gunned by the IRA on the premises. He was strong and fit and was a champion boxer in his youth and he managed to struggle down the stairs and out onto the footpath outside where he died. He had taken five bullets, according to reports.

The newspapers reported that he had been double dealing. He was arrested after an IRA bank raid and he cooperated with the police by giving them details of other IRA operations in return for his freedom. Not long after his death, I phoned one of the other names that were on my list. We had been friends at school and I knew that he was an active member of Sinn Féin, (the political wing of the IRA,) and arranged to meet him. I told him of my meeting with Billy Wright and what I had done subsequently. "I had carried the .45 pistol the morning I went to see him, and I was prepared to use it if needs be. He may or may not have delivered my message and I want you to relay it for me just in case." I repeated what I had told Billy. "Tell your people that I'm carrying and I won't go down without a fight." Not too long after our meeting, I got a phone call from one of the other names on the list. He wanted me to meet him in Slattery's Pub in Terenure, on the South Side of Dublin.

I didn't know what was planned, so I spoke to the Battalion Intelligence Officer. He looked at me in amazement, telling me that he knew nothing of my previous conversations with the Brigade Commander. He felt that it was too heavy for him to deal with, and he arranged for me to speak to the Brigade IO. We sat down in the living room of his house, which wasn't very far from where I lived. I went through the whole story again with him. He acted as if he heard it all before but it was obvious to me that he hadn't. "So what do you want me to do?" he asked when I'd finished speaking.

"I'd like you to arrange cover for me while I'm in the pub and if someone could watch my car so that it's not interfered with I'd appreciate that."

"I can't do that," he said with a look of disdain, "Sure you're only a civilian." That remark was typical of the regular. It was their way of putting down the amateur. The problem was that this amateur had no respect for the so-called professional. They had proven themselves unworthy of the name, in my opinion. The one and only opportunity the army had to resolve the partition issue once and for all was blown because they were unfit and unready.

"So the commission I hold from the President is of no worth. Is that what you're telling me?" I said with raised eyebrows. He also gave the distinct impression that I was just a telltale and I wondered just where his loyalties lay. "Do you have any suggestions?" I asked.

"Go into the Garda Station in Terenure and tell them that the law is likely to be broken and get them to arrange to come in and get you if you're not out by a specified time."

"That's it?" I said in disgust.

"That's all I can do for you," he said, as I got up to leave. The meeting had been arranged for the following Friday and I called the senior NCO's around me on Thursday in barracks. Without going into too much detail, I asked them if they would be prepared to be there the following night. Not one of the six I spoke to was prepared to oblige. The officers were no better, with one exception. His name is Sean Sherwin. He later became the youngest member of the Dáil and is now the National Organiser for the Fianna Fáil Party. He proved to be a true friend, and we are still very close today. I help him in whatever way I can and will continue to do so as long as I live. The Garda behind the desk in the station looked at me as if I was off my head, when

I tried to get him to make the necessary arrangements, without telling him anything of value. He wasn't entertaining me at all until I told him that I was a lieutenant from Griffith barracks, and to get the arrangements in place good and quick.

"Is this political?" he asked.

"It could be," I said. "Just do as I'm asking, right!"

He then said that he would take care of it.

My adversary sat at a table in the lounge, drinking a glass of Guinness. I gestured to a young waiter and ordered a pint also as I sat down on the opposite side of the table. I noticed that Sean was sitting at the end of the bar with an excellent view of everything. "Look… there seems to have been some misunderstanding," he said. "We were told by Billy Wright that you had been talking to the *Special Branch*, so naturally we got a little uptight about things. We since found out that he was in fact, their *Gillie*, and that's been taken care of." As he spoke to me, he constantly looked about and nodded at the people sitting at other tables.

That got up my nose and so I said, "Do you think I'm some sort of idiot? I know what you're at and I will not be intimidated. Do you think that I'd be foolish enough to come in here without arranging cover myself? Now cut the crap; and by the way, if I'm not out of here at nine o'clock on the dot, I've arranged for a squad of Gardaí to come in and get me."

He was flabbergasted. "There was no need to do that," he said, looking distinctly nervous.

"I didn't know what you had planned and I wasn't about to take any chances. Now let's get something straight. Whatever Billy Wright told you is a load of rubbish. I don't know where he got my name from, or in what context he used it. But this much I can tell you, he was one of yours and he was the one feeding the SB with information. So how can you believe anything that he told you?"

"Yeah… well that's what my people say as well, so I'm here to clear the air. We don't have a problem with you."

I checked my watch, "Before I go, let me give you a word of advice; tell your guys to learn to keep their mouths shut, then you'll have fewer problems. Also… I happen to be a commissioned officer in the Defence Forces. If one of yours spilled his guts to me, or any of my colleagues, we would be duty bound to report it. So you can forget about the *Informer* thing. That label, in my opinion, is reserved strictly for your gang. By the way, how come the SB gave my name to Billy Wright?"

"They traded it with him in exchange for information he gave them on the *movement*. They reckoned it would divert us from finding out about him. In any event, we have our own guys in the Gardaí and in the Army, too."

With that, I got up and left the pub, vowing to myself again that no matter what information came my way in future, it would stay with me. I wondered again about the Intelligence Officer whom I'd had the recent meeting with. I also deeply regretted reporting what information I had gotten in the first place. My life had been put at risk for nothing and there would not be a repeat performance… ever.

There was a Garda sergeant and a colleague standing at the edge of the footpath across the road. I went over and identified myself, thanked them for being there and told them that the matter had been cleared up, so there was no need to hang about any longer. I went over to my car, checked it out before getting in and being satisfied that it hadn't been interfered with, I drove home. I wondered as I drove how the hell the SB got my name in the first place. Then I remembered what the Colonel said about them telling him that I was a member of the IRA. He must've given them my name. I remember my own CO telling me that the regular army didn't trust us reserves. So it wouldn't have been too difficult for a Garda officer to convince the Colonel that I needed investigating. Not very bright, I thought and I promised myself that from now on I would take my own advice and keep my mouth shut. The threat may or may not have disappeared, but I wasn't taking any chances; so I continued to carry the .45 revolver in the glove compartment of the car just in case. I didn't trust the buggers.

Chapter Seventeen

Love at Last

Linda became pregnant and we moved into rented rooms in Bray, County Wicklow. We lived in an old Georgian house that had been converted into flats. The ceilings were very high and fireplace was tiny. We used to sit at the fire in the evenings with our coats around our shoulders to keep some heat in our backs. It was infested with mice, too. But we were deliriously happy. Our daughter Tara was born, and brought no end of joy into our lives. She was bright and beautiful, just like her mother. We moved out of there after six months or so, and moved into a rented bungalow on Bray Head. It was idyllic. We walked along the promenade in the evenings and enjoyed visiting the local cinema. Linda's sisters came to visit, which brightened our weekends tremendously. When I asked them if they would be in trouble with their parents for visiting us, they laughed and said, "Who cares?"

Linda's father arrived for a visit just before Christmas and asked her to come with him to see her mother, and to bring the baby. He accepted a lift from me and when I stopped the car outside of his house, he asked me to come in.

"It would be better if I didn't," I said. But he insisted and reluctantly I complied. His wife was very cool with me and I didn't blame her. But I appreciated what he'd done. He didn't believe in holding a grudge and I held him in great regard for that. We became very good friends eventually. I always enjoyed being in his company. He insisted that her mother accept the situation, after he asked me to sign a piece of paper stating that I would look after their daughter. That I did gladly.

———∿———

Within the week, I received a phone call from the administration officer in the barracks. He asked me if I could call in the next day at twelve. "What's up?" I asked.

"Nothing much, I'll speak to you when you get here," he said. I arrived as arranged and he told me that we had an appointment with the Brigade Commander in Collins barracks. We got into his car, but I was still none the wiser as to why the Brigade CO wanted to speak to me. It was raining heavily and I carried my rolled umbrella with me as I took a seat in front of his desk.

"You called into the Garda Station in Terenure two nights ago and used your rank to get the Garda on duty to arrange some sort of cover for you. Is that true?"

"It is, Sir," I said.

"Who the hell told you that you could do that? he demanded.

I told him about my meeting with the Brigade IO and his suggestion to me.

"How dare you," he roared, his face getting as red as a beetroot. "You're only a civilian."

"Would you repeat what you just said?" I asked as I rested my chin on my umbrella.

"You're a civilian" he roared again.

"In that case, I don't have to sit here and listen to your bullshit, do I?" I got up and walked out, slamming his office door as I went.

The Admin officer caught up with me. He had been standing behind my chair. "The *Pig* has never been spoken to like that before," he laughed, "He'll never get over it, congratulations." "Thanks a whole bunch, Ado," I said smiling. The Admin Officer's name was Adrian but we all referred to him as "Ado the Ad'm Officer." We both giggled like kids all the way back to the barracks.

"You might have told me what was in store," I said, as we stood in the doorway of the block where his office was located. "By the way you referred to him as the *Pig*. Where does that come from?"

"That's a nickname he's had since he was in the military college."

"Well… he's a pig by name and a pig by nature," I said as I walked away.

The next day, Thursday, I reported into barracks as usual to be told that I was wanted in the CO's office. "More bloody trouble," I thought as I climbed the stairs to the second floor of the block. I knocked and a voice invited me in. It was the Admin officer again. The CO was nowhere to be seen.

"Sorry about this, but I've been told to take you off all security duties." He was a nice guy and we got along very well and this caused him considerable embarrassment. I knew that he had nothing to do with that decision, and he was following orders.

"Right," I said, "Well tell whoever is responsible for issuing that order if I'm not re-instated by Sunday morning I'll go to the Newspapers on Monday. They will be interested to hear the whole story, I have no doubt."

The following Sunday I was sent for again. This time the CO was there himself. "I hear you want to resume security duties," he said with a smile.

"Yes sir," I replied saluting. "Well, you're reinstated as of now. The captain will arrange for a time that's convenient for you."

I thanked him and he shook my hand before he went back into his own office. I was back on duty the following weekend. I received the first of many phone threats that night. The switch put through a caller who had asked to speak to the Orderly Officer. I picked up the receiver and said hello. "We're coming to get you," the voice said.

"Well, come on then," was my reply, "I haven't had any fun all day." Whoever it was at the other end slammed the phoned down. That didn't worry me in the slightest. Only cowards would use that method to try to intimidate. If the IRA were going to do anything serious, they would just get on with it.

One of the phone calls that I got was from the Brigade Commander. By the sound of his voice, he was obviously having a good night in the mess. "Turn out the guard and get ready, they're on their way to take the barracks."

"Right Sir," I said and hung up. The phone rang again almost immediately. It was a commandant ringing from the mess where the Brigade CO was drinking.

"Ignore that last order," he said, "The commander is a little the worse for wear."

I acknowledged his call without further comment and got back to doing my job. It didn't stop me from thinking that all the regulars were good for was drinking themselves into oblivion.

For years after the outbreak of the Troubles, I branded the Taoiseach Jack Lynch as, "Jittery Jack." I thought he had made the decision not to send the army across the border. I was wrong, and I apologise for that now. The jitters were coming from those who were being paid to defend our people. The millions that had been spent in training an army would've been better spent elsewhere. The reason I had joined the force in the first place was in the hope that an opportunity might arise to do something about the North. That opportunity presented itself in 1969 and the army was found wanting. It would be unfair to brand all of the army as incompetent and unwilling. The commander of our troops on United Nations service in Cyprus had his men on stand-to, expecting the call to return, so I've been told. When that didn't happen, he threw his cap on the ground and kicked it around like a football in utter frustration. The Irish are great on Foreign Service. Our reputation on UN service is second to none. But while we risk life and limb helping others, we failed miserably at home. The British Prime Minister Harold Wilson, admitted some time ago that he had held off sending the British Army into the North for a full two weeks to give us time to go in and take it. We failed to take advantage of that gap… to our shame. The pity of it is that no one was held to account for the ineptitude that was evident at all levels. If anyone should claim that we hadn't the numbers or that we are too small a nation to go to war, then look at the Israelis I say, and that argument is nullified.

—⟋⟍—

We were desperately short of funds at home. The duties I did in barracks brought in the princely sum of £8.00 for twenty-four hours. That helped a little, but not much. So Linda decided to go back to work. She soon got a job, but it was in Inchicore and that meant a long drive for us as it was in Dublin 12. We put Tara into a crèche in Templeogue. We quickly realised that we needed to move again, and we rented a house in Walkinstown, not too far from Linda's workplace. Summer came in pleasantly and we settled in well. The neighbours were nice, but kept to themselves. One night, just after we had gone to bed, there was a terrible racket going on outside our house. Male voices could be heard swearing loudly. A neighbour from two doors away asked if they might be quiet, as she had school-going children who needed their sleep. She was told where to go in no uncertain terms. I climbed out of bed, pulled on my jeans and reached under the mattress for the gun. Tucking it into my waistband, I made my way down the stairs. They could see me coming through the frosted glass of the hall door.

"Let's get the bastard," one of them shouted as I opened the door. Two of them came running up the driveway.

I pulled out the .45 and cocked it. "Take another step, yeh bastard, and I'll blow your effen brains all over the road," I said, pointing it at the head of the lead guy. He let out a roar and stopped in his tracks, staring at what I had in my hand.

"He's got a gun," he roared, turning on his heel and followed by his mates, ran off down the road. All went quiet again and I retired for the night. Next morning, as I backed the car out of the drive with the window lowered so I could see properly one of the young boys from the house two doors away was standing looking at me.

"Good morning," he smiled.

"Good morning," I replied.

"Was that a real gun you had last night?"

"What gun?" I asked, smiling back.

"Oh, say no more," he said, winking and he turned on his heel and ran off. There was never a problem in the area after that, and people nodded a greeting whenever they saw me. The message had gone out again, "Don't mess with the Sheridans."

Realising that the house in Tallaght was empty and that I was still paying the mortgage on it, we decided to move in. It suited our needs for a time until a new estate opened in Old Bawn Tallaght, and we bought a house there. That got us away from the prying eyes of the neighbours at our last address. The only person that knew of our situation on the new estate was a work friend of Linda, who happened to buy the house right next door to us. Everything looked and seemed normal. People just accepted us as another married couple, and Linda had a friend nearby to talk to over a cup of coffee.

My father arrived home just about then and he stayed with Linda and me. We sat up talking until the early hours of the morning. I related the whole business to him regarding Billy Wright, and asked him if I was wrong in doing what I did. "My only concern was that I didn't want to see us involved in another Civil War. I know that while you didn't fall out with my uncle Jim, you still don't speak to your uncle's side of the family," I said.

"No," he said, "You did what was right. Now let me have the names of the individuals that were threatening you. I'm having a meeting with some of my old comrades, and I'll see to it that this business is finished with, once and for all. If it isn't, we'll see to them if anything happens to you. By the way, there's a particular reason why I decided to stay with you and Linda. I want the family to get the message that I approve of her, and as far as I am concerned, she is now your wife."

That meant more to me than anything. I have always loved my parents, and he and I had a special relationship; so it was wonderful knowing that we were not going to fall out over my broken marriage.

Our neighbours were very friendly. They were mostly young couples trying their best to make a life for themselves. We had been there for quite some time when I was approached by a few of the local men one evening. "Does that barking dog not bother you?" one of them asked. "It barks all night long and it's directly opposite your house. Do you not hear it?"

I had heard the barking dog in the mornings when I left home for work, and in the evenings when I returned, but never at night, I told them.

"Holy Moses," they said, "You must die when you go to sleep."

I was due to leave home at six o'clock the next morning to travel to Cork on business. So I went to bed at ten, read for a while, and fell asleep. At midnight, the barking dog woke me and my head was buzzing. I lay there for a few minutes, trying to get back to sleep. It kept on and on, until finally I got fed up and got out of bed. Linda was awake also, and she asked me what I was doing. "Just going to the toilet," I told her. Having finished there, I went into the back bedroom and took my gun out of its hiding place. I tucked it under my pyjama top. The window, which tilted, was partly open because of the warm night that we were having. I pushed it further open and took the gun out and fired. A sheet of flame three feet long roared from the muzzle and the cordite hit the glass and poured back into the bedroom.

Linda, who was dozing, let out a scream with the fright. "What are you at?" she roared?

"Getting us a good night's sleep," I laughed as I tried to get rid of the smoke before the police arrived.

Next morning, the neighbours who had complained to me the previous evening were waiting at the end of my driveway. "Did you hear the bang last night?" one of them asked.

"What bang?" I asked trying to remain straight faced.

"It was you, you fecker," he laughed, "I was just about to sit on the loo when it happened, and I almost jumped into the bath with fright. Did you kill the dog?"

"No... I used a blank, this time, and you can tell that idiot who owns the dog that I'll be coming after him next, if my sleep is disturbed again." I had in fact used a blank cartridge. It wasn't the dog's fault that he was being left out all through the night, every night, and I wasn't about to punish him for that. The owner got sense and took him in from then on.

Our daughter, Aisling, was born on the 13th October 1975. The years seemed to be flying by. She was, like Tara, a beautiful quiet child and she brought much joy into our lives. Tara loved to play with her and mind her, as though she was her own live doll.

My father decided to pay us a visit just before Christmas in 1976. He was delighted to hold our new baby and to play with Tara. We sat up late one night, discussing family matters and having a general chit-chat. Then at around 3 a.m. as we were about to retire for the night, he asked me if I would do him a favour. I assured him that I would and told him all he needed to do was ask.

"Well okay," he said, looking a little bit embarrassed. "I've been told by the doctor that I've only got about six months to live. I've got cancer of the prostate and they cannot do anything more for me."

I sat looking at him dumbfounded and with my mouth hanging open. "Are you sure dad?" I finally managed to utter.

"Yes," he said. "I've been to see the undertaker and made all the arrangements." He then gave me the name and address, etc., of the undertaker and he produced a "Will" from his jacket pocket.

"I'm really sorry, Dad," I said, "But you can rely on me to carry out your wishes."

"I knew that, Son. That's why I came to see you. I'll be happy to go and meet up with your Ma again, so don't be worrying about me."

That's what I would expect from a "Hero;" no fuss and all arrangements in place. My regard for him was further heightened and I wished that I would have the courage to do as he had done when my turn came.

Seven months later in July, my eldest sister Alice, phoned me to say that he had died. I quickly arranged time off work and booked a flight to Manchester. Things will be different this time round, I thought to myself as I sat waiting to board my flight. Some of the family had blamed me for the sudden death of my mother. If she had not been forced to return to England, if my ex-wife had treated her with respect, if I had paid more attention, things might have been different is what I was told. I don't know if "The blame game" is peculiar to Irish families, but whenever an unexpected death occurs, the family has to blame someone. I took all of the flak following the death of my mother, despite the fact that none of the family living in Dublin had offered to accommodate my parents when they decided to leave my home.

My younger brother Bill met me at Manchester airport and took me to his home. He and his wife Margaret are the most hospitable people I know. I was to spend the next week with them. Burials take a lot longer to arrange in England. When a person dies in Ireland, they will be buried within forty-eight hours. So I decided to use the time by calling a family council to discuss my father's wishes. I asked that only the Sheridan's attend. That was a mistake. It offended Alice's husband. That was far from my intention but since none of the family said anything, the thought of offending just didn't cross my mind.

The meeting began with Paddy, my eldest brother pacing up and down the room in my father's flat, laying down the law.

"Alice is to get all of my father's possessions and you'll do as I say," he said, getting a nod of approval from Alice.

"Just hold on a minute," I said as I stood up.

"Who the hell do you think you are?" he snapped.

"Let me tell you who I'm not. I'm not the kid you used to give sixpence to for mending punctures on your bike. So just you sit down and listen for a change."

He was stunned. "Right, then let's hear what you have to say."

I produced my father's will and began to read from it. When I had finished, I told them all about my father's visit and his last request. He had left a small sum of money and requested that it be divided equally among all of us. My eldest sister began to cry. She felt that all of the money should be hers because she looked after my parents when they returned to England. Others disagreed. So I quickly thought of a solution that should satisfy all present. "Look, let's distribute the funds as outlined in the will. Then if anyone wants to donate their share to Alice, put the money in an envelope and get it to her. If you leave your name off, no one will be exposed or embarrassed and Alice cannot blame anyone for holding onto their share."

Everyone thought that this was a good idea. Except for Alice that is, and she got really up tight when I informed her that my father's Rolex watch was to be given to my brother Bill. My father and Bill had never got on very well. No one knew why, least of all Bill himself. So I reckoned that my father wanted to make amends when he decided to give him his watch. Alice got even more upset with this latest piece of news and began to berate me. I assured her that all I was doing was carrying out my father's wishes and that I had no responsibility for the contents of his will. Her husband, Frank, took a distinct disliking to me after he had been told what had transpired. He was the one wearing the watch at the time.

However, before the money could be withdrawn from my father's account, my sister went to a lawyer and he had the account frozen until matters had been resolved. That in turn meant that I had to see a lawyer also, and between the jigs and the reels, no one got anything. In the end, it all went to the lawyers in fees.

The funeral took place on an unusually hot July day. After the church service, the cortege drove past the flats were my father had lived. There lined along the pavement were the old people from the club he belonged to and as we passed one of his old army comrades came to attention and saluted. What a wonderful gesture. It brought tears to my eyes.

We were kept waiting for over an hour at the cemetery before the priest arrived. By that time, there was a distinct odour coming from the coffin. I assumed that he had been delayed on urgent business. But Bill told me later that someone informed him that the priest had gone to his home to have breakfast after the church ceremony. Had I known that at the time, I would've carried out the burial myself. His arrogance and lack of respect left me breathless.

The years since my mother's death had made me a stronger, more determined man with a very keen sense of fair play. I was determined to do what was needed to achieve what had been asked of me. That's the way I am, and I'm not too pushed if it makes me unpopular in certain quarters. My father had recognized my leadership qualities in the same way as my commanding officer had done. I'm very proud of him and I hope that he was a little bit proud of me.

Nine Months in Wicklow.

Linda had expressed a wish to live in a cottage in the country, and we began to look around at weekends. We found one in a small town in County Wicklow and moved there shortly afterwards. Just before we moved in however, someone tried to burn it down. They set fire to the curtains but as luck would have it, someone else saw the flames soon afterwards, and called the fire brigade. They responded very quickly and the damage was kept to the minimum. Our insurance company sent an assessor, and he quickly arranged for the damage to be repaired. It was summer when we moved in and the surrounds looked very picturesque. There was a small stream running past one side of it, with a cemetery on the other side. No noisy neighbours there then!

There was a large field at the back with horses running loose in it. However, at the far side of the field was a small estate, on which lived a couple of troublemakers. They let it be known that they didn't like Dubliners; they would sit in the field at the back of the house, and call my wife names as she hung out the washing. With this problem and following the fire, I decided to buy further insurance, so I bought a German shepherd guard dog. The £450 that I paid for him included training. He was worth every penny, and when we were out of the house he was left inside. I dearly hoped that the person who tried to burn the house would break in while he was there. When we were home, I had him on a long leash outside. So we knew whenever anyone even approached the place, and that turned out to be quite frequent.

I got to know the pub where these guys went for a drink and decided to pay a visit. I tucked the gun into its usual place, and wore my Mac as I sat down at the bar. I never drink bottled Guinness, but this night I made an exception and ordered one. An older man came and sat beside me. "Are you from Dublin?" he asked, having heard my accent when I ordered my drink.

"Yes," I said, and explained that I had recently moved into the town.

"Be careful," he said, "There's a bad bunch of people living at the back of you."

"I've already met a few of them," I said, and almost immediately a guy appeared at my side and pushed against me. I grabbed the neck of the bottle and swung it across his face. "Get back, yeh bastard, or I'll ram this down your throat." He stepped back, looking sideways at his mates and waiting for them to make their move. I put the bottle on the bar and held my coat open. "Go ahead… who wants to be first?" I asked through gritted teeth. They froze and began to back off. "Now let's get something straight, you lot. The first one of you that bothers my family or me again will be buried in that cemetery by the side of my house." I finished my drink and bidding the older man a good night, I left the bar. As soon as I got home, I hid the gun in its safe place. The message got home; don't mess with the Sheridans.

Next morning, I had a call from the local Garda sergeant. I fully expected him and invited him into the sitting room. "Do you have a gun?" he asked.

"Nothing more than what you see on the wall," I answered, nodding at the two replica muskets that were hanging over the fireplace.

"I wouldn't leave those there," he said.

"They're only plastic," I said, as I took one down for him to inspect.

"Yeah, I see, but don't leave them up there anyway. Nosy people will see them through the window and break in to get them, thinking that they're real. They certainly look real," he said.

"So you expect that we will have problems of that nature do you?"

"Well the crowd up the back field are all intermarried, and there's more than a few head cases among them."

"All right, sergeant," I said, and took both of the pistols off the wall. "I'll put them away." Something that I've noticed over the years whenever I've come up against criminals is when you get the better of them, the first people they look to for help is the police. The sergeant hadn't called on a neighbourly visit to welcome us to Wicklow. He had received a call from one of the head bangers to tell him that I had a gun.

"By the way, sergeant, while you're here we can clear up another matter," I said.

"And what would that be?" he asked.

"I had a call from my sister-in-law in Birmingham regarding a visit she had from her local murder squad. It seems that some maker of pornographic films was found murdered, and they wanted to question me about it."

"Do you go over to Birmingham regularly?" he asked.

"As a matter of fact I do. I attend sales meetings in Cardiff and I usually fly into Birmingham the day before the meeting, and stay with my brother and his wife."

"And did you murder this guy?" he asked, smiling.

"Not a chance," I said, "And if I did, do you think I'd bring it up with you? They must be scraping the bottom of the barrel anyway. From what my sister-in-law told me, the description of the suspect was of a guy much older than me and he had a beard and moustache. In any event, I am not involved, nor have I ever been in pornography."

"Where would they have gotten your name and address from?" he asked.

"I have no idea," I said, thinking of my ex-wife. She would be bad enough to hear of a thing like that and phone the police help line. "Hell hath no fury," is certainly true. I don't know what went on as a result of our conversation, but I heard no more afterwards.

Winter came and the small stream by the side of the house became a raging torrent. The house had no damp-proofing, and it was cold, damp, and miserable, and it was infested with mice. We decided to get the hell out of there, and we put it up for sale in the New Year, once the winter was over. We had been there only nine months when we sold it. But we made a profit, and we moved back to dear old Dublin.

Back in Dublin.

The relationship with Linda's mother had vastly improved and we noticed that there was a house for sale on the same avenue where she lived, so we went after it. It proved to be very sound and warm. It needed a lot of work to brighten it up, both inside and out, and we set about making it cosy and to our liking. A while after we moved in, our son Philip was born on the 19th April 1979. After much discussion about what his name should be, my wife agreed on Philip. At first I wanted to call him Oisín, but Linda wouldn't hear of it. So since I'm a student of Military History, we settled on Philip... after the US cavalry general who distinguished himself in the American Civil War.

The Northern problem continued to worsen, with the one side trying to outdo the other in the awfulness of their atrocities. I must admit that I seriously considered offering my services to the IRA, but I soon dispensed with that notion when I read and saw pictures on television of the scene of carnage that was "Blood Friday." I couldn't believe my eyes when I saw a fireman lifting the remains of a human being on a shovel. So I continued to do duties in barracks and whenever I had the time,

I volunteered for border duty also. It was a pleasure to be in charge of mixed regular and reserve patrols. The lads worked well together, and the experience was good for both sides.

As with my experience in civilian life, I seemed to attract trouble. (Perhaps it was down to the fact that I look soft and an easy touch.) It seemed like every day, on almost every patrol, there was an incident of one sort or another. One of the regular officers swore that I had brought friends up from Dublin to create problems to make me look good in the eyes of the senior ranks. I assured him that I hadn't, and he asked me if he could take the next patrol. I gave it to him willingly, as I was feeling in need of a rest. We were patrolling round the clock, without sufficient numbers of troops. So we were working four hours on, and four hours off. My colleague came back from his patrol without experiencing any problems. I took the next one and was on the radio to HQ within half an hour, reporting a problem. We were nobody's friends in the area that had been dubbed "Bandit Country" by Merlyn Rees, the British MP, and Secretary of State for Northern Ireland. It was exciting however, and I realised that I was happiest doing just what I was doing at that moment.

Normally a first lieutenant, (I had been promoted after two years in the previous rank,) would have to wait at least ten years before he would be considered for a captaincy. But as things stood, the army was seriously short of senior officers, so I was nominated for a captain's course. It was run by the Military College, and it turned out to be very interesting. No longer were the instructors confined to the rigid tactical instruction that I had experienced on the potential officer's course. We worked fourteen hours per day, fighting and patrolling, day and night. One evening after the day's work, we were back in our billet cleaning up and getting ready for the next day, when one of the guys decided to have a go at me. "I hear that you're a Karate Expert," he said.

"No, I practice it, and Judo," I replied. "There are no *experts*, in my view. There's always somebody who can take the expert down."

This particular guy could be a severe "pain in the neck," particularly when he had a few drinks in him. But here we were, stone cold sober, and he began to push things to the point where something needed to be done to shut him up. A few of the other guys were egging him on also. "Look," I said, "I'll show you something if you promise to behave yourself in future."

"Go on then," he said, all satisfied with himself that he was about to show me up. I happened to have some 4.5 inch blocks of timber in the boot of my car, which were leftovers from a previous demonstration. I went and got them, and pulling two stools together, I set the blocks of timber across them. He had been insisting that he could do anything that I could do, so I offered him first go at breaking it with his hand. He got into position and raised his hand. I was sure that he would do it, if only to prove his point. But as his hand came down he stopped. "You're just trying to hurt me," he said. "Let's see you do it first."

He stepped away and I raised my hand, focused on the point of impact, and swung my hand. The timber broke with a crash. The others clapped their hands and turned their attention to him. "Let's see you do it," they chided.

This guy was the captain of a first class rugby team, and he was tough as nails. He looked at them and then at me. "F… off," he said, "I've a game to play next week and I am not taking any chances."

"Right," I said, "Then let me show you this, and afterwards I don't want to hear any more out of you." I put one block on top of the other. "That's five inches you're looking at now." I swung my hand and the block smashed. "Now tell me, how thick are your testicles?"

"Wha… what do you mean?" he said.

"I reckon they're about this thick," I said showing him a space that I had created with my thumb and forefinger. "The next time you bother me, that is what will happen to them," I said, pointing to the broken blocks. The lads all cheered and clapped again, and gave him a terrible time for the rest of the night. Later in the mess, I bought him a pint and we shook hands. We're still friends today. The course was conducted over fourteen weekends, following two full weeks in the field. It was intense but very satisfying. And he learned not to mess with the Sheridans.

Meanwhile, my job was going very well, also. I had landed the single largest account in the whole of Europe, and as a result became highly unpopular with the General Manager. I was called over to London for a meeting with him. He complained that I was earning more than him and that wouldn't do. He wanted to readjust my target figures upwards. "If I had lost that account would you adjust the figures downwards? I asked.

"Well, no," he said hesitantly.

"Well, bugger off with yourself and tell the other twenty guys operating in this market to get off their arses and try to match what I've just done. By the way, am I not right in assuming that you get an overriding commission on what the sales force produce?"

"What's that to do with you? he asked.

"Well I believe that I'm putting more money in your pocket that anyone else on the sales force. So you ought to be thanking me."

He was livid and as I left the meeting, I reckoned that he would exact revenge at some future date.

It wasn't long in coming. A few weeks later, two area managers arrived over to see me. After working with me all day, they invited Linda and me to join them for dinner that evening. We met in the lounge of the Shelbourne Hotel and had a couple of drinks while it was decided where we would eat. I excused myself and went down to the basement to visit the toilet. When I got back, one of them asked me for my car keys.

"What do you want the keys for? I asked.

"We've ordered a taxi to take you home. We're going to buy Linda a dinner that you wouldn't be able to afford."

"How do you feel about that, Linda? I asked.

"I told them that they didn't know what they were letting themselves in for, but they ignored my warning."

I looked at my watch. It read 7:45 p.m. "The last plane has just left for London. You pair be on the first flight in the morning and don't ever come back to this country. I'll be here at nine o'clock to check that you've gone. If you're still here, I'll send you home in a box. Do I make myself clear?" I said slowly and deliberately while I looked them both in the eye. They could see that I meant every word. I was back at the hotel next morning as promised, to see if they had left. They had and as far as I know they have never been back.

There was no employment legislation to deal with that sort of harassment in those days. I would've taken the appropriate action otherwise. The whole experience left a sour taste in my mouth and turned me against employers generally. Oh, I continued to work and do a good job, but I lost any trust I might've had for bosses from then on.

Being removed from the main scene, (I worked from home and represented three separate divisions of the company,) I couldn't prove that any of what had taken place. However, I can testify to the fact that some of the sales forces at least, were rewarded for not reaching target. One of them was actually awarded the "Salesman of the Year" trophy at the annual conference. He wasn't within a mile of my figures. But Arthur, my immediate boss, with something of an embarrassed look, told me that the general manager wanted to boost the guy's confidence. The following year, having had my target increased threefold, my figures were 189 percent of target, and the award went to a man who had exceeded his target by just 1 percent. Arthur blew his top and protested in the strongest possible terms. He was promoted sideways for his trouble, and the two that I had run out of Ireland were promoted over his head. I resigned shortly afterwards. Arthur, who was an ex-marine commando sergeant and a Yorkshire man, was honest and straight talking. We hit it off from the first day we met. We had many enjoyable evenings together in company with Linda, and there was never a hint of any impropriety. I was told later that he got on a plane to the United States, and complained about his treatment to the main men in the parent company. Resulting from his visit, the general manager and the divisional director were sacked, and he was promoted to European Manager; Research & Development. A couple of years later, the company established a main office in Dublin. I received a phone call one afternoon inviting me to come and discuss a possible opening with them. The day before the appointed time however, the interview was cancelled without explanation. The two guys that I had run out of the country were still in position and I suspect that they had a hand in things.

CHAPTER EIGHTEEN

STABILITY ONCE AGAIN

I had joined a company based in Wales that offered a new challenge and where I was surrounded by friendly staff, and decent management. The company manufactured a range of steel products for the construction industry. This was in total contrast to my previous trade. I was a lithographer who had moved on to selling printing products. But I was up to the challenge, and enjoyed working with the new company so much that I decided I would finish out my working life with them. The products that they manufactured were new and innovative. It was exciting to visit an architect's office and introduce the staff to new products that really piqued their interest. I travelled over to Cardiff regularly for meetings, which were usually held on Friday. During my visits, I took the opportunity to visit my brother Bill and his wife Margaret, who lived in Manchester. On one occasion, Graham, my boss, asked me if I intended to visit my brother. I confirmed that I did, and he told me he would arrange with the representative for that area to give me a lift. Generally, I used the train when I flew into Cardiff and flew out of Manchester.

Following the meeting the new Rep came over to me, and told me that Graham had instructed him to take me to Manchester. I told him that I would get the train as usual, if it were inconvenient for him. "No," he said, "I was told and I'd better do as the boss says." It would've been better for me if I had used the train, because all this guy did was complain to me all the way up the motorway. At one stage, he said he didn't know what sort of a risk he might be taking, because I could be an IRA bomber. (The IRA had recently begun to plant bombs in the UK.) I told him to cop onto himself and to be careful of his tongue. He dropped me in Piccadilly where Bill was waiting for me. We had a good laugh when I told him about the "moany bugger" who had just dropped me off. My boss wasn't a bit pleased when I told him about this. He really let the guy have a piece of his mind.

Bill is my junior by two years. He is a painter and decorator and was very fit as a result. He also managed a football team for his local pub. He phoned me on Wednesday to say that a guy on the opposing team from Sunday's match had issued a serious threat. Now, Bill is well able to look after himself when it comes to physical stuff. But this guy had repeatedly threatened to "blow his kneecaps off." Bill didn't know how to handle it, so he phoned me.

The team stood by and listened to this without doing anything about it. But then, one could hardly blame them if the guy seemed to be serious. The landlord of the pub was very concerned also and asked Bill what he was going to do about the threat. He said, "I've made a phone call and there'll be somebody here in forty-eight hours to take care of things."

After dinner, we excused ourselves to Margaret and headed down to the pub. As we walked in to the lounge, a hush fell on the crowd and they separated like something you'd see in a Western movie. The landlord came to me and I ordered two pints and asked him where the "smart ass" was.

"He's not one of my regulars," he said, all concerned. "He drinks in the Royal Oak."

"Why didn't any of you lot do something about him when he was here?" I asked.

"He sounded very determined and we thought he was out of his head, particularly as the argument was over nothing," the landlord whined.

"So you all just let him away with it, isn't that right?"

There was a hush again and he said that he didn't want trouble.

"We don't look for trouble, nor do we want it, and there won't be any here tonight," I said. "It's more than a little disappointing, however, when no one was prepared to at least phone the police and report the other guy." Before I left Bill that Sunday, I got the address and other details of the offender from him. I told him that I'd phone him later in the week and give him a night when I wanted him to be sure that he could account for every minute of his time. We shook hands as usual at the airport departures ramp. I thanked him and Margaret for a lovely weekend and reminded him of what I'd said earlier.

When I got home, I phoned a couple of ex-army friends. They had trained under me in the Reserve, and after serving their time, left and joined the Irish Guards. They had served in Aden and one of them had been wounded in action. They had been ambushed while on patrol and had been rescued, just as their ammunition had run out. I explained what had happened with Bill and what I had in mind to do about it. They agreed to help, and I arranged to meet them in Manchester the following Friday. They would travel up from London and pick me up at the airport.

When we arrived at the address, one of my friends knocked on his hall door and asked if he owned a car with the registration number... he confirmed that he did.

"My friend has run into it, would you mind having a look?"

He got his coat and came outside to see what damage had been done. He didn't suspect a thing, as my friend is good at mimicking an English accent. When he saw that there was no damage to the car and that there were two more of us waiting there, he realised that he was in trouble.

"What's this all about?" he said, trying to tough it out.

I explained why we were there.

"I was just kidding," he said nervously.

"I don't believe that," I said.

"Who're you?" he demanded to know.

"Someone who doesn't take threats lightly," I said, as I delivered the first blow. Before he could gather his thoughts, I hit him again and again. I had arranged with my friends to watch my back and make sure that no one else interfered. They left me to it, and when I'd finished, one of my friends phoned for an ambulance.

Next week, the police came calling on my brother, wanting to know if he knew anything about the assault. He asked what day and time they were speaking of. They told him and he was able to produce witnesses in the local pub where the threats had been issued.

"We know that you arranged for him to be done," they said.

"Well go ahead and charge me then," he told them. "Look, let's get something straight, if it had been me who issued the threat, you'd have had a phone call, and I would've been hauled in by the scruff of my neck. Why? Because I'm Irish, that's why. That guy obviously made one threat too many and he's paid the price. So unless you've proof that I was involved, you can bugger off and leave me alone."

They knew that he was in the clear. They had checked with the guys in the pub and had gotten confirmation that he was with the football team, discussing tactics for the game on Sunday. Before the police left, they told him that the guy who made the threat would be in hospital for quite a while. So, another one had learned not to mess with the Sheridans.

My job was going well. I had built the business up to a level that the directors were happy with. My future looked assured, and then as we entered the 80s, the construction industry hit a recession. Tradesmen were leaving in droves to work in Germany, and to a lesser extent the building sites in London. The chairman chose this time to sell the company to one of the world's largest conglomerates. Despite assurances to the contrary, they sent in a *Hatchet Man*, and it was decided to appoint a Merchant Stockist in Ireland, and I was made redundant. I phoned the marketing director and asked him about the assurance he had given me just a week or so previously, that my job was not in jeopardy. He asked me to fly over to see him. I did and he offered me a job in the export department. It would mean my spending six weeks at a time in the Middle East, and Africa. I accepted, and the plans were put in place for me to make the switch at the end of the month.

One of the areas I worked in was Nigeria. What a hellhole that country is. Everybody, from government officials down, is on the take. It was dangerous for whites and there was a constant worry about bandits. One day as I travelled along the motorway, my driver suddenly pulled up and stuck the car in reverse. "What are you doing?" I asked.

"Sorry Sir," he said, "There's bandits up ahead." The robbers had set up a roadblock on a main highway and were robbing whoever happened to come their way. I thanked my driver as he drove off the off-ramp that we had just passed a moment or two ago.

I fell in love with Egypt. What a contrast to Nigeria. I've been back there many times on holiday and just love their culture. I also worked in the whole of the Middle-East area. Saudi Arabia was very interesting. I enjoyed the honesty of its people. Well, wouldn't you be honest if you were in danger of losing your hand for thieving?

Conversion.

Although I had given up practising my religion, I hadn't given up on God. I still prayed every day and asked for guidance. Then one Friday evening after returning from Cork on business, I was laid out on the settee at home after my dinner and watching television, when the doorbell rang. Linda was in the kitchen tidying up and nearest to the door, so she answered it. The sitting room door opened and she put her head round the opening and said that there were two young men who wished to talk to me. Political matters had been cleared up, and I didn't take any precautions as I made my way to the door. They looked and dressed like salesmen. Before they could say anything I told them that I had an encyclopaedia and more books than I could read so "No, thanks."

They smiled broadly, saying that they weren't selling anything. "Have you heard of the "Mormons?" they asked.

"Aren't they the people that only deal in gold?" I asked.

They laughed, and said no, but could they have fifteen minutes of our time to deliver a message. It was a cold night and I felt a little sorry for them, so I invited them in. They told us of a man called Joseph Smith who'd had a vision in which he saw God the father, and His son Jesus Christ. They showed us a film-strip, depicting this vision and afterwards asked if we believed that there were such things as visions in modern times. How could I disagree, when I believed that there had been visions at Lourdes and Fatima? I couldn't explain what had happened to me, but I just knew that what I had just seen and heard was truth. A wonderful feeling of peace fell upon me. I felt as if I was floating on air and I wanted to know more.

They left after the fifteen minutes was up, but we made a further appointment so that Linda and I could learn more. Linda didn't feel the same as I did, but was nevertheless impressed by what they said and was willing to listen further. They brought peace and tranquillity back into my life. I hadn't slept at all well since my marriage break up; my job was under threat, and my army career was in absolute turmoil. Over the next weeks and months, as I learned more of The Church of Jesus Christ of Latter-day Saints, I came to realise that this was the church that I had dreamed about for so long. My whole life changed and I wanted to put things in order, and marry my partner. From now on, nothing fazed me, and I was inspired to write the following:

I've travelled far and travelled wide:
With no companion by my side:
In tobacco and drink I sought in vain:
But found no comfort, only pain:
Then at home one evening at my chore:
A knock sounded at my front door:
I opened, and there in the night:
Stood two young men smiling bright:
We're Mormons they said and
Bade me goodnight:
We've come to preach the one true God:
May we come in? I gave a nod:
And as they spoke, before my eyes:
I saw the truth, there was no disguise:
Now I'm happy and content:
To share that truth is my intent.

While I was happy with the world for the first time in a long time, I was to discover that the world wasn't happy with me. Family and friends alike thought that I had lost the plot when I told them about my new found happiness. Not only had I given up swearing, I no longer took alcohol, tea, or coffee. Some thought that if I was left to it that I'd soon get over it, like a bad dose of a cold. Others took it upon themselves to reclaim me before I fell too far. "Are you going to condemn me for living a cleaner life than I had ever led before?" I asked my family and friends. They tut-tutted, and shook their heads. It's strange to hear the things that people come out with in this sort of situation. People who are Roman Catholic really know very little about their own religion. I can testify to that. After all, I was one myself. If anything, I was better acquainted than most of my peers, because I had won a religion competition at school. It was open to the thousand or so boys that attended there, and I took first prize. But here were people, who knew little of their own religion and absolutely nothing of this new religion that I was looking into, advising me and talking absolute nonsense. The missionaries had invited me to be baptised, but I declined regretfully, because Linda and I were not married. I decided to do something about that situation, and set about putting the wheels in motion to correct that situation as soon as possible. Five years later, I went to court in Birmingham got a Decree Nisi, and six weeks after that received confirmation of the Divorce. I proposed to Linda and we were married soon afterwards. We moved to a house in County Wicklow and lost contact with the missionaries for a few years. We would come in contact with new ones at a later stage.

—⁓—

Around this time, the battalion spent two weeks on camp in Kilworth Camp in County Cork. The battalion CO was known as *Jackass*. It was well earned. He took a dislike to me, due I suspected, to complaints he was hearing from my company CO. He had been drafted in from "D" company and brought with him the prejudice that existed between our two outfits. I was due to be promoted to second in command of the company and he tried his best to block that. There was nothing that he, or anyone could do, in fact. I had the seniority; I had put in the hours and had done the relevant courses. So the promotion would be automatic unless he could find a way to block it. He certainly tried. The method he tried was insulting to my intelligence, and I let him know that in no uncertain terms. But more about that later.

I found myself on orderly officer duties every second day. This meant that I would be on duty for twenty-four hours then resting for twenty-four hours and back on duty again for the same period. On one particular night, as I went to check that the guards were alert, I noticed Jackass standing in the front door of his billet, urinating into the road. He was too lazy to walk to the latrines. Having just completed my rounds, I entered the orderly officer's office and sat down to make an entry in the diary.

The door burst open and the Jackass was stood there with his greatcoat over his pyjamas. "Why aren't you out checking the guard instead of sitting here on your arse?" he roared.

Calmly and deliberately I pointed to my head. "I have just come back from a patrol, and you will notice that I'm still wearing my greatcoat and cap. When I've completed my entry in the diary, I will be back out again… Sir." The emphasis on "Sir" bore the message, "Get back to bed, you ignorant jackass or I'll put you to sleep right here."

Next morning after writing up my report and handing in my pistol, I was on my way to bed when I met my company CO. "Where are you going?" he asked.

"I'm off to bed; I was on duty last night."

"Right," he said, looking at his watch (it was gone nine o'clock at this stage), "Get a few hours, I want you on the range at one o'clock." There was no reason for him to behave in that way toward me. I had always been loyal and supportive of him, despite the fact that I had no respect for him. A couple of years earlier, one of our lads had been killed while riding a motorbike. At least that's what I thought until my CO told me that the car that ran him down was driven by a prominent Sinn Fein member. The young passenger he had in the car with him apparently admitted to police immediately after the accident that the driver had deliberately driven the car at our lad because he was in uniform. When I asked why we weren't insisting that the police charge the driver, he gave me a lame excuse. The lad who had been killed had been a good servant of the state and had married just a week before.

"I won't be on camp," I told him. "I'm going to have a shower and then I'm heading into Fermoy. I'm entitled to my time off and if you don't like it, I suggest you charge me when I get back." After showering and getting into my civilian clothes, I headed towards the camp gates in my car. Just before I reached the exit, one of the sergeants called out to me. I stopped the car and he asked if I was heading into town. I confirmed that I was, and he asked if he and a quartermaster sergeant could hitch a lift. I said that they'd be welcome. When we got to Fermoy, they asked me what I was intending to do. "I'm going to find a bar and relax and have a skinfull," I said.

"Would you mind if we join you?" they asked.

"Not at all," I said and we found a cozy little place and spent all day there, right up until eleven o'clock that night. I dropped them back at the camp gates and I drove to the officer's mess across the road. As I was about to enter the bar, a commandant came out. He was on his way to the toilet.

"Ah, Eamonn, how are you?" he asked, all smiles.

"I'm in rare form, Sir. Is the Jackass in the bar?"

He had known me for many years and he could tell that I wasn't enquiring about the CO's health. He also knew what was going on and how unjust it was. So he grabbed my arms and pinned me against the wall. "I know what you're going to do and I'm appealing to you to leave it and go to bed."

"Look, Sir," I said, "I've had enough of him and it's time to get things sorted out."

"Not now," he pleaded. "Please go to bed and sleep on it at least."

I finally agreed but only because I wouldn't want anyone thinking that I needed *Dutch Courage* to face him.

Next day, I was on orderly officer duty again and after drawing my pistol, I was on my way across the camp square to inspect and arm my guard. It was pouring rain and that didn't help my mood. I had my trench coat over my best uniform, unbuttoned because of the bulk of my pistol. Before I had taken half a dozen steps onto the square, I met the CO of "B" company. He was a hard drinker and it was obvious that he was looking for trouble. "Where're you going to?" he asked with venom.

I pulled my coat open and pointed to the pistol. "Don't get me annoyed, Sir, or I'll be tempted to draw this and use it, now bugger off with yourself."

He could see that I meant business and quickly disappeared into a billet. The Jackass was an ignorant swine and he tried his best to get me to resign. Every dirty detail that he could dream up was slung at me. But I dug my heels in, the more he tried, until finally he moved on. He was promoted to Lieutenant Colonel after camp and replaced by the Brigade Intelligence Officer. Yes, you guessed it, the one that I'd had the problem with in the past when asking for cover. Things were about to get even more interesting. One might be forgiven for asking why, if I was a volunteer and on reserve, did I not just quit. All I can say is that I'm not a quitter and the more people try to get at me, the more I'll stay around, if only to get up their noses by being there. It didn't work for Jackass and it wouldn't work for this guy either.

I met the new CO while I was on duty back in barracks in Dublin. He came into the officer's mess where I was based and sat down near to where I was sitting. My father had given me a cutting from a very old newspaper that had been inserted by a solicitor. It asked for any relatives of the late Helen Sheridan to make contact concerning an unclaimed fortune. I was working on the family genealogy in an attempt to establish a link and had the documents spread out in front of me. My intention was to use the quiet hours to good effect. My father claimed that there was a Helen in our family in the 1800s, and that his father had worked for years in an attempt to prove this. But, because the IRA had destroyed the National Records Office during the Civil

War, he was unsuccessful. So my father thought that I might have better luck.

The CO asked me what I was doing and I began to relate the story. Helen was a teenage girl living on the family farm in County Cavan. One day, while she was feeding the chickens in the yard, a troop of soldiers appeared at the gate. The officer in charge (was named Robert Dudley Blake, later to become Colonel Blake), had been attracted by her sweet singing voice. It was a summer morning and all seemed well with the world. They spoke for a while and the officer was so smitten by her that he asked if he could come back and visit her again. She obviously liked his manner and agreed. After a short courtship, they eloped to the Gorbells in Glasgow and married. The Gorbells is an integral part of Glasgow City today, and hasn't enjoyed the best of publicity in recent years. But at that time it was a just a sleepy backwater.

Robert's family, who still live in Twisel Castle in Northumberland were not at all pleased that he should marry an Irish peasant girl. They rowed with him and he parted from them. But not before taking his share of the family fortune. He set about moulding Helen into a woman who would be accepted in the society that he was used to mixing in. He paid for her to attend a finishing school in Switzerland and before long, she returned with the education and the sophistication that was expected of a lady of means. Robert was considerably older than Helen, and knowing that it was likely that he would die before her, he made certain in his Will that his fortune would go to her. He stipulated specifically that none of his money was to go to the Blake's. He died, and Helen then set about buying up lands and properties that belonged to the Blake family. She amassed an even greater fortune and died intestate. Because there was no heir named in Helen's will and no mention of family, the law firm placed an advertisement in the Irish newspapers seeking a relative. That was the cutting that my father had handed me, that in turn had been given to him by his father. She had, it seems, destroyed all evidence of her background when she was with Robert, perhaps because of the way in which his family reacted to their marriage.

She obviously didn't want to cause him any embarrassment with his friends. My investigations proved that Robert and Helen did in fact marry. They are shown on the Blake family tree. And the money that Helen left now sits unclaimed in the British Treasury. The last time I checked, it amounted to £300,000,000. During my investigations, I found that distant and near relatives would not cooperate with me by providing any information or documentation that they might have. I've witnessed the greed that shows in certain family members' eyes at the mention of money. They deliberately held back on providing information. They were no doubt thinking that I wouldn't share the money with them if I managed to get my hands on it.

The CO looked at me as though I was deliberately trying to be superior to him. So he related a story about his family who had a vast cattle ranch in Argentina. "They have been exporting beef for over a hundred years and would be worth more than the amount you mentioned."

"Right, you bugger," I thought, "so that's how it's going to be is it?"

He left himself open soon afterwards. He brought up the business of service in uniform and was bragging about the years that had been put in by his family in the Irish Army and how he had served with the United Nations.

I countered with, "Oh, isn't that nice. My father served in two real wars."

"What do you mean by that?" he asked?

"He served in the War of Independence and then went on to serve with the 8th Army during the Second World War." His face grew red as a beetroot and he got up from the table and strode off. "There will be trouble ahead," went through my mind as he disappeared out of the door.

—m—

My trips abroad, whilst enjoyable for me, were nevertheless having a detrimental effect on my family. I was in Nigeria when Linda informed me that my dog Stag had been killed. He was never allowed out unless he was on a lead. I had been advised never to allow him to make friends with anyone except family. My son, who was only four years of age at the time, opened the gate into the back garden where he was totally enclosed. Stag ran past him down the driveway, out onto the road and straight under a passing bus. He was killed outright. All of the family were upset, and I swore that I would never have another dog. My friend had gone, and I felt so badly about it that I just couldn't go through the trauma again. There were other problems that arose, and disasters always seem to happen when I was far away from home and could do nothing about it, except advise Linda what to do for the best. So I made the decision to resign from my job.

I had been exploring the possibility of moving to the United States and on my way back from the Middle East I arranged to fly on to the USA. A friend met me at LAX airport and took me to his home in Colton, seventy or so miles south of Los Angeles.

The first company I approached seeking work was a medium-sized printer's. The owner was impressed with my experience, and we agreed a package, and a time for me to take up the position of Works Manager. I had a month to persuade my wife to agree to the move, decide what to do about the house, and take up my new position with the new company. We decided to rent the house and make sure that we were happy with our new surroundings. This proved to be a wise decision, as things turned out.

When I reported to work, the owner reneged on our agreement regarding wages. He knew that I was there illegally, and took advantage by dropping the agreed salary by ten thousand dollars. I also found that I was working a double shift without extra pay. I pointed out to him that he had broken our agreement, and I wasn't happy with that. He reacted by bringing in the local police Lieutenant of Detectives to interview me. I later discovered that his reason for this was because he had been shot by a hired gunman while working in a local company, due to his bad behaviour. He was a senior manager with the local cement works at the time and made life so unbearable for the workers, it is alleged that the union hired a hit man to sort him out. I wasn't surprised to hear this. He was shot several times and only barely survived. The resulting compensation provided the funds, which allowed him to buy the printing works. He obviously thought that he might be at risk again, and decided to take out insurance in advance this time.

My wife became pregnant shortly after we arrived and she was terribly worried about the expense of having a baby in the United States. My employer had reneged on the medical arrangements also. After four months, we decided to return home, much to the disappointment of our children. They loved the idea of being able to come home from school and jump into the pool at the apartment complex where we lived. I sympathised with them, as it certainly appealed to me also. But this in no way compensated for the fact that it was impossible to relax and leave the children to play on their own. We had to take it in turns to watch the kids at all times, for fear of kidnappers. It was frightening to see the number of photos of missing kids on the notice board of the local supermarket. Every milk carton carried a picture of a missing child also. A dark brown fog could often be seen coming from the direction of Los Angeles. This was the pollution caused by the thousands of cars that used the highways every day. The people were very helpful and friendly, and they did everything they could to persuade us to stay when they heard that we had decided to return home. There was no way that I was going to continue working for the company I was with, anyway.

Just as I was wondering what would be the best thing to do for my family, I got a phone call from an ex-customer in Ireland. He asked me to return home and offered me a job with his company as Sales Director. I accepted, resigned immediately, and made arrangements to return home. It seemed as though the Lord had answered our prayers. Linda was delighted, the kids were disappointed, and I was philosophical. But I'd had enough of travelling and decided that I would stay at home in future, come what may. We visited friends in Salt Lake City and while we were there, we spent a day in the Temple. What a wonderful experience it was, too. Although we had been through the Temples in London and Los Angeles, the Salt Lake visit was special. Not just because it was in the area of Church Headquarters, but because of its age and unique design. We stopped off in Atlanta on our way home, and visited the Temple there also. Temples are a unique place, where Mormons carry out baptisms-by-proxy on behalf of their deceased relatives. They are sacred places and are regarded as being literally the "House of the Lord." The peace that I had experienced during the visit of the first missionaries that called to our home returned. I resolved to live in accordance with church teachings, and to do my best to hold onto the peace of mind that I was experiencing.

Back to Dublin again…

On my return to Dublin, I resumed parading with the reserve; and I decided to have the religion section of my army record changed. My company CO, when I told him about this, suggested that I might like to talk to a Jesuit priest friend of his. "Thanks, but no thanks," I said, "Do you not think that I'm mature enough to make up my own mind?"

He then made arrangements for me to speak to the Battalion CO. When I entered his office, he bared his teeth at me like a dog.

"What's this about?" he demanded.

"It's about my right to have my record changed, Sir," I said.

He looked at my CO, shrugged his shoulders, and dismissed me with a look of disgust on his face. I was due to fill the vacancy of second-in-command of the company. My CO arrived back in the company office and put it to me that a sergeant, who had passed the potential officers course and was awaiting promotion to the officer ranks, should fill the vacancy.

"You'll be the de facto second in command, and he'll get his promotion," he told me.

I looked at him for a long few seconds. "Do you think I'm stupid, as well as a traitor" I asked.

"I don't understand," he said.

"Let me make something clear to you then. I am due the promotion and if you or anybody else tries to deny me that, I will take a redress-of-wrongs case against you. If that doesn't work, I will go the newspapers. There is much more behind this than even you realise. I know that I will be regarded as a traitor for

277

changing my religion; and I'll make an example of you and the Battalion CO if you discriminate against me on those grounds. Why can't the new second lieutenant take over the vacancy that I leave behind?"

He had no answer to that. Needless to remark, I was officially promoted to the vacant position shortly afterwards, and the newly promoted man took over my position as platoon commander.

More problems followed. The next year on camp in Gormanstown, County Meath, I marched the company down to church on Sunday morning. When we reached the chapel, the platoon sergeant came to me and asked if the men had to attend Mass.

"No," I told him, "All you're obliged to do is be paraded to the church. That complies with the regulations, but you are not obliged to attend."

"Right, Sir," he said and announced this to the men. Almost all of them broke off after dismissal and went in various directions. Very few of them went into the church. Shortly afterwards I was visited by two senior officers and accused of stopping the men going to Mass. I informed them that the facts would prove otherwise, and to go ahead and charge me if they so wished. Nothing further was done about it.

However, I did have a run-in with the chaplain at a later date. I was orderly officer again and having finished my lunch, I retired to a corner of the bar in the mess. There was nowhere else for me to go, as the ante-room, (where the Orderly Officer would normally be when not on tour,) was full of air corps officers, celebrating some event. I was sitting quietly reading the newspaper and minding my own business when a young air corps officer came over to me. "The chaplain would like to meet you," he said, nodding his head in the direction of where he was sitting.

I got up and followed him across the room. The chaplain was sitting with another young officer. "What's your name?" he asked as he took my extended hand.

"Sheridan, father," I said.

"Where are you from?"

"Dublin," I said.

"You're not a Dubliner," he said.

"I was born in the Rotunda Hospital at the top of O'Connell Street and you can't get more Dublin than that."

"Well, your father wasn't from Dublin," he said.

"He was also born in the same hospital as myself," I smiled.

"Well, your grandfather wasn't from Dublin," he said getting a little agitated.

"No, he was from County Cavan," I said.

"See, I told you that you weren't from Dublin," he said, looking at the other two and grinning.

"How long does someone have to live somewhere to qualify as a local?" I asked frowning.

He didn't like my question. "I'm drinking brandy," he said.

I put my hand in my pocket and pulled out what amounted to a few pence in change. "Congratulations," I said, "I haven't enough to buy a lemonade!" His face suddenly looked as though I had just slapped him. I excused myself, and went back to my newspaper. The other three asked the barman for a bottle of spirits and left the mess.

Later that evening, the two young air corps officers arrived in the mess. They had been drinking all afternoon in the priest's house. They demanded to know why I wasn't answering the telephone, and it was obvious that they were looking for trouble from their demeanour.

"The phone hasn't rung while I've been here," I told them.

One of them picked up the receiver. "There's no line," he said, "It hasn't been switched over from the camp exchange."

"That's not my job," I said. "Now, if you know how to do that, then I suggest you get on and do it." Both of them approached me menacingly.

Just at that moment, two of my colleagues came through the doorway and saw what was happening. Both of them got between me and the other two. "What's going on here?" one of them demanded.

"Get out of my way Frank," I said, "You're spoiling my fun." The other colleague happened to be the one who had been on

the captain's course with me, and was the one to whom I'd given the karate demonstration.

"Do you realise what'll happen to you if you try it on with him?" he said. Before the young guys could ask what he meant, he told them about the demonstration he witnessed on camp the previous year. "Get out of here quick if you value your health," he told them.

They almost ran back down the road to the priest's house. He had obviously been egging them on. Frank and Jimmy, my two friends, had a good laugh about the matter. They wanted to know what I would've done if they hadn't arrived on the scene.

"Do you think I would've soiled my hands on them when I was carrying a pistol?" I asked smiling.

"You're one mad bugger, and that's a fact," said Frank. Next day, the news was all over the camp. The two young air corps officers were not to be seen again while I was around.

The camp commander must've gotten wind of what had happened, because he asked me if I would be willing to give a demonstration of unarmed combat at a concert, that was to be held the following Thursday. During my time in England, I had learned the arts of Judo and Aikido, and since I had returned to Ireland, I studied Karate. The senior officers were amazed to see how a weapon could be taken from an attacker with the minimum of effort. Not many years later, the Ranger wing of the army was founded, and unarmed combat was included in their training.

Chapter Nineteen

REDUNDANT

On returning to work after camp, I had a problem with my boss. When I checked, I found that my co-director and the plant manager had conspired against me. Being the organised person that I was, I had been leaving a schedule of calls at the office so that they could contact me if needed. There were no mobile phones in the cars at that time. They had been phoning my customers ahead of my arriving, and taking their orders. They then claimed that they were doing all the work. I was being accused of doing nothing. My boss was in no mood for listening to me, so we parted. For the first time in my life, I found myself without a job to go to.

The immediate effect of being told that your services are no longer required is one of shock and disbelief, followed by confusion and disorientation. It is all the more traumatic when it happens at forty-nine years of age. My immediate thoughts were for my very pregnant wife and our three children. The children had been used to their father always having a current registered car. Now I would be arriving home without one.

I kept asking myself on my way home what I had done to deserve such treatment. The market was severely depressed but I was getting my fair share, plus a bit more... so why me? My ego was completely shattered and I had terrible forebodings about the future. I felt bitter about my treatment, coupled with helplessness, despondency, and loss of self-respect.

Having gathered my thoughts before I reached home—and so as not to worry my wife in her condition—I assured her that I would soon be back at work. After all, I was very experienced and that had to count for something. I seriously considered taking legal action against my ex-employer, but I soon discovered that I was powerless. I wasn't a member of a trade union, my directorship was non-executive, and I wasn't entitled to redundancy.

I cursed the luck of my employer, and got on with sending my CV to various employment agencies. I scanned the newspapers and after two weeks without a reply to my various letters, I decided that I'd better sign on at the labour exchange. Never having to go anywhere near a labour exchange in my life before now, I didn't know what to expect. That first morning was fine and bright, as I made my way to Werburg Street in the city centre. I was dressed in a crisp white shirt and wore light blue summer slacks with a red leather belt. All eyes turned my way as I crossed the cavernous hall to the enquiry counter. There were lines of unshaven, unsmiling, and shabbily dressed men with bored blank expressions, shuffling toward steel cages where they were being attended to by equally bored people behind the bars. The whole place was dirty and dull, and in dire need of redecorating. There was a piece of pencil, tied to the bars to prevent people from robbing it. By the time I had filled in the necessary forms, I was feeling depressed myself and a little dehumanised.

Imagine my dismay when I was told that I was only entitled to assistance, and not unemployment benefit. I was short of the requisite number of credits because I had been out of the country. My wife and our three and a half children would have to survive on £98.00 per week. I felt embarrassed, degraded, and ashamed.

Research points to the high level of stress that managers experience when they find themselves unemployed. This is brought about by the fact that they believed that they had been managing their job so well, and the deep level of commitment they had. We all tend to live beyond our means when we're working. It's so easy to run credit cards up to their limit. Being overly committed financially adds to the stress. As the weeks turned into months, the feelings of chronic anxiety, depression, and hopelessness began to manifest themselves physically. My duodenal ulcer gave me considerable pain, and my wife found that her psoriasis was in a bad state.

Our living standards began to suffer. At first, we lived off what savings we had to try and maintain the standard that we'd been used to. But we soon found that we were having to cash in insurance policies, and at a considerable loss.

Beans on toast replaced steak and onions. We cut back on light and fuel, things that had always been taken for granted, and there was no social life. We began to avoid friends and family alike, in case we'd be invited to functions that we couldn't afford. On one occasion, I was late in paying money into my account at the bank, and they refused to pay my mortgage. This was despite the fact that I had been dealing with them for twenty years, and had paid off several loans faithfully over those years. I was told that I should've arranged for an overdraft. But they would not facilitate overdrafts to the unemployed. We were quickly becoming non-persons.

As a consequence of all of this, my ulcer perforated and I was rushed to hospital on Christmas Day, 1986. The surgeon who performed the operation told me afterwards that I was lucky to survive. Needless to remark, I was unable to attend the dole office, so I wrote a note authorising my wife to collect my money. But bureaucracy raised its ugly head and she was refused. They advised her to see the Health Board Officer in our area. He turned out to be very kind and understanding, and saw to it that she had sufficient to survive on. I had previously been subjected to a "means test," and one would have thought that this would have been sufficient to allow my wife to collect the money due to me. But it appeared that the dole office was only too happy to offload us onto another department. I came to bitterly resent the whole system.

Before I had fully recovered, I went on the offensive. I set about ringing friends, and one of them gave me three names of companies to contact. Two of these offered me employment.

The surgeon had told me that I wouldn't survive another attack on my health of the kind that I just had. So this made me more determined than ever to succeed. My old fighting spirit returned and it paid off.

I'm delighted to say that I wasn't tempted to seek solace in alcohol or drugs My belief in the Almighty and His saving grace stood to me throughout. The church stepped in and offered help, once those in authority found out about our plight. We were provided with fuel, and light, and anything else we needed until we were back on our feet again. As soon as the situation righted itself, I saw to it that the church was repaid.

One thing that stood out glaringly through all of this was the fact that I had no formal documentation or qualifications. I was highly technical, with the ability to impart technical information clearly and concisely. But I didn't have a certificate to my name. Employers take advantage of individuals in that situation. They couldn't possibly pay higher wages to someone without the "bits of paper," to show that they are professionals. I suffered as a result. Not just financially, but psychologically as well. And after being patronised, one evening, by one of my colleagues in the officer's mess, I vowed to change all that. I discussed my problem in this regard with my wife, and as soon as we had recovered financially from our situation, I set about seeking the formal qualifications that were needed to get the higher salary, etc. Then one evening on my return from work, my wife handed me an advertisement from the newspaper. It invited people such as me to get in touch with the college and discuss the possibility of studying for a Degree.

The senior lecturer at the National College of Industrial Relations sat across the desk from me on the appointed evening of the interview. He introduced himself as Michael Barry, and what a kind and inspiring man he turned out to be. We discussed my situation, and the experience that I had in industry. We discussed many things, and then he said he would accept me onto the course. I almost jumped up and kissed him. But I restrained myself, and thanked him graciously. An hour had gone by in what seemed only minutes. We spent the next thirty minutes or so, just chatting. He asked me if I had any other interests. I mentioned the fact that I was a Captain in the Army Reserve.

"Well why didn't you tell me that at the very beginning," he said a little exasperated. "If you had, I would've accepted you there and then. It never fails to amaze me that Irishmen have a habit of hiding their light under a bushel. I don't know why they do that. I'm sure you fought long and hard to reach the rank that you hold. Am I right?"

"Yes, that and the Fellowship I earned with the Institute of Sales and Marketing Management just recently."

I won't repeat what he called me. But we hit it off very well, and he gave me a starting date for lectures and welcomed me to the college.

Five years of hard studying at night brought me a second-class Bachelor's Degree in Human Resource Management. The degree is in the humanities and it is very wide ranging. One of the subjects is anthropology. I found it very interesting. A Jesuit priest taught the subject. One evening, he was discussing the ways in which people seek to make themselves important. He handed out a form with various suggestions and professions mentioned. He then asked the group what class did we belong to using the criteria outlined on the sheet.

"Working class and proud of it," I said when he got to me.

"But according to the information you supplied, you're middle class," he said.

"As far as I'm concerned, Sir, if one has to work for a living then you're working class."

He shook his head and moved on to the next subject, that of status-seeking people. "Our Taoiseach, Charlie Haughey likes status," he said. "The next thing he'll go for will be to have his head on a stamp."

"If he put his backside on it, we'd all get a chance to lick it," I said. The class disintegrated in hysterics. He did his best to mask his amusement and gave me a very stern look. It was a hard grind most of the time… but there were some lighter moments. Coupled with the Degree, I also qualified as a Member of the Institute for Personnel Consultants. I had new business cards printed with B.A.F. Inst. S.M.M. M.I.P.C., but despite what the senior lecturer said about flaunting the qualifications, I couldn't bring myself to use them. I settled in the end for BA.

The qualifications did the trick. I secured a job in sales with a company that distributed printing trade supplies. Later on, I was head-hunted by a very large printing company that wanted to set up a sales department. That proved to be a wrong move, so I found a job as Plant Manager with a rival company. A few years later I was head-hunted once again. This time by a previous boss who had set up a Printing Trade House. He was a good man but he ran out of cash and the company went into liquidation. I found myself redundant once again. However, it wasn't long before I was back at work. My reputation as a successful salesman was well known and I was in demand for a change. The years soon flew by. I worked until I was sixty-eight, and decided that I had had enough. There were other things I wanted to do. Linda gave birth to Ross, our last son, twenty-one years ago and the last of our children. I was prompted to dedicate a poem to her. It goes:

> *I awake at dawn and in the half-light*
> *Look upon her countenance:*
> *She sleeps serene, this girl I met*
> *When seventeen:*
> *She's forty now and slightly plump*
> *Caused by bump and bump*
> *And bump and bump:*
> *Four beautiful kids we love so much*
> *She wakes and smiles we kiss, we touch:*
> *Some people marry just for life*
> *But her and me are married for eternity:*
> *We don't just think, but know for sure*
> *A crown is ours if we endure:*
> *The trials and tribulations of this life*
> *This girl... my lover... and my wife.*
> *We endured and we're still together after forty years*
> *and still in love.*

EPILOGUE

My life has been varied, and I believe, interesting. I've never got into the "cudda-shudda" philosophy. Choices are placed before us throughout our lives. I believe it's all right to look back at times and wonder what might have happened, if we had chosen a different path. But it's important not to get maudlin if things haven't quite worked out the way we'd have liked. It's true that money doesn't buy happiness. My wife and I were never happier than when we were struggling to survive in rented rooms and living on chicken soup. Why? Because we were so much in love that nothing else mattered and we were working together for better things.

We meet certain people along life's path who affect and influence us. I will always remember the ones who showed kindness and unselfishness. My parents were wonderful examples of unstinting love. My mother in particular proved herself worthy of sainthood by her devotion to raising such a large family in such economically challenging circumstances. Not to mention her raising a child that wasn't hers. My pal Jimmy Johnston always remained faithful. He died suddenly and unexpectedly in 2009 and I miss him. My commanding officer, Commandant Dessie Byrne in the 20th Battalion, who recognised the leadership potential in me and insisted I attend the interview for potential officers. During the five years I spent studying for my Degree, I couldn't attend to my duties in the army reserve as often as I would've liked. I had been given the job of battalion adjutant. He's the senior staff officer in a battalion and he is not required to attend as often as a company officer. I enjoyed it for a while, but because I'm an all or nothing man, I decided to retire. So at fifty-five years of age I resigned with the rank of captain.

I am also indebted to my boss in Birmingham, Mister Eric Balfrey, an officer and a gentleman. The senior lecturer at the National College of Ireland, Michael Barry, who stated that it is important for us to be remembered when we die, and what better way to do this than to write a book. I promised to remember Don Bluth, the animator. He set up an animation company in Dublin. But it was through our church that we met and became friends. I hope you're happy Don. I want to pay special thanks to my editor Anne Younger without whose help this work would not have been published., and last but not least, my family whom I love dearly. I also include here the children of my first marriage. I want you to know that I tried to locate you for months on end. Finally, discovering your address, I met Éamonn and Martin while on my way to knock on your door. I decided to back off when I saw how scared you were of me. I then tried writing to Catherine after I received divorce proceedings from your Mom's solicitor. I asked in my letter that she phone my brother, Gerry's house or make contact through my solicitor. She phoned and made it plain to my brother's wife that you wanted nothing to do with me. I'm sorry for all that has happened and for the hurt I caused you. Please try to find it in your hearts to forgive.

I have learned many lessons during my life. There are three things that are most important, in my opinion. First is faith in the Lord Jesus Christ, second is forgiveness; for if we can't forgive I believe it shows in our countenance. We become ugly, literally. The third lesson is to keep getting back up when life knocks you down and try again. Never give up.

Always remember what I taught you, be proud of your country and your name. And remember the motto, "Don't mess with the Sheridans."

Lightning Source UK Ltd.
Milton Keynes UK

178225UK00001B/47/P